The SEASONS

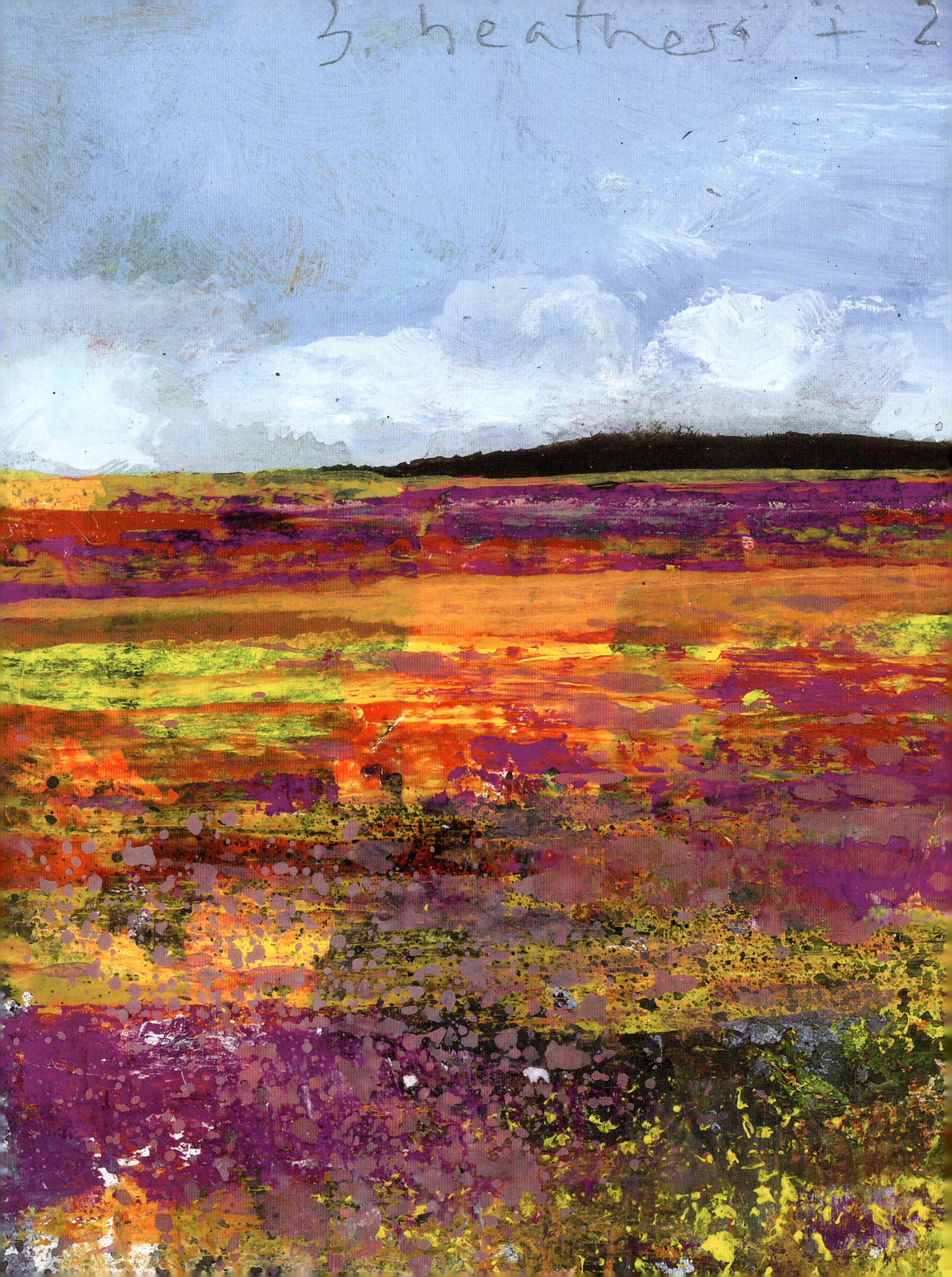

3. heather # 2

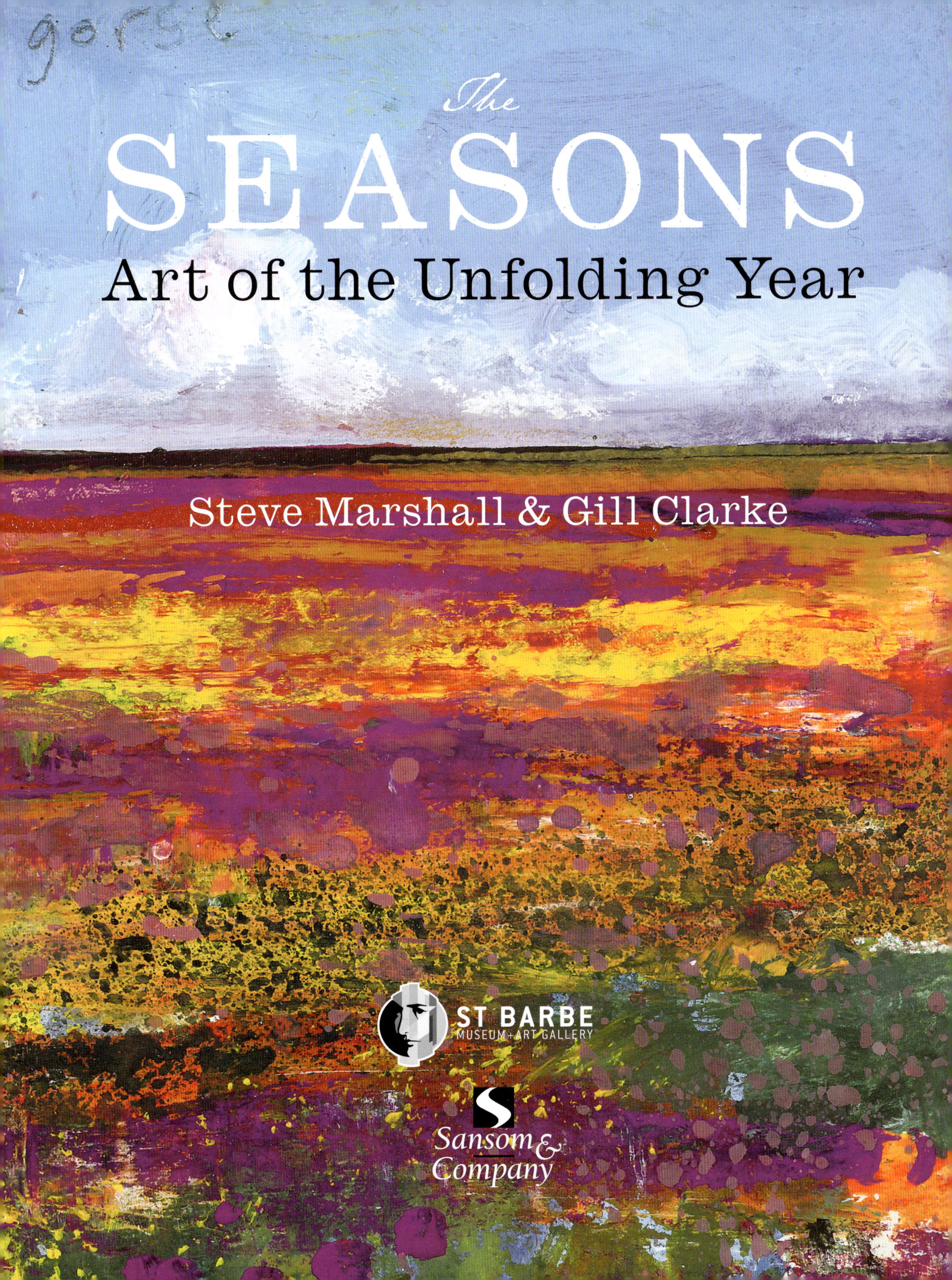

The SEASONS
Art of the Unfolding Year

Steve Marshall & Gill Clarke

ST BARBE
MUSEUM + ART GALLERY

Sansom & Company

First published in 2020 by Sansom and Company,
a publishing imprint of Redcliffe Press Ltd.,
81g Pembroke Road, Bristol BS8 3EA
www.sansomandcompany.co.uk · info@sansomandcompany.co.uk

ISBN 978-1-911408-69-7

Published in conjunction with 'The Seasons' exhibition
at St Barbe Museum and Art Gallery, Lymington
11 September 2020–10 January 2021

British Library Cataloguing-in-Publication Data
A catalogue record for this book is available from the British Library.

Design and typesetting by E&P Design

Printed and bound by Akcent Media

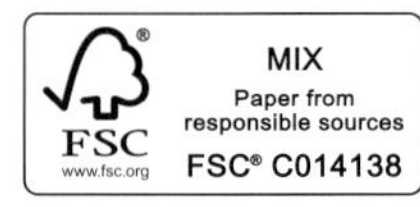 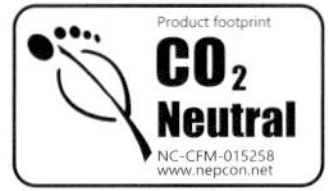

Sansom & Company is committed to being an environmentally friendly
publisher. This book is made from Forest Stewardship Council® certified paper.

Frontispiece: Kurt Jackson, *Three of heather and two of gorse* (detail)

CONTENTS

SPONSOR'S FOREWORD

The last decade has seen a huge rise in the popularity of nature writing with such writers as Richard Mabey, Robert Macfarlane and Helen Macdonald very much to the fore. This has also led to the rediscovery of past classics; elegiac texts by Nan Shepard, Richard Jeffries, Adrian Bell, W.H. Hudson and Edward Thomas to name but a few.

What is striking about the more recent books is that, compared to the older texts, there is much less emphasis on the seasons. However, this exhibition splendidly shows how nature and, at least historically, man's activities have always been intrinsically linked to the rhythm of the seasons. One of the exhibition highlights is Clare Leighton's *The Farmer's Year*, published as a sumptuous book in 1933. Two years later she published *Four Hedges: A Gardener's Chronicle* putting beyond doubt her empathy for the seasons and their central influence on the natural world.

Nowadays we are much less attuned to the seasons, although in our temperate climate they are surely one of creation's greatest gifts. Certainly, we are conscious of the weather and the variation in daylight hours, but central heating, air conditioning, year-round availability of weather sensitive foodstuffs all conspire to mask seasonality. And that is before the undoubted impacts of climate change as alluded to in the text.

This fine catalogue was largely written during the Coronavirus lockdown. To the extent that the lockdown had any upside at all then, for those of us fortunate enough to be able to access the countryside, it has surely reinvigorated our interaction with nature and the joys of a British spring. As sponsor of this catalogue and as a lender to the exhibition, I heartily commend the efforts of authors and curators and I hope all visitors will enjoy the show.

Stuart Southall

INTRODUCTION

This book and the exhibition that accompanies it are intended as a celebration of the changing seasons at a time when many of us are becoming increasingly remote from the natural rhythms of the year. When the project was initiated it seemed that our predominantly urban western society together with the dominance of digital communication in our busy lives left little room for appreciating the small wonders of the turning year. One of the results of the Coronavirus outbreak was that suddenly we had the time to stand and stare and during lockdown notice the arrival of spring and the promise it holds, as flowers appeared, leaves unfurled and birdsong filled the unnaturally quiet air. These momentous events hopefully will lead to positive change in many aspects of national life including a greater appreciation of the natural environment and the many threats it faces. As climate change continues to affect the weather and natural phenomena associated with each season their traditional boundaries are becoming increasingly blurred. The breadth of imagery contained in this book seeks to draw attention to the joys of each season while they can still be appreciated. Perhaps it may also encourage further consideration of what we each might do to ensure the cycle continues in some recognisable form.

The seasons occur because the tilt in the Earth's axis causes different parts of the planet to receive the sun's most direct rays at different times of the year. Here in the northern hemisphere it is summer when the North Pole is tilted towards the sun, when the South Pole tilts to the sun we have our winter. Understanding the progress of the seasons has always been crucial to humanity in terms of food and survival. The alignment of monuments such as Stonehenge, where stones were placed to mark the summer and winter solstices, and the huge amount of labour and planning which went into their construction reflects the vital importance that ancient peoples placed on understanding and marking key dates in the seasonal calendar. The uncertainties of weather and climate meant that festivals were often held at these points in the year and offerings made to ensure that nature's cycle would continue and spring would follow winter once again.

This book opens with winter, which ushers in the start of the new year. We have used the three months traditionally allocated to each season (December, January and February for winter and so on) although there is overlap and of course how wintry or autumnal a month might feel varies from year to year. For each season an introductory text sets out some of its main features, based around the themes of calendar and traditions, weather, landscape and plants, animals and farming. In order to give a sense of the richness of material that has been created in response to each season we have also referenced works that are not included in the exhibition. In these cases we have included details of the collections in which they can be found to encourage readers to explore further. Each seasonal introduction is prefaced with an excerpt from John Clare's poem 'The Shepherd's Calendar' which, although written almost two hundred years ago, describes seasonal events that are still familiar today. Many of the sources referenced in these sections have been chosen because they are viewed as classic texts and originate from the same era as much of the art work, most were also illustrated by artists whose work is featured in the exhibition. Among the supporting images are photographs from the St Barbe Museum collection that reflect seasonal events in the New Forest area.

These texts are followed by a catalogue of the works included in the exhibition to represent each season. It is an almost boundless topic: clearly there are many signifiers of seasonality and we have tried to include some of the notable features and some less appreciated aspects of the turning year. We have chosen artists who had a particular understanding of the way nature, landscape and agriculture was transformed as the months progressed, so as to offer an appreciation of these phenomena through the filter of their experience and imagination. To give the exhibition a distinct focus and identity we have only considered British artists from the twentieth and twenty-first centuries and the material largely relates to the south of England, near to our venue. The exhibition's subject matter is primarily rural because this is where the signs of seasonal change are most apparent and diverse. We have also included representations of gardens, which along with city parks, are the places where many people experience seasonality on a day to day basis. One of our key themes is agriculture. Farming has a great impact on the appearance of the rural landscape and the annual cycle of work on the land has long underpinned the natural rhythm of the seasons in the countryside. In the early 1900s farming methods continued to reflect age-old traditions, the key jobs were the same as those illustrated in the Luttrell Psalter in the fourteenth century: ploughing, harrowing, sowing, weeding, reaping. These timeless tasks remained attractive to the artists featured here but while rural landscapes continue to inspire new generations of painters, the highly mechanised world of modern agriculture has a much reduced appeal.

Seasonal change was a notable subject in the first half of the twentieth century but from the 1950s Abstract Expressionism and the art movements that followed made landscape and particularly rural life unfashionable. From the 1960s Land Artists made a very direct connection with the seasons: Andy Goldsworthy (b. 1956) created ephemeral artworks from fallen leaves and ice, David Nash's (b. 1945) *Ash Dome* was a living sculpture that grew and changed with the seasons and there were references to nature's

cycle in the walks of Richard Long (b. 1945) and Hamish Fulton (b. 1946). But the representation of rural landscapes and seasonality in more traditional media was not re-established until the Brotherhood of Ruralists, including Peter Blake (b. 1932), David Inshaw (b. 1943) and Annie Ovenden (b. 1945), rediscovered the landscapes of Wessex in the 1970s. Today concerns about climate change and ecological disaster have made the countryside and stewardship of the land a compelling subject once again. These peaks and troughs in the popularity of seasonal change as a subject for art are reflected in the exhibition material.

The content of both exhibition and accompanying book reflect a time when people were generally more in tune with the land and the changing seasons, a situation in many locations in urgent need of rediscovery if the damaging effects of climate change, habitat destruction, pollution, declining soil fertility and industrial-scale farming are to be avoided. Ignoring these factors risks the disappearance of those seasonal indicators, so attractive and emotive to artists and writers across the centuries, and our lives and those of future generations will be the poorer for it.

Steve Marshall (sm) and Gill Clarke (gc)

WINTER

Withering and keen the Winter comes,
While Comfort flies to close-shut rooms,
And sees the snow in feathers pass
Winnowing by the window-glass;
Whilst unfelt tempests howl and beat
Above his head in chimney-seat.

John Clare · The Shepherd's Calendar · 1827

Winter is a season of short days and darkness, when nature appears dormant or even dead. Consequently it has been a time for seeking comfort and company around the warmth of the hearth. Midwinter festivals were intended to lighten the dark and mark the turning point of the year at the winter solstice, which falls around 21 December. This sense of cosy communal celebration is beautifully captured by Robin Tanner's etching *Christmas* (p. 33) where light spills from the houses and carols are sung by lantern light. Visually winter is often depicted as a season of snow and ice as in John Nash's illustration for December in *Almanack of Hope* (fig. 1), a time for building snowmen, snowball fights and ice skating (fig. 2). In fact such weather is rare in the south where rain and wind is more usual – the word winter actually has its root in old Germanic words meaning wet or water, it is literally the wet season. Sunshine is either absent or weak. In *The Downs in Winter* (fig. 4), Eric Ravilious skilfully evoked watery light filtered through passing clouds, bringing gentle warmth to an otherwise desolate scene of hedge-less fields and an abandoned farm roller. Yet even in the depths of winter there are always signs that spring is not so far away: in January buds begin to grow, catkins hang on hazel branches and the thrush is heard again. By February the days are noticeably longer, frogspawn appears in ponds, tawny owls hoot to mark their territory and the blackbird is in full song. Valentine's Day was traditionally believed to be the day birds chose their mates.

The transformation of landscape under snowfall has made the snow scene a popular subject for artists. In James McIntosh Patrick's (1907–1998) highly detailed panorama *Winter in Angus* (1935, Tate Collection) even the distant mountains are in sharp focus in the cold, still air. Adrian Allinson's (1890–1959) fondness for dramatic lighting brings a childlike sense of wonder to *Winter Magic* (Brighton and Hove Museums and Art Galleries Collection). Robert Gibbings' (1889–1958) snow-covered roof-tops are cleverly suggested by simple geometric shapes in the wood engraving *Dublin Under Snow* (1918, Ashmolean Museum Collection). January is often the coldest month, particularly in the north and east with freezing winds blow-ing in from Siberia or cold air descending from the Arctic. In some years February may bring the worst weather (the storms and flooding of 2020 being a case in point) but in others it can be sunny and mild. The variability of the British climate and the very localised weather we sometimes experience perhaps explains the national obsession with the elements.

Stripped of their leaves, it is possible to appreciate the intricate and individually unique structure of deciduous trees. Artists have long been drawn to trees as subject matter, whether for their symbolic connotations, or to give structure and a sense of scale to landscapes, or as portraits of individual specimens. Bare winter trees dominate John Aldridge's bleak, snow-covered landscape *Winter* (p. 17) and lend an eerie atmosphere to Graham Sutherland's *Cottage in Dorset, Wood End* (p. 21). The sometimes unsettling presence of leafless trees is powerfully expressed in Edward Burra's (1905–1976) watercolour *Blasted Oak* (1942, Arts Council Collection) and Edward McKnight Kauffer's (1890–1954) Shell poster *The New Forest* (1931, Shell Art Collection). In Clare Leighton's wood engraving for February from *The Farmer's Year*, curving branches provide movement and energy in a scene of winter lopping (p. 28), while in Stanley Badmin's *The Old Ash* (fig. 3)

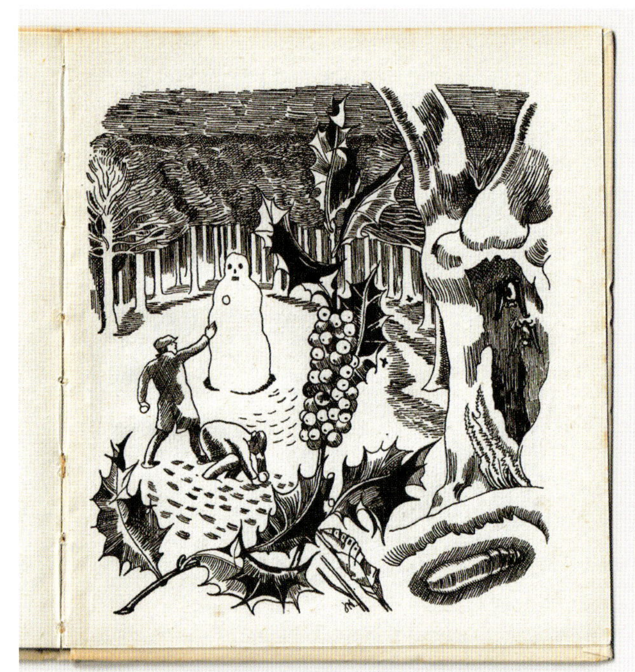

FIG. 1 · **John Nash** (1893–1977) · *December*
illustration for *Almanack of Hope*, poems by John Pudney, 1944

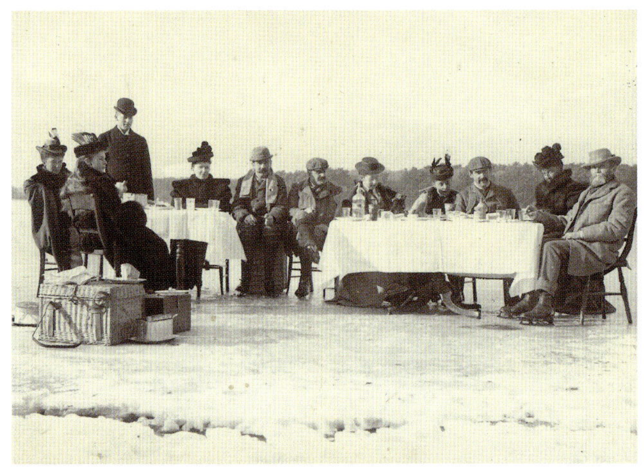

FIG. 2 · Lunch party on the ice at Sowley Pond, near Lymington, winter of 1894–5
St Barbe Museum and Art Gallery Collection

the fresh growth sprouting from an ancient pollard gives
a sense of renewal and hope. When trees are bare, green
or golden clumps of evergreen mistletoe are clearly visible.
Mistletoe carries sticky berries from November to December
and is brought into homes for Christmas and New Year traditions that reflect its long associations with fertility, peace
and good luck (p. 32).

To survive the winter many flowering plants die back to their
roots, while some survive only as seed. Evelyn Dunbar's *Winter
Garden* (p. 22) shows leafless trees and bare soil, yet there is
a sense of ground being prepared for new life come the spring.
Winter is not devoid of flowers, the snowdrop (p. 34) makes a
welcome appearance in January and February. On the heath
the bright yellow and intensely fragrant gorse flowers appear
from January, although they do show sporadically throughout
the year; as the saying goes: 'when gorse is out of bloom, kissing
is out of season'. In Frederick Golden Short's painting (p. 24) a
scattering of flowers enliven the drab tones of the New Forest in
winter. From January the buttercup yellow of lesser celandines
brighten woodland walks, stream banks and hedgerows. In his
poem 'The Year's Awakening' (1910) Thomas Hardy marvelled
over the appearance of the crocus, demonstrating nature's
uncanny knowledge of the right moment to spring into life:

> *How do you know, deep underground,*
> *Hid in your bed from sight and sound,*
> *Without a turn in temperature,*
> *With weather life can scarce endure,*
> *That light has won a fraction's strength,*
> *And day put on some moments' length,*
> *Whereof in merest rote will come,*
> *Weeks hence, mild airs that do not numb;*
> *O crocus root, how do you know,*
> *How do you know?*

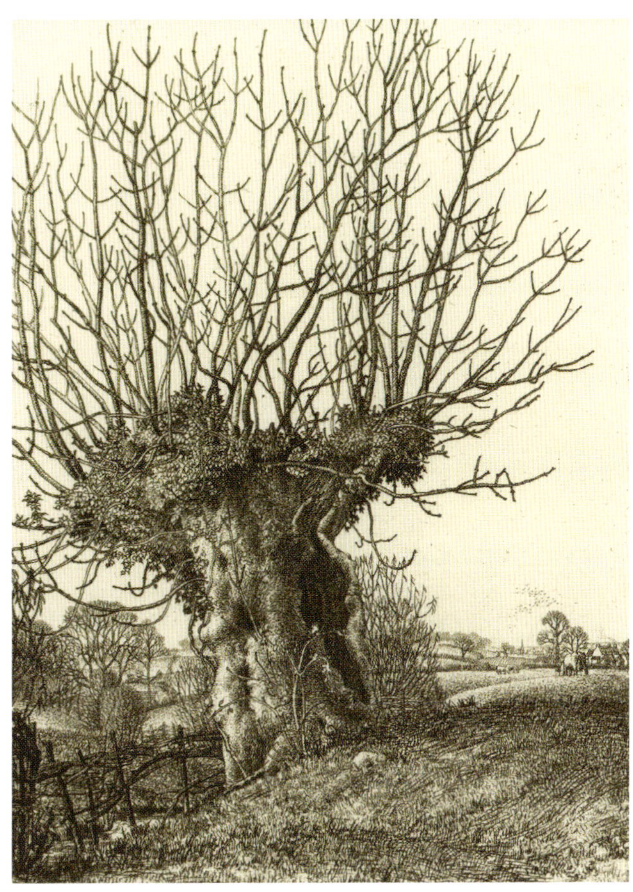

FIG. 3 • **Stanley Roy Badmin** (1906–1989) • *The Old Ash*
1929 • etching
Stuart Southall Collection/© estate of the artist

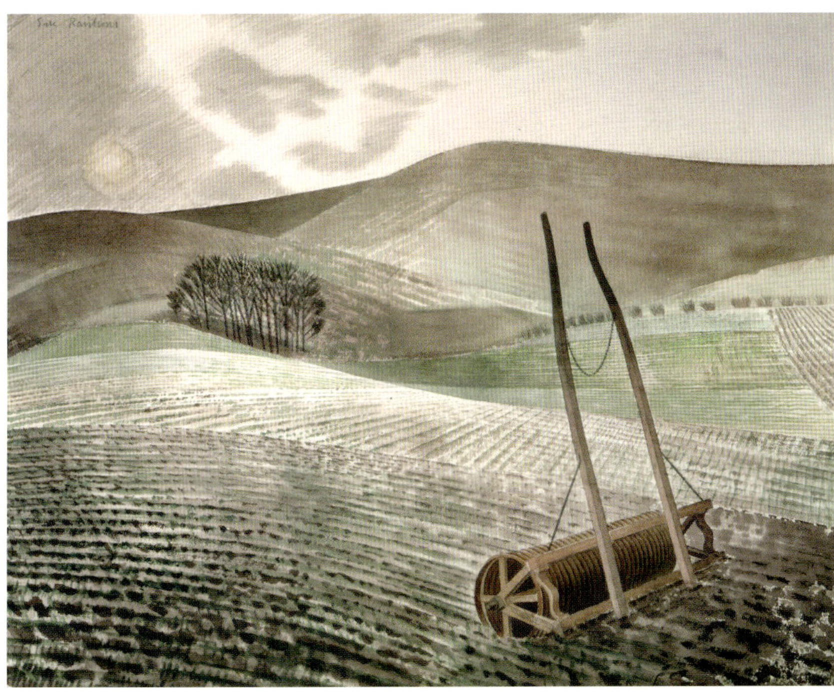

FIG. 4 • **Eric Ravilious** (1903–1942)
The Downs in Winter
1934 • watercolour on paper
Towner Art Gallery, Eastbourne, East Sussex/
Bridgeman Images

Winter can be a hard time for wildlife. Food might be buried under snow or locked beneath frozen ground. Flocks of field-fares and redwings may be seen searching for food in urban gardens in particularly harsh weather. Iced ponds like those seen in John Nash's *Wild Garden, Winter* (p. 15) are a problem for hungry herons and other birds looking for a drink. Prolonged cold weather can be disastrous for small birds that lose their body heat more rapidly. In order to survive long-tailed tits, sparrows, starlings and wagtails will roost together and dozens of wrens will cram themselves into the same bird box.[1] Small mammals such as hedgehogs, dormice and bats hibernate, while frogs, toads and newts go into a state of torpor under rocks or at the bottom of a pond. Bumble bees and some butterflies also hibernate but may be seen on warm days. The absence of these creatures during winter can reinforce the sense of monotony and drabness in a land-scape drained of life and colour.

Winter was often thought of as a quieter time for the farmer, but there were always tasks that required attention. In *Men and the Fields* (1939) Adrian Bell (1901–1980) wrote about his experiences as he travelled across southern England and Wales. He had been a farmer in East Anglia and had a keen understanding of the seasons' influence on agriculture. Of winter he commented: 'It is the dead season: the days are short, yet the farmer must be as busy as ever in his mind. There are innumerable jobs need doing which there is no time for when the farm work is going forward'.[2] In the past when threshing had been done by hand it would have occupied farm workers for most of the winter. Grain was separated from the stalks and husks by beating it with flails. The remains were winnowed in a breeze to remove the rest of the chaff. The corn was collected in sacks ready for planting or selling on to a seed merchant and the straw would be used as litter in animal pens. George Clausen (1852–1944) recorded the last stages of this process in a pair of etchings *Dressing Wheat* (fig. 5), which shows men feeding a hand-cranked sifting machine, and *Filling Sacks*. Clausen created a series of drawings, paintings and etchings which explored the effects of light and shadow on the magnificent architecture of historic barns. A sense of timeless activity in an almost church-like setting can be seen in *Interior of an Old Barn* (1908, Royal Academy Collection).

These arduous jobs disappeared with the arrival of the threshing machine. In *The Life of the Fields* (1884) the nature writer Richard Jefferies (1848–1887) commented that these machines, once the cause of riots, were now just another part of the rural landscape and had become a proper subject for the artist: 'It is so accepted that the fields would seem to lack something if it were absent. It is as natural as the ricks: things grow old so soon in the fields'.[3] Clearing ditches to make sure that fields drained properly was another important activity at this time of year. The maintenance of hedges was also a winter job. A well laid hedge would keep livestock in (or out); if left it would grow tall and gaps would appear at the bottom. Hedge laying was a skilled task and became a popular subject for printmakers. Robin Tanner's *Wiltshire Hedger* (p. 29) is seen wielding his bill hook, while Stanley Anderson's *Hedge Laying* (1945, Royal Academy Collection) shows the hedger, having made his cut at the base, pulling the blackthorn branch that will be woven between stakes to build a robust barrier.

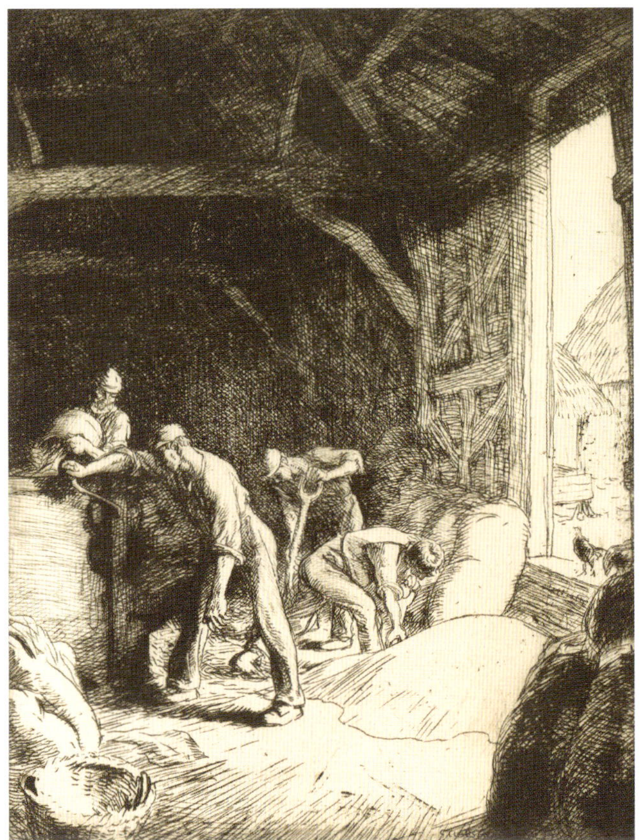

FIG. 5 · **Sir George Clausen** (1852–1944) · *Dressing Wheat* *c.* 1912–21 · etching
Stuart Southall Collection/© estate of the artist

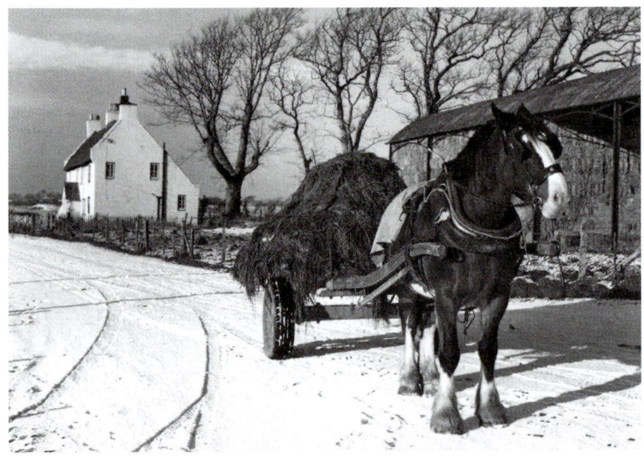

FIG. 6 · Horse with a cart of winter fodder at Vidle Van Farm, Keyhaven
St Barbe Museum and Art Gallery Collection

Hedging was also a subject for one of John Nash's lithographic illustrations for Adrian Bell's *Men and the Fields*. Ploughing begun in the autumn would traditionally be finished by Christmas; after that icy weather might make the soil too hard to work. Heavy rain would make it too wet, although the arrival of the tractor made this less of a problem. Once the earth had been turned, winter frosts were useful for breaking up clods of soil. Winter was also a time to spread fertilising muck on the fields.

Livestock needed feeding throughout the winter when the grass in pastures was not growing. Cattle and sheep might be given a kale field with moveable enclosures to ensure they cleared each section thoroughly, helpfully manuring the ground, before moving on to the next area. Once hurdles were used for this purpose but by the time C.F. Tunnicliffe was illustrating the Ladybird *What to Look For* series at the beginning of the 1960s an electric fence was a much less laborious solution.[4] Tunnicliffe's etching *A Hard Winter* (p. 25) shows sheep being fed cabbages in a snow-covered field. Mangolds were stored in clamps for the winter and over time their starches would turn into sugar making them a sweet and popular meal with livestock (p. 31). Stanley Badmin illustrated a mangold clamp being made in warm autumnal colours for the Puffin book *Farm Crops in Britain* and also depicted potatoes being preserved in the same way in the etching *Potato Clamps* (p. 30).[5] Evelyn Dunbar, while working as an Official War Artist, painted Land Girls grading potatoes retrieved from a clamp in *Potato Sorting, Berwick* (1943, Manchester Art Gallery Collection). Dunbar's depiction of this vital wartime harvest was part of a wider commission she received to portray the agricultural work of the Women's Land Army.[6] Hay was usually the most vital source of winter feed (fig. 6). Candlemas on 2 February marked the midpoint between the winter solstice and the spring equinox, so farmers would hope to still have half their hay left at this time. It was also thought that good weather at Candlemas foretold a long winter. Clare Leighton's wood engraving of early lambing from *The Farmer's Year* (p. 27) shows a partially cut rick in the background.

Candlemas shared its timing with the pagan Celtic festival of Imbolc, which marked the start of the lambing season and the stirring of new life in spring. Late winter and early spring was the busiest time of year for the shepherd who made sure that birthing went smoothly, found foster mothers for orphan lambs and hand-reared them when necessary. In *Farmer's Glory* (1932) A.G. Street (1892–1966) explained that on his father's farm half the arable land was given over to corn but the rest was devoted to providing year-round feed for sheep. He recalled a labourer grumbling: 'All we do do … is run about and sweat atter they blasted sheep. We be either lambing 'em, runnin 'em, marken 'em, shearing 'em, dipping 'em or some other foolishness. And they can have all the grub we do grow, and God knows how much it do cost the Guvnor fer cake'.[7] The book's beautifully engraved illustrations by Gwen Raverat suggest an altogether calmer atmosphere (fig. 7). **SM**

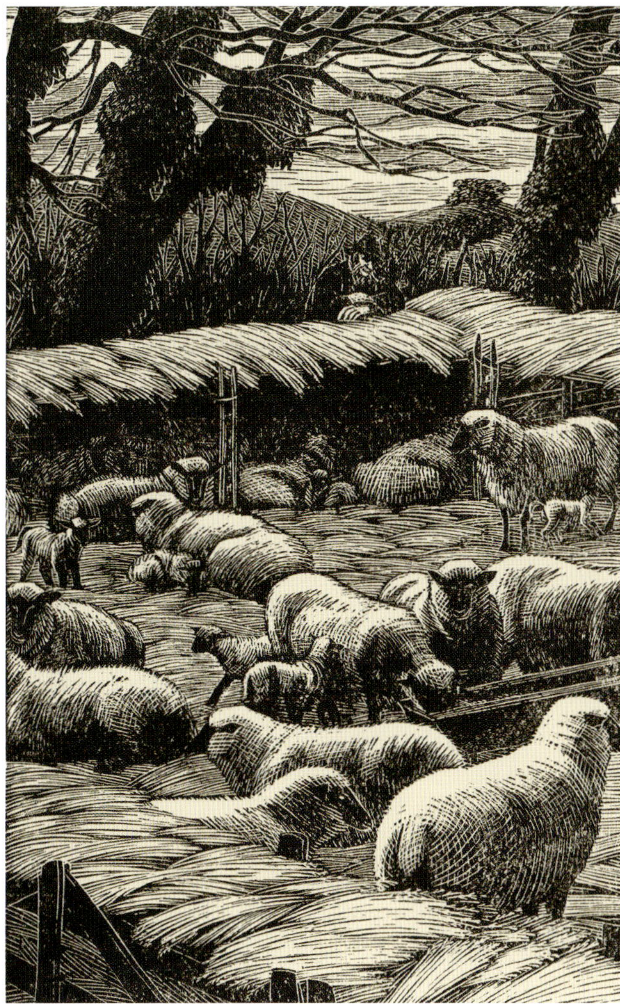

FIG. 7 · **Gwen Raverat** (1885–1957) · *Lambing Fold*
illustration for *Farmer's Glory* by A.G. Street, 1934

1. www.bto.org/understanding-birds/species-focus/wren (accessed 24 March 2020)
2. Bell, A. (1939), *Men and the Fields*, Batsford, p. 139
3. Jefferies, R. (1884), *The Life of the Fields*, Lutterworth Press edition 1947, illustrated by Agnes Miller Parker, p. 151
4. Watson, G.L. (1960), *What to Look For in Autumn*, Ladybird Books, p. 45
5. Stapledon, G. (1955), *Farm Crops in Britain*, Penguin Books Ltd., p. 13
6. Clarke, G. (2006), *Evelyn Dunbar: War and Country*, Sansom & Company, p. 116
7. Street, A.G. (1932), *Farmer's Glory*, Faber and Faber, 1934 edition, pp. 33–4

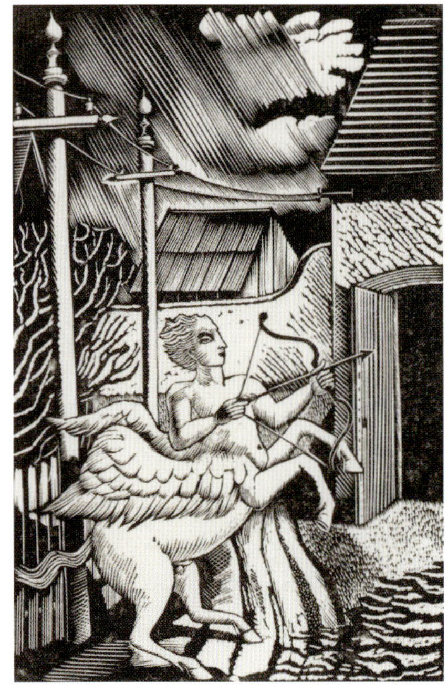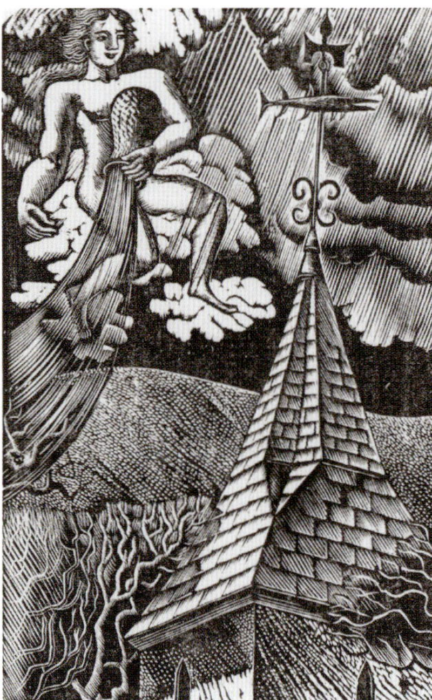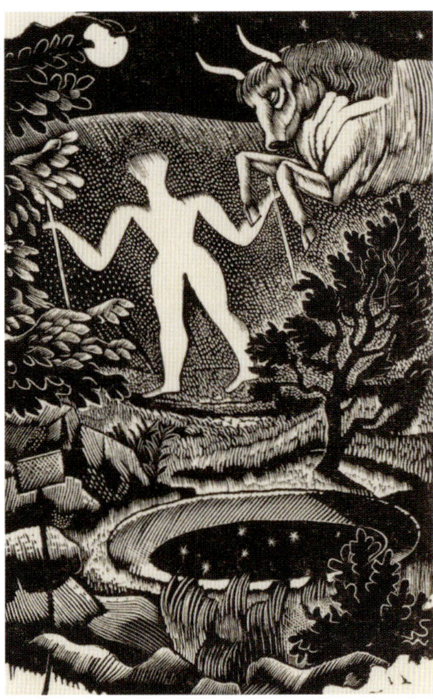

Eric Ravilious (1903–1942)

December, February and *May*

1928 · wood engravings · 100 x 63 mm (each) · from *Almanack 1929 with Twelve Designs Engraved on Wood*

Julian Francis Collection

Almanacs, in one form or another, have been with us for millennia, reflecting a desire for certainty or at least some inkling of how the year might unfold. These were books that not only set out the key dates in the calendar (including astronomical events and moveable feasts such as Easter) but also provided astrological forecasts for the year. In the uncertain but vital business of farming, where timing and seasonal weather patterns were crucial, almanacs became all but indispensible and in Britain by the eighteenth century they were outselling the Bible.[1] They advised on the best times for planting, auspicious days for important activities or decisions, unlucky days to be wary of and long range weather forecasts, all based on the movement of the stars and phases of the moon.

By the time Eric Ravilious was commissioned to provide illustrations for the Lanston Monotype Corporation's *Almanack* in 1929 such prognostications had largely given way to more practical concerns. But by including figures representing the signs of the zodiac in scenes of the Sussex countryside Ravilious recaptured some of the old mystical tradition of astrological powers influencing daily life. His awareness of this heritage is shown in the preface where he writes: 'The deities who became symbolised in the planets were thought to govern the change of the seasons and thus the agricultural labours of each month'.[2] Ravilious established his reputation as a wood engraver before becoming better known as a painter of watercolour landscapes. As well as commercial work like the Lanston commission he provided illustrations for a number of Golden Cockerel Press books such as Shakespeare's *Twelfth Night* (1932) and *The Writings of Gilbert White of Selborne* (1938). He was also responsible for the design used on the cover of the *Wisden Cricketers' Almanack* – the 'bible' of the summer game. **SM**

1. Groom, N. (2013), *The Seasons: A Celebration of the English Year*, Atlantic Books, 2014 edition, p. 57
2. Ravilious, E. (1929), *Preface by the Engraver* in *Almanack 1929 with Twelve Designs Engraved on Wood*, Lanston Monotype Corporation, 1928, unpaginated

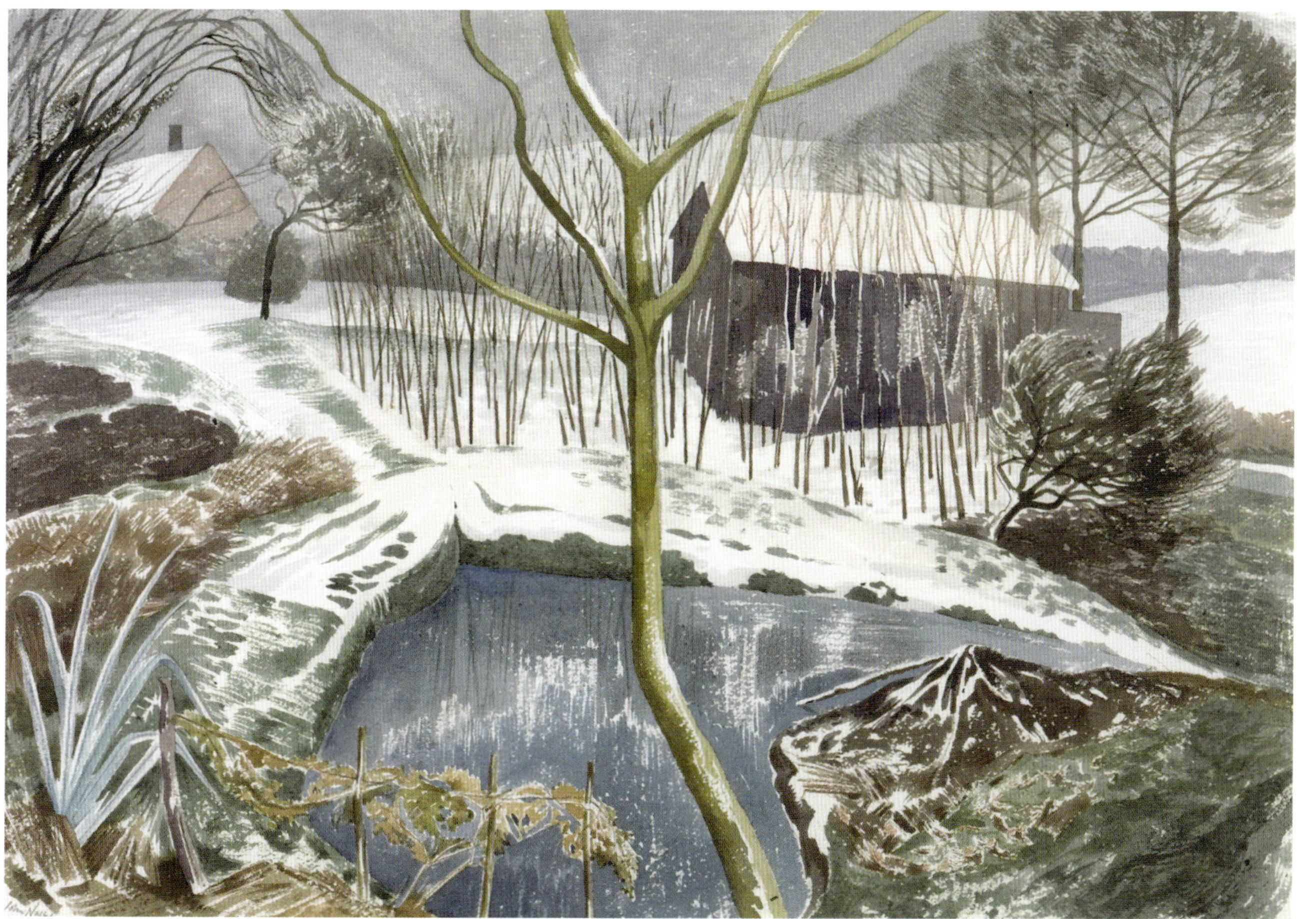

John Nash (1893–1977)

Wild Garden, Winter

1959 · watercolour · 406 x 571 mm

Tate: presented by the Trustees of the Chantrey
Bequest 1959 · photograph © Tate · image
© The John Nash Estate/Bridgeman Images

During the Second World War John Nash served with the Royal Marines as
an Official War Artist and also engaged in more secretive work in camouflage,
deception and aircraft identification. Discharged in 1944, he moved with his wife
Christine to Bottengoms farmhouse, a virtually derelict building near Wormingford
in Essex. The surrounding landscapes of the Stour valley on the Suffolk-Essex border
were very much 'Constable country' but over the next thirty years Nash made them
his own. During the summer he would head off on painting expeditions across
Britain with artist friends such as Edward Bawden (1903–1989), but in winter
it was Bottengoms and the surrounding country that occupied him.

Wild Garden, Winter shows one of the ponds in the Bottengoms garden. Nash was
a keen plantsman and had overseen the rescue of the garden from years of neglect.
He viewed its layout and planting as one of his most satisfying achievements. This
watercolour combines two favourite subjects: a pond and a snowy landscape seen on
an overcast day. Nash enjoyed capturing the subtlety of the colours he experienced
on such occasions and it is perhaps the balance of light and tone that makes this
such a convincing and meditative depiction of winter. Details such as the reflec-
tions of densely planted saplings on the surface of the frozen pond, the shapes
of individual trees and the brick gable of the farmhouse are carefully observed but
are complimentary rather than competing elements in the composition. A few years
earlier Nash had painted the same pond in sunshine (*Frozen Ponds*, 1953, private
collection) viewed from above with snow-covered fields as the backdrop.[1] SM

1. Lambirth, A. (2019), *John Nash: Artist & Countryman*, Unicorn Press, p. 212

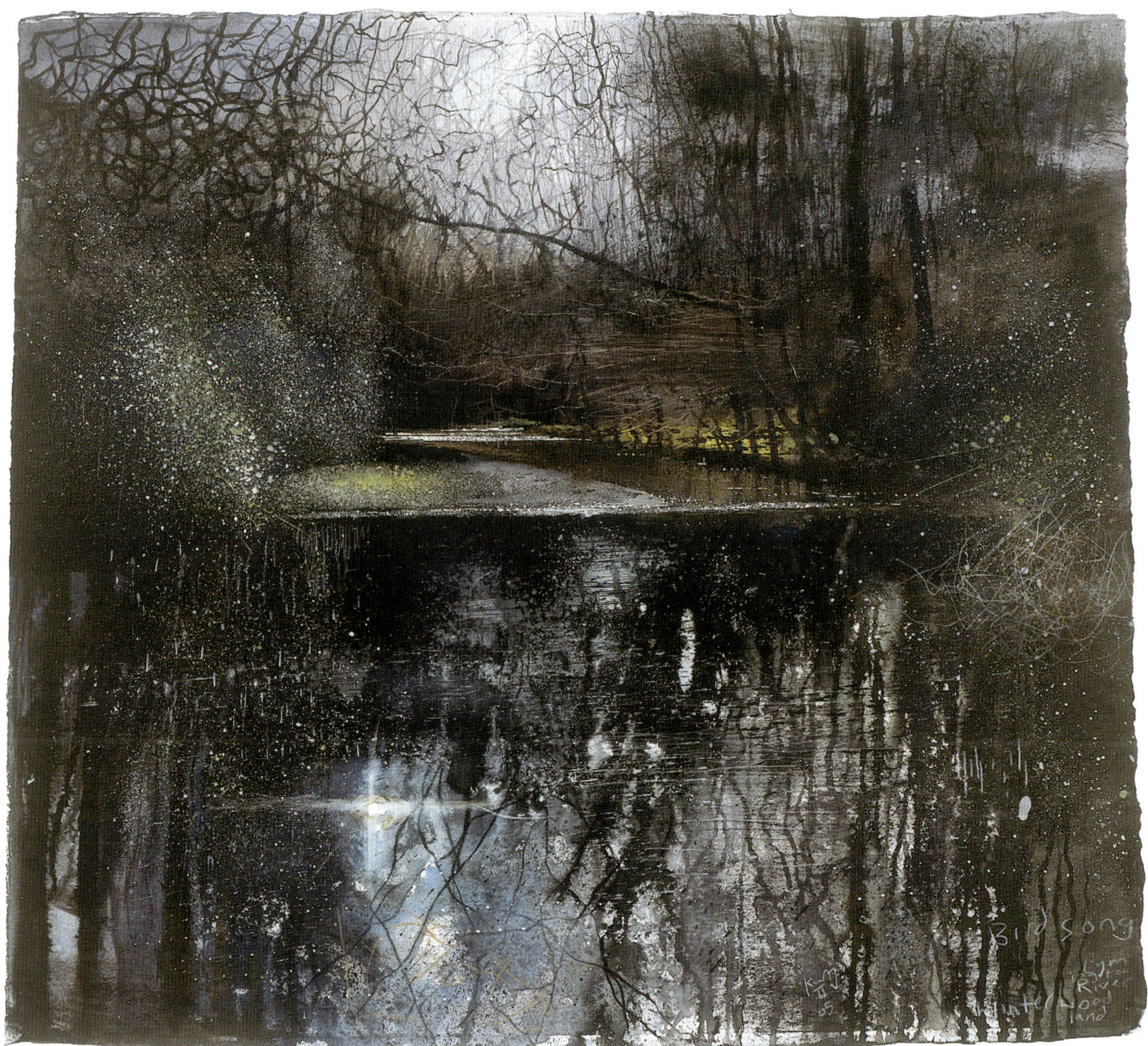

Kurt Jackson (b. 1961)

Bird song, Lymington River, winter woodland, Feb. 2005

2005 • mixed media • 570 x 620 mm

St Barbe Museum and Art Gallery Collection
image © the artist

The trees are showing their bare bones, their true form after shedding their clothes; the only real colour is now in the last bits of foliage left rusting above and below, the reds and browns and orange, tawny and russet, a spectrum of earth and fire in the dark woodland. I sit with my back against the bole of an oak, her corrugated bark rigid against my spine, my legs sprawled in the damp leaf litter. My brush follows these now visible undulating boughs and branches, twisting and snaking, each bend echoing the phrases of the song thrush that repeat and reinvent themselves rising up into the canopy. **Kurt Jackson**

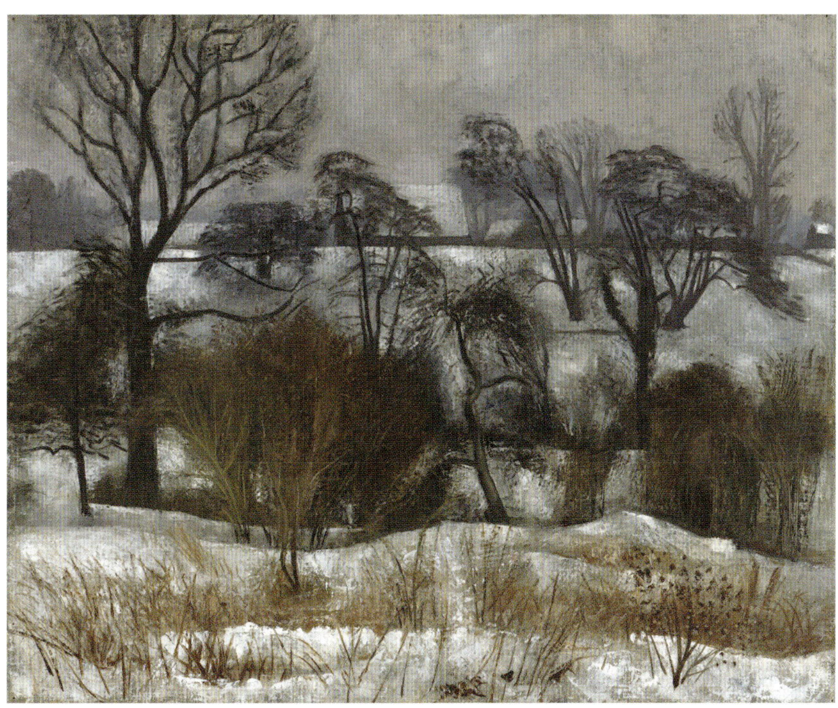

John Aldridge (1905–1983)

Winter

1947 • oil on canvas • 510 x 610 mm

Gardens and gardening were two passionate interests of John Aldridge and were a recurring topic in his paintings. His friend the poet John Betjeman (1906–1984) whom he met when both were students at Oxford University in the 1920s described him as 'the gardener's artist'. Aldridge's move to the village of Great Bardfield in north west Essex and his purchase of 'Place House' in 1933 enabled him to develop his horticultural expertise and create a garden that became much admired. He was to remain in this flourishing artistic community initially collaborating with Edward Bawden (1903–1989), himself a knowledgeable gardener, on a series of wallpaper designs. Aldridge was also in contact with other keen artist plantsmen including near neighbours Cedric Morris (p. 60) and John Nash (p. 15).

The landscape and rural scenes close to Aldridge's home featured in and inspired his work and he would often be seen working *en plein air* on his portable easel. The delicate and muted tones of *Winter* with its bare trees and heavy snow convey a sense of the bitter seasonal cold, conditions that no doubt favoured working in the warmth of his studio. During the year Aldridge, an accomplished draughtsman provided illustrations for *Adam was a Ploughman* by C. Henry Warren (1895–1966), the well-known author and broadcaster on the English countryside, the book largely based on rural Essex was dedicated 'To the Memory of Thomas Hennell, artist, poet, countryman'.

A number of highly popular selling exhibitions were held in Great Bardfield in the mid-1950s when summer visitors flocked to see modernist artworks in the homes of artists. 'Place House' with its extensive gardens together with Aldridge's somewhat conservative oil paintings and rugs knitted by his first wife Lucie were a particular draw. He told the reporter Nevile Wallis from *The Observer* that 'people seem to prefer this domestic informality to galleries'.[1] **GC**

1. Aldridge quoted in *The Observer*, 17 July 1955, p. 6

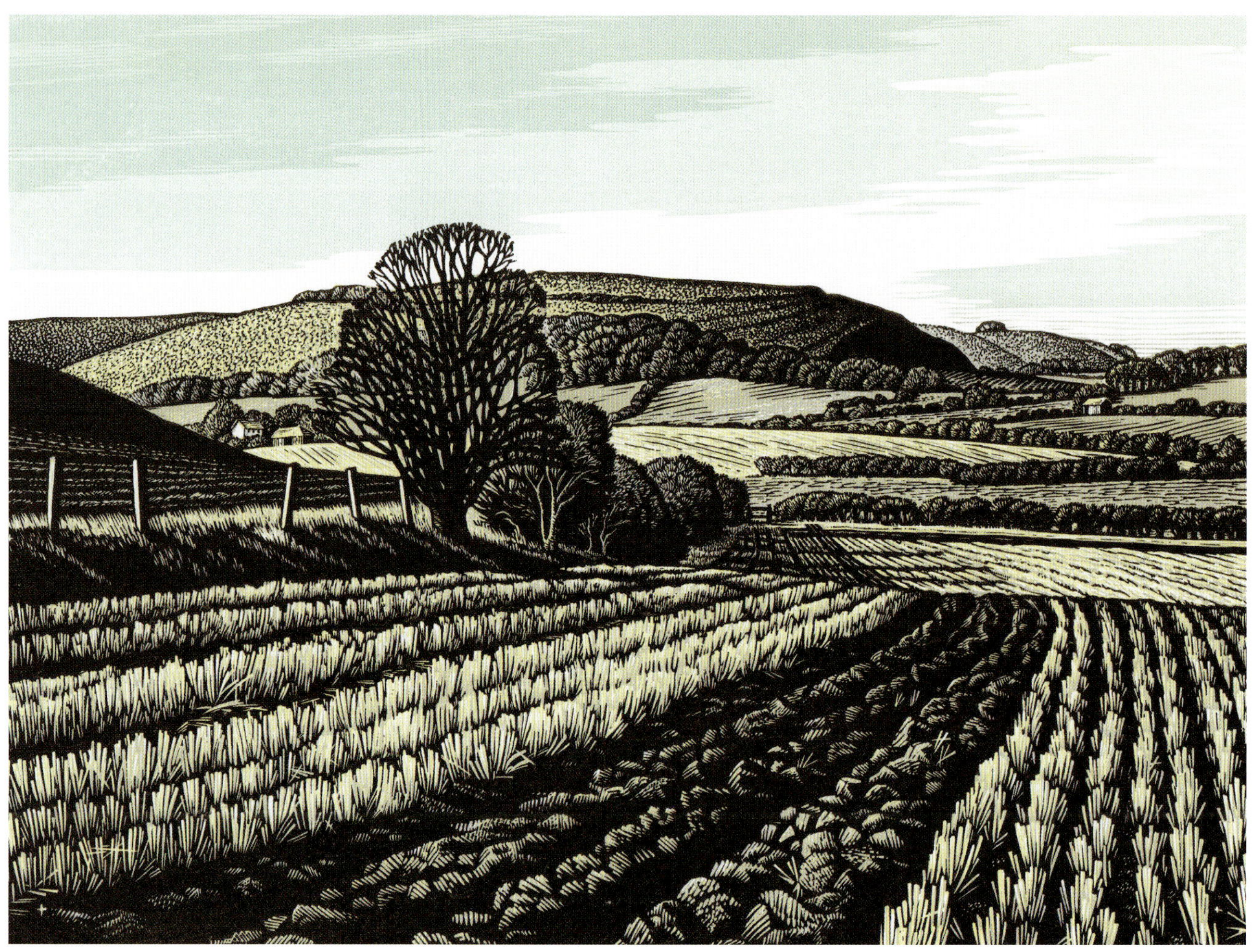

Howard Phipps (b. 1954)

Winter Stubble Fields

2004 · linocut · 230 x 300 mm

collection of the artist · image © the artist

Winkelbury is a massive Iron Age promontory hill fort that thrusts out from a chalk ridge on the edge of Cranborne Chase in Wiltshire. The distant hill is Win Green, with its distinctive clump of beech trees. It is one of the highest points in this area which has been a rich source of inspiration for me over a number of years. The downs here are particularly dramatic with steep-sided coombes which have precluded intensive agriculture, and consequently reminders of remote human history are still apparent.

The hill fort is observed here from the head of the Ebble Valley, and the first springs that develop into the Ebble chalk stream rise in the lower fields in winter. Working on location on a winter morning I made a watercolour study, from which I developed this linocut. I liked the shapes and patterns within the stubble fields, in addition they made for a contrast with the timeless, rounded form of the hill fort defined by the low winter light, just picking out the ramparts. The hedgerow and first marks of the plough through the pale stubble serve to take the viewer's eye into the picture. I have drawn in these fields on a number of occasions and subsequently made a wood engraving of this landscape from a different vantage point in autumn.

The linocut was printed, using an Albion hand press, from three separately cut blocks: a key block for the black (and the upper most part of the sky colour), and a further three colours from the two other blocks, parts of each colour are super-imposed one on another at the printing stage. The key block is printed last.

Howard Phipps

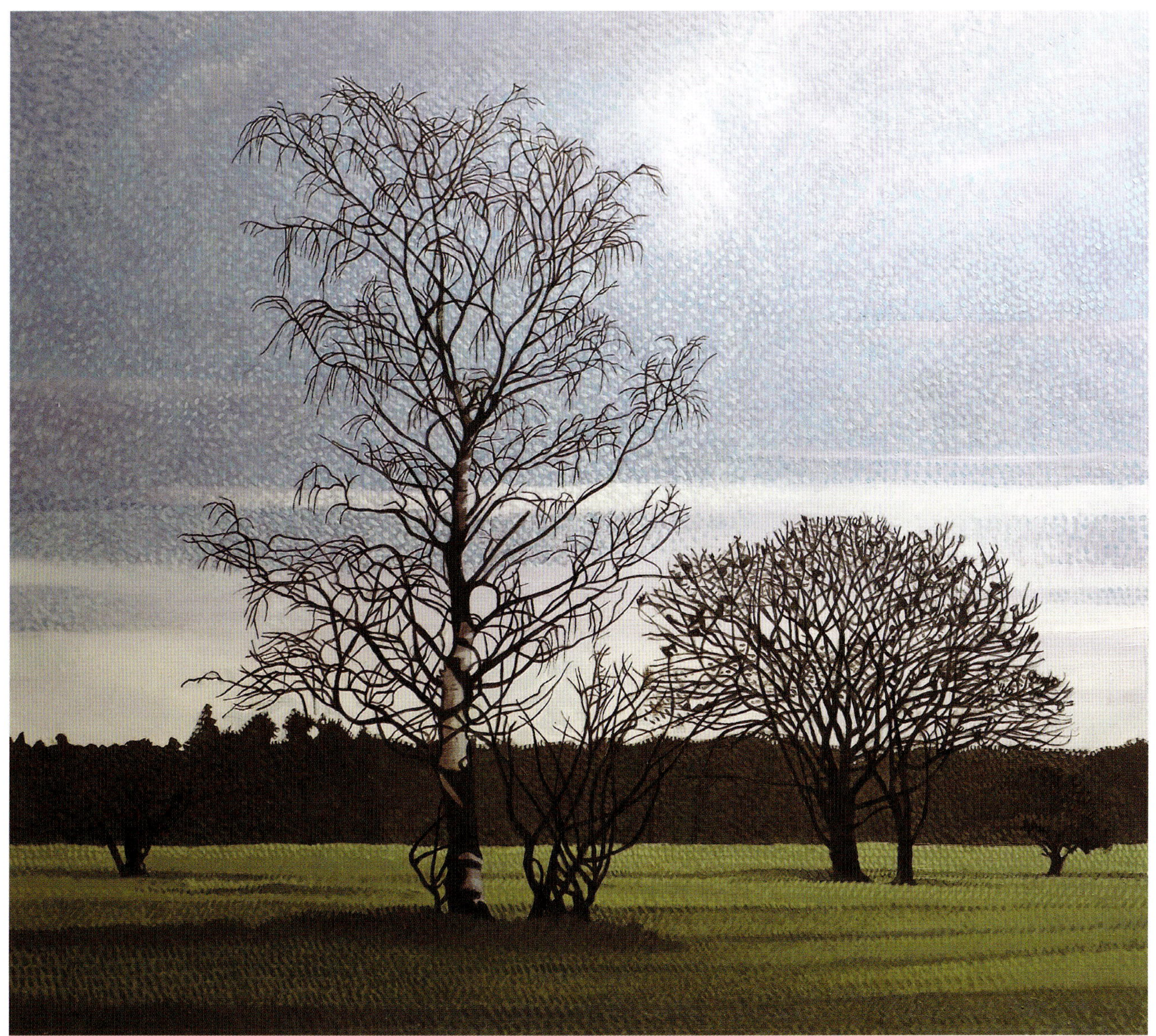

Annie Ovenden (b. 1945)

Clearing in the New Forest

oil on board · 457 x 508 mm

collection of the artist · image © the artist

Driving home yesterday I noticed little yellow dots appearing in the hedgerows. Exciting! The primroses are waking from their winter sleep. Spring is on its way.

Subtle, slow changes to start with, sometimes barely noticeable but as the days grow into weeks, as stormy short days turn long and sunny my artist's palette requires subtle changes too.

For example in winter the sun sits low in the sky casting long shadows, defining contours, hills and valleys needing more ultramarine, alizarin and burnt umber than green. The trees etch their bare branch patterns against the skyline's varying tones of greys. **Annie Ovenden**

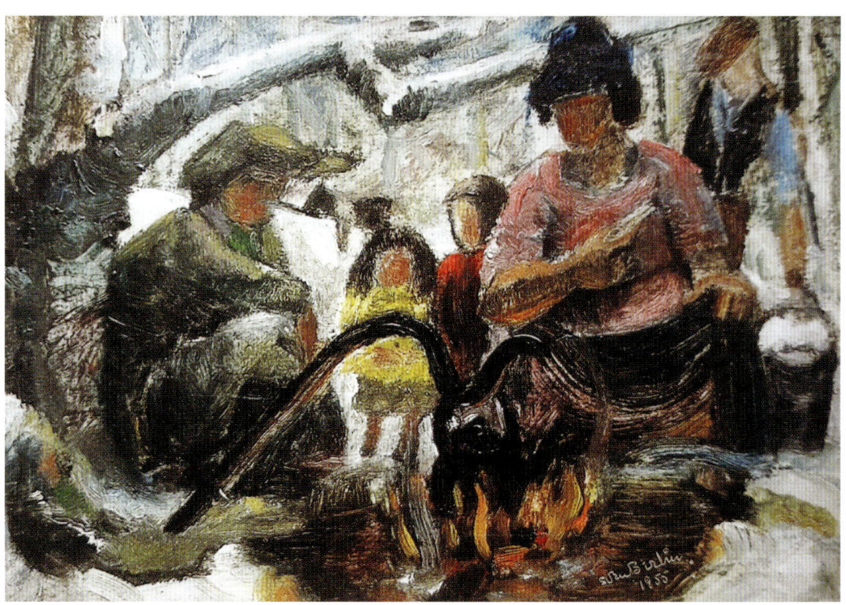

Sven Berlin (1911–1999)

Gypsies in the Snow

1955 · oil on canvas · 255 x 345 mm

private collection · image © The Estate of Sven Berlin

Tired of the increasingly acrimonious divisions between the abstract and figurative artists in St Ives, Sven Berlin and his wife Juanita (1925–2012) left Cornwall for the New Forest in 1953. After an arduous two-month journey in a Gypsy wagon they camped near Minstead just as winter was arriving. With little money, battling illness and nursing a sick child it was a harsh introduction to the itinerant life. However, their saving grace was the support of the local Gypsy community, who showed them how to survive, let them join flower and peg selling expeditions and even paid them to decorate wagons and make signs.[1] As a teenager Berlin had been spellbound by an encounter with a New Forest Gypsy and he now returned to the compound at Shave Green in which Gypsies who would not accept council housing were forced to live. Berlin was accepted to a remarkable degree and was given un-usual freedom to draw and paint them. His portraits of their lives under the trees in the 'green cathedral' of the New Forest is a remarkable record of a dying way of life.

Many of Berlin's paintings of Shave Green are marked by the green, aqueous light created by the canopy of beech and oak leaves. Life there in summer might seem idyllic but the winters were hard as the Gypsies were forbidden to create any structure with walls or floor and so lived in tents and wagons. This painting shows a group gathered around an open fire, a kettle warming over the flames. In his memoir of these years *Dromengro: Man of the Road* Berlin wrote: 'I had seen them here in the snow ... when each figure of man or woman or child stood out as in a Lowry painting, the colours iridescent, the flames of the fires burning bright orange'.[2] **SM**

1. Juanita Casey (2003), *Life with Sven: The Wagon Years* in *Sven Berlin: Paintings from Shave Green 1953–1970*, St Barbe Museum and Art Gallery, p. 13
2. Berlin, S. (1971), *Dromengro: Man of the Road*, Collins, p. 114

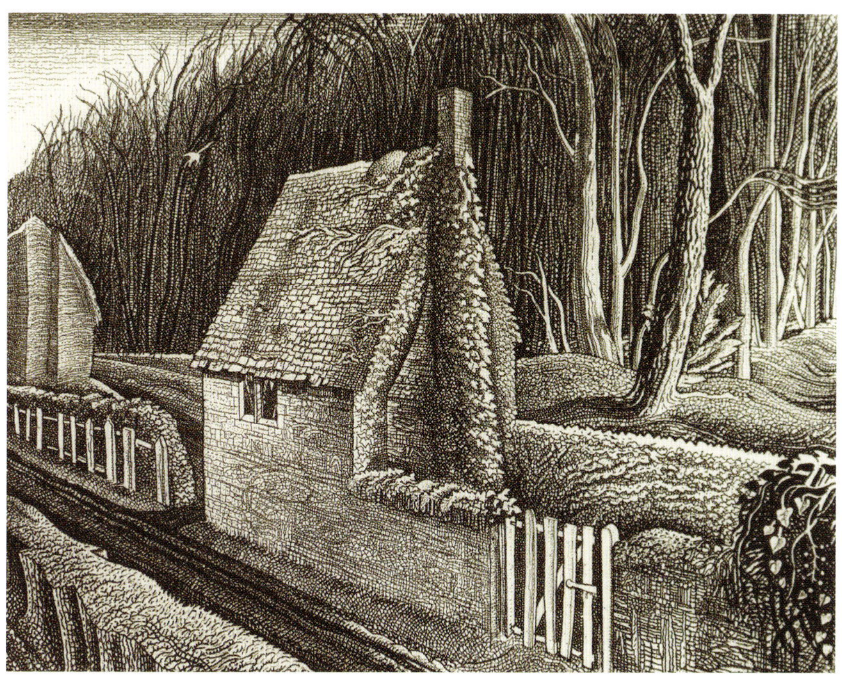

Graham Sutherland
(1903–1980)

Cottage in Dorset, Wood End

1929 · etching · 117 x 125 mm

Landscape and the effects of time and weather were significant themes in the work of Graham Sutherland. *Cottage in Dorset, Wood End* draws on elements of these while offering glimpses of his later more distinctive style as he moved away from the pastoral tradition of earlier etchings such as *Cray Fields* (p. 75) to establish his own visual landscape. This evolving approach is evidenced in the shape and movement of the row of trees as they wave their bare unnaturally twisted boughs in the chill winter wind. Sutherland evokes a sense of unease, as a solitary stylised bird flies across the dreary landscape. This is no cosy cottage in the woods with smoke rising gently, the scene is devoid of life save ivy rambling up the chimney. It was for Sutherland a time of loss – his only son died in July 1929 aged just three months.

Cottage in Dorset, Wood End was made shortly before he more or less abandoned the medium in 1930, owing to the collapse of the market for contemporary etchings in England. Sutherland turned instead to painting and poster design for Shell-Mex and London Underground, finding inspiration in the mid-thirties and intermittently throughout his life from the wild and dramatic landscape of Pembrokeshire in west Wales.

Sutherland's enduring interest in the links between art and nature were explored in the last decade of his life when he returned to printmaking. Between October 1976 and May 1977, he made a close study of the mysterious lifecycle of bees and detailed the processes of growth and change in the hive through a series of aquatints of the world's most important pollinator of food crops. **GC**

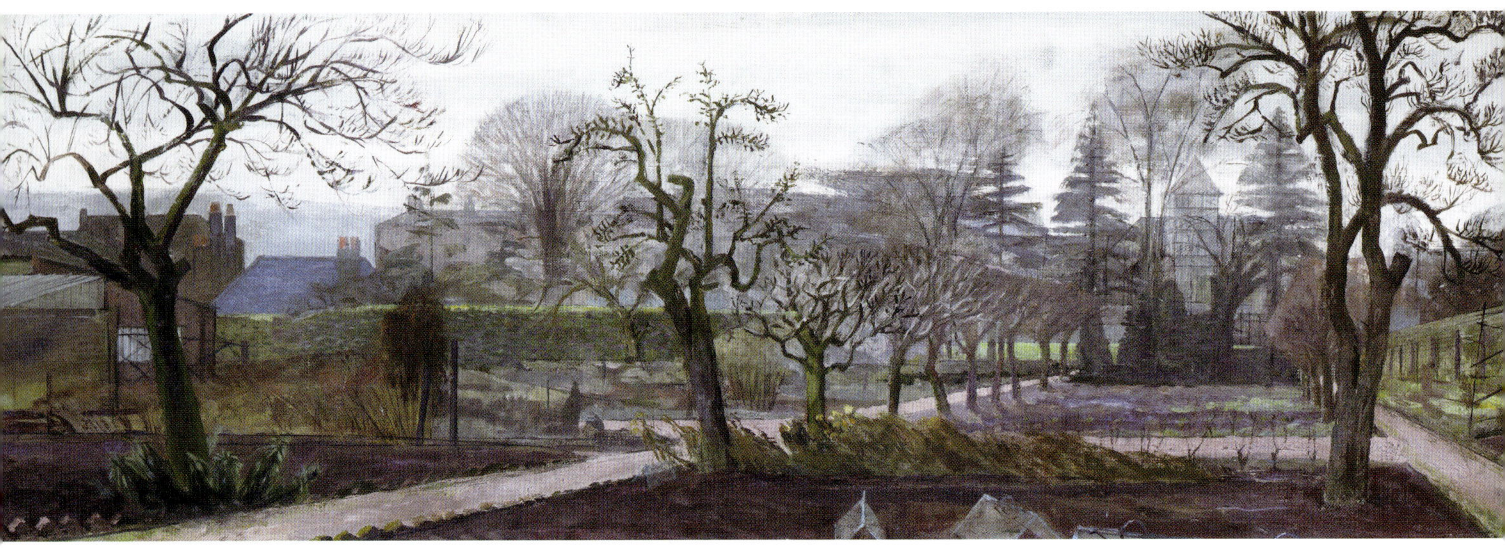

Evelyn Dunbar (1906–1960)

Winter Garden

1929–37 · oil on canvas · 305 x 914 mm

Tate · photograph © Tate

The inspiration for much of Evelyn Dunbar's early work lay in her devotion to nature and the natural world, and in particular the garden, which was deeply rooted in her affection for the Kentish landscape.[1] Dunbar's great interest in plants and flowers and her understanding of their various stages of development and the impact of the season is much in evidence in *Winter Garden*.

Dunbar worked intermittently on *Winter Garden* for some eight years, commencing in the late 1920s before she went to London as a student, finally completing it in 1937. The painting, with its complex composition, retains a freshness and vitality which is enhanced by the low tone to reflect the soft winter light. *Winter Garden* depicted the extensive Dunbar family garden at The Cedars, Strood, near Rochester in Kent. Its vagaries were well known to her and this personal connection enlivens the painting. The garden was both well planned and maintained, and designed with the different seasons in mind, and in spite of the enforced lethargy of winter there is feeling of ethereal beauty about the garden. As the light fades, the gardener can still look forward with confidence and optimism to the arrival of spring and the first bulbs breaking through the soil. **GC**

1. See *Evelyn Dunbar: War and Country* and in particular the chapter 'Country and Garden Life Illustrated: An Intimate Relationship' where I explored Dunbar's interests in gardens and gardening. I remain indebted to the late Dr John Sansom for his enthusiasm in publishing this first biography in 2006 and to St Barbe Museum and Art Gallery for hosting the Dunbar retrospective exhibition I guest curated in the same year.

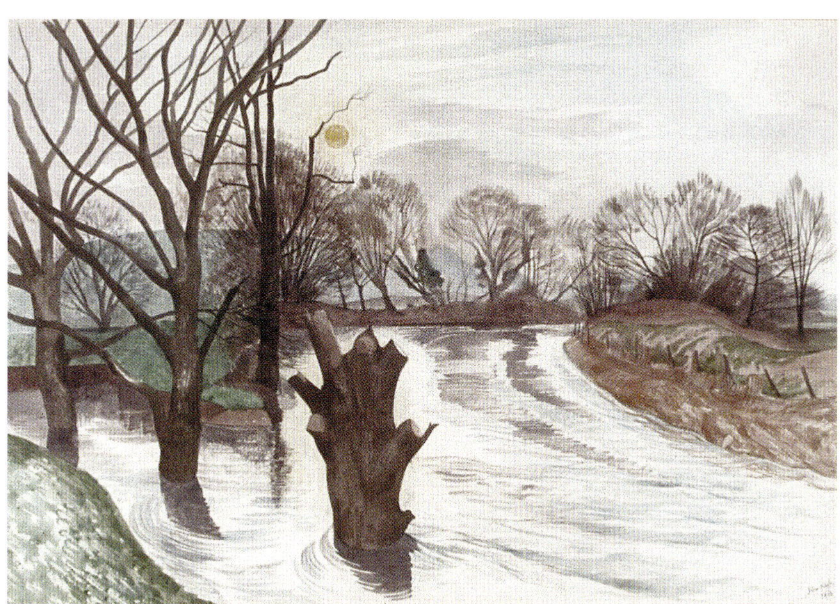

John Nash (1893–1977)

Flood at Wormingford

1960 · watercolour

UK Government Art Collection · image © Crown
Copyright: UK Government Art Collection

Although John Nash settled at Wormingford in 1944 he had initially discovered the area just after the First World War, returning again in the early 1920s and renting a bungalow at Wormingford Mill in 1929. East Anglia made a lasting impression which he explained to the author and Tate Gallery Director John Rothenstein (1901–1992): 'Compared with the west it's more brilliant in atmosphere, and it's subtler, less obviously dramatic'.[1] The British countryside was Nash's primary subject matter throughout his life and his paintings express a strong connection and love of this world. His preference for the subtle and less dramatic makes his work no less engaging, indeed he found poetry in subjects that, apparently mundane and ordinary, might have been passed over by another artist. He would immerse himself in familiar settings and tease out the details that appealed to him: 'Half a haystack interests me now just as much as a wide stretch of country'.[2] Knowing the landscape so well Nash was also able to appreciate and capture its changing character across the seasons.

Flood at Wormingford was painted in the winter of 1960 when East Anglia and other parts of the country had been hit by severe flooding, with roads turned into rivers and houses inundated with water. Here the worst of the weather seems to have passed and weak sunlight returns. Nash had a particular interest in water: rivers, streams, ditches, canals, quaysides and ponds of all shapes and sizes are recurring features in his work. The transformation of a nearby landscape into a lake must have been a welcome diversion during one of the wettest years on record. Nash's interest in the shapes of bare trees and the play of the wintry light on the floodwaters evokes a typically calm and reflective scene. **SM**

1. Rothenstein, Sir John (1983), *John Nash*, Macdonald & Co., pp. 72–3
2. Rothenstein, Sir John (1956), *Modern Painters: Lewis to Moore*, Eyre & Spottswoode, p. 243

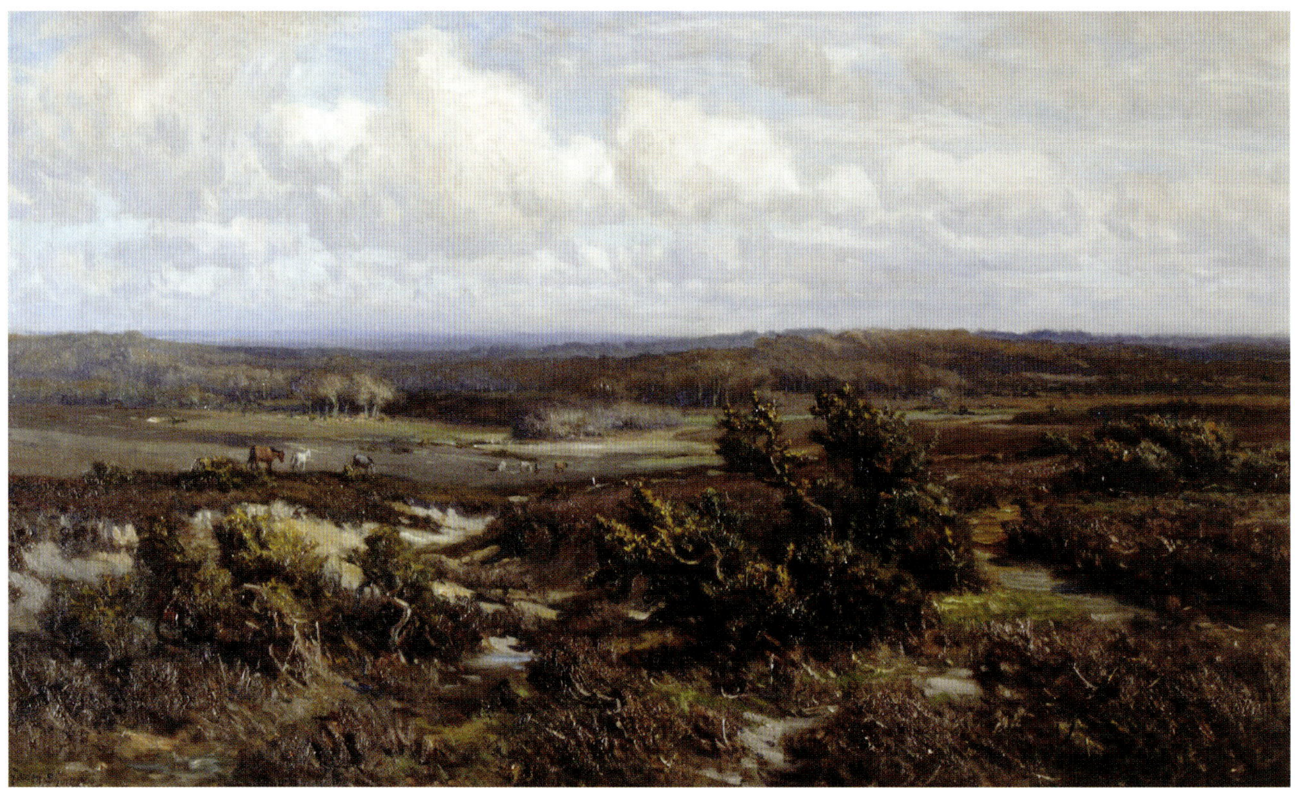

Frederick Golden Short
(1863–1936)

New Forest

1900 • oil on canvas • 470 x 762 mm

Southampton City Art Gallery • image
© Southampton City Art Gallery/Bridgeman Images

Short was born at Lyndhurst and studied at Southampton Art School. Although he made painting expeditions to Devon and Cornwall the vast majority of his work was based around his New Forest home. Outside of this area he is mainly known through the illustrations he provided for Francis George Heath's books *Autumnal Leaves* (1881), a walking tour of parts of the New Forest, and *Sylvan Winter* (1886). In the latter Heath praised Short for 'a touch which no mere art-training could give'.[1] Certainly Short knew the Forest and its trees as well as anyone and was a familiar local figure cycling with his paints and easel strapped to his back in search of fresh subjects. He never tired of its heaths and glades, capturing their changing character across the seasons.

This painting is among Short's larger and more impressive works and reflects his unparalleled ability to capture the colours of the New Forest in varying qualities of light. Here the purple heather blooms of summer are long gone and the ponies move across a landscape of browns and ochres and yet Short conveys the spirit of warmth and optimism that a clear bright day towards the end of winter can bring. Patches of sunlight slipping between the passing clouds highlight a distant stand of trees and catch the first new flowers on the gorse bushes, while the blue sky is reflected in scattered puddles. **SM**

1. Heath, F.G. (1886), *Sylvan Winter*, K.P. Trench, p. ix

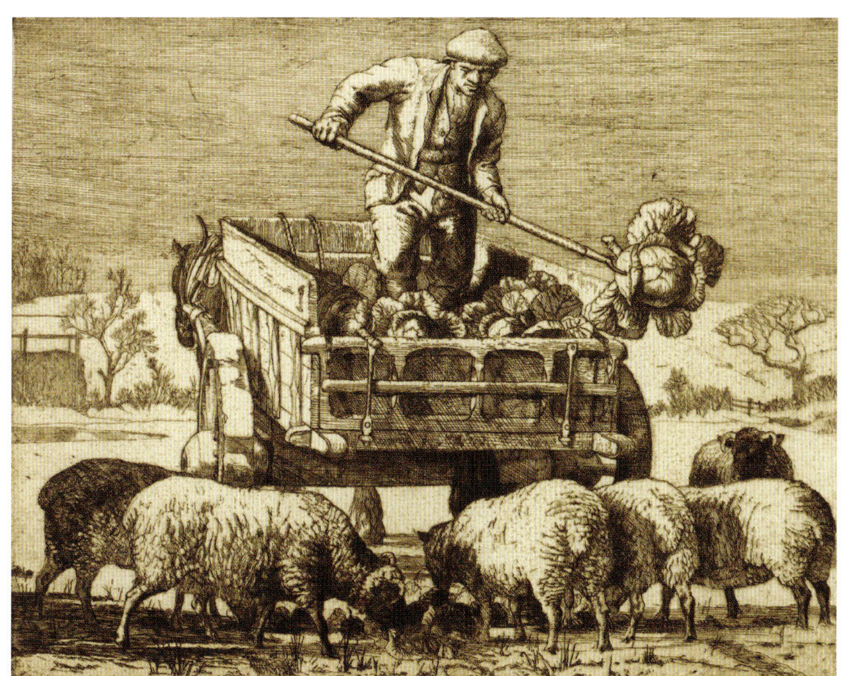

Charles Tunnicliffe
(1901–1979)

A Hard Winter

1928 · etching · 227 x 277 mm

Stuart Southall Collection · image reproduced by
kind permission of The Estate of C.F. Tunnicliffe

Although Tunnicliffe's work as an illustrator is well known, the watercolours
he submitted each year for the Royal Academy's Summer Exhibition and the
etchings and wood engravings he produced as works of art in their own right are
less familiar. Tunnicliffe attended the Macclesfield School of Art in Cheshire aged
just fourteen, later winning a scholarship to the Royal College of Art in London.
After graduating in 1924 he was encouraged to stay on to study printmaking, his
aptitude brought some success in the last days of the etching boom before the
market for prints vanished during the Great Depression. Tunnicliffe's family ran a
farm at Sutton Lane Ends near Macclesfield and this was his day to day experience
from birth until he left for London nineteen years later. Although he decided to
become an artist rather than continue the family business he retained a fascination
for agricultural work and it provided the subject matter for many of his prints and
book illustrations.

In *My Country Book* Tunnicliffe explains that while these formative years did not
make him an artist they shaped his interests because they were: 'spent in the heart
of the country, in close contact with animals and birds, with farms and farmers
and their ways of life, and all the thousand and one jobs which a farmer has to do'.[1]
His intimate understanding of the countryside and the activity that unfolded there
across the seasons is reflected in his convincing depictions of agricultural work.
Tunnicliffe was certainly not sentimental, some etchings present an unflinching
record of slaughtering a pig, but his affection for the ordinary tasks of farming
shines through in this scene of cabbages being fed to hungry sheep while snow
covers the grass. **SM**

1. Tunnicliffe, C.F. (1942), *My Country Book*, The Studio, p. 7

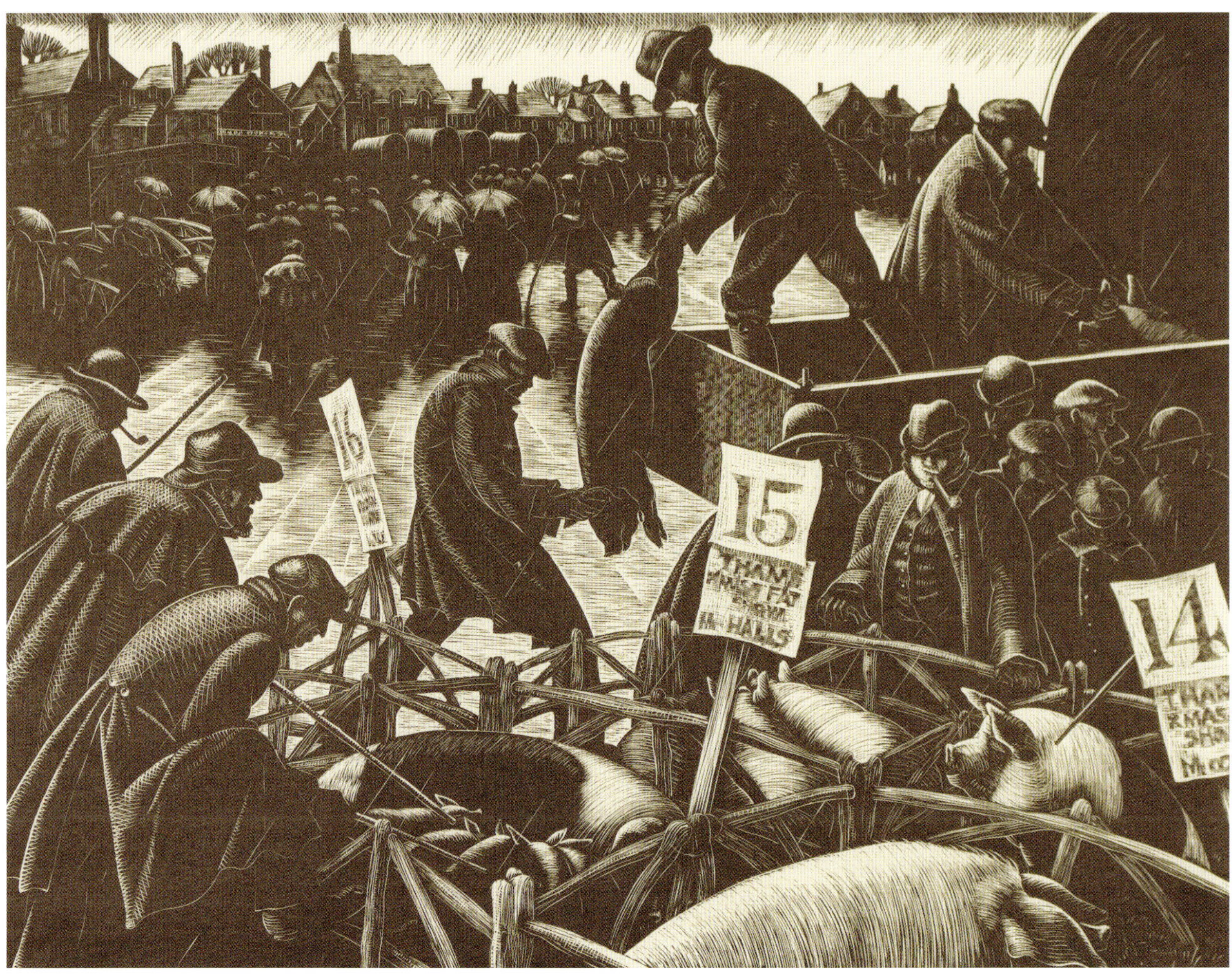

Clare Leighton (1898–1989)

December

1933 • wood engraving • 204 x 262 mm
from *The Farmer's Year*

Stuart Southall Collection • Clare Leighton's
wood engravings are reproduced courtesy
of the artist's estate

Clare Leighton studied at Brighton College of Art and the Slade School of Fine
Art before learning wood engraving with Noel Rooke at the Central School of Arts
and Crafts. She became one of the most prolific and successful book illustrators
of her day, happy to work with commercial publishers rather than private presses
so that her work was available to a far wider audience. Her affinity for nature and
rural life made Leighton an ideal candidate for her first major commission to
illustrate Thomas Hardy's *Return of the Native* (published in Britain and America
in 1929). Her most notable publications were those she wrote and illustrated including *The Farmer's Year* (1933), an unsentimental look at life on the land, *Four
Hedges* (1935), the story of a year in her garden, and *Country Matters* (1937),
where she looked at the lives of her neighbours in the Chiltern countryside.

The Farmer's Year: A Calendar of English Husbandry was a labour of love that
featured a large scale engraving for each month with a facing text and decorated
initial letter. The book proved extremely popular, running to three English editions
and an American one in just three months.[1] *December – The Fat Stock Market*
is the last chapter and engraving in the book, but appears first in our seasonal
sequence. In her text Leighton explains how the farming community had been
up before dawn to prepare their vehicles and animals for market and describes
the chaos created by escaped pigs and cows. The seriousness with which the
foreground figures study the livestock confirms the importance of this pre-
Christmas sale to the local farmers. A handful of incredibly fine lines suggest
the rain for which capes have been donned and umbrellas opened. **SM**

1. Selborne, J. (1998), *British Wood-Engraved Book Illustration 1904–1940: A Break with Tradition*,
The British Library/Oak Knoll Press, p. 378, n. 32

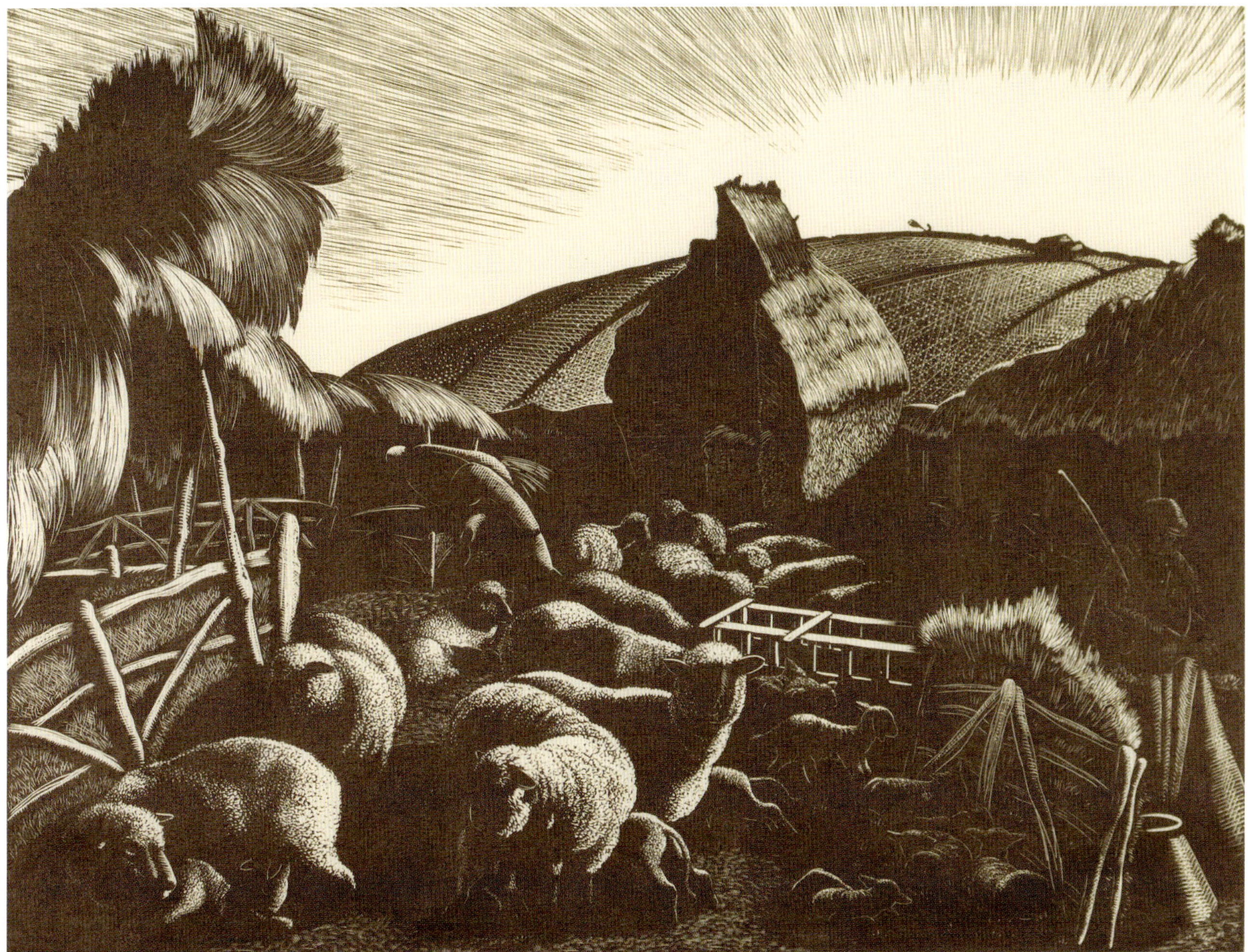

Clare Leighton (1898–1989)

January

1933 • wood engraving • 204 x 266 mm
from *The Farmer's Year*

One of the key features of Leighton's engravings are the large areas of black with thin, faint lines used to suggest form. It was therefore vital that the inking of the blocks was not heavy-handed or all these subtle details would be lost, something that Leighton quickly realised as she began working with a variety of publishers and printers. Happily her work with Collins on *The Farmer's Year* delivered the necessary subtlety. The technique is used in this print to contrast the deep shadows in the sheep pen against the glare of the sun rising over the distant hill. Just a few marks suggest the shepherd, ewes and lambs emerging from the gloom as dawn breaks over a peaceful scene of early lambing:

> *It was weather such as this that was making the shepherd so serene. The few hours of pale winter sunshine stroked the backs of the weighty sheep and gilded the straw of the rick that was in the lambing pen to be cut for bedding.*[1]

SM

1. Leighton, C. (1933/2012), *The Farmer's Year: A Calendar of English Husbandry*, Little Toller Books, p. 8

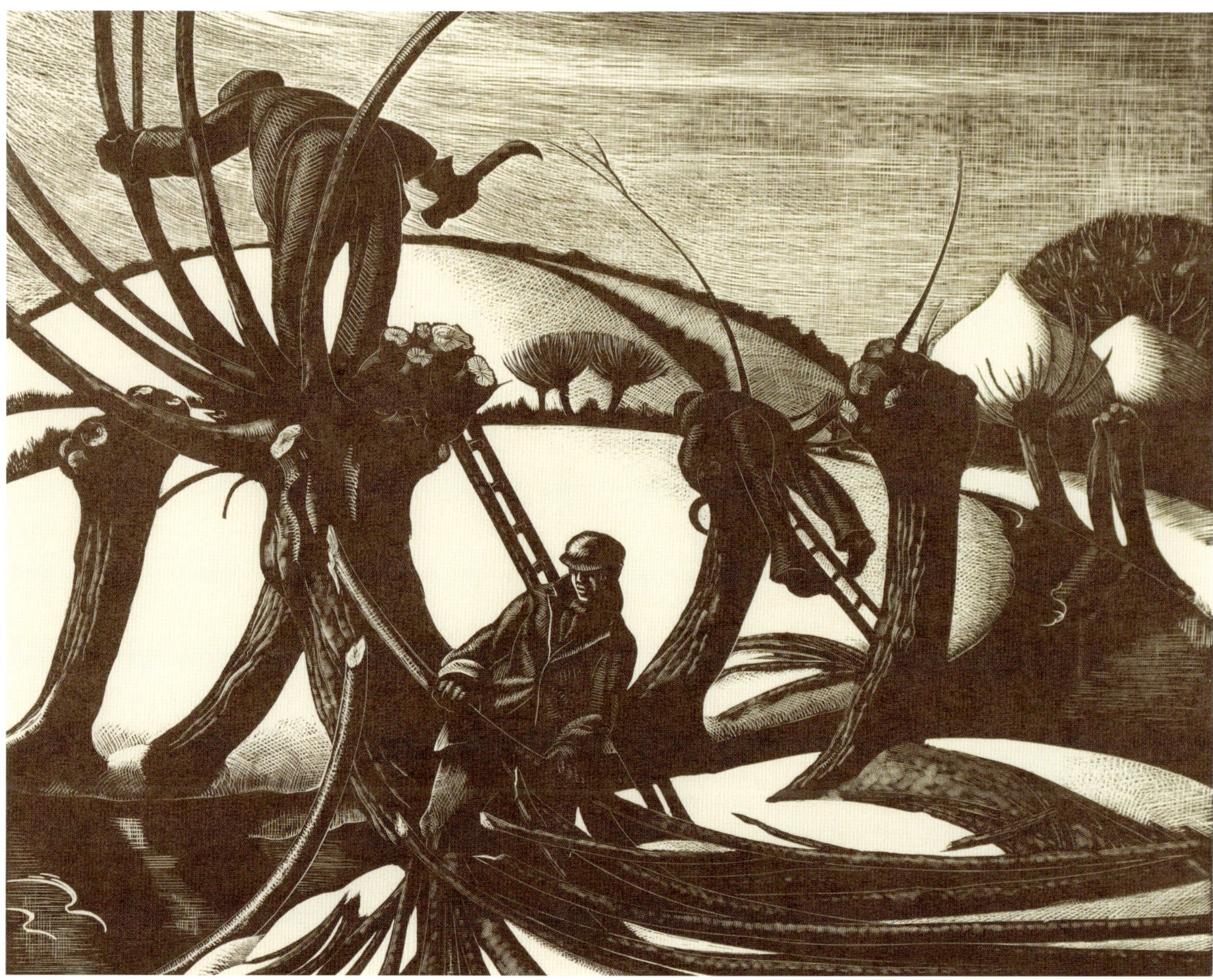

Clare Leighton (1898–1989)

February

1933 • wood engraving • 203 x 253 mm
from *The Farmer's Year*

Stuart Southall Collection • Clare Leighton's
wood engravings are reproduced courtesy
of the artist's estate

Lopping, the engraving for February in Leighton's *The Farmer's Year* is perhaps the most striking of the set. The snow-covered landscape gives Leighton an opportunity for strong contrasts with the areas of unembellished black and the arcs of the willow branches. As Leighton explains:

> *Hedging and ditching, lopping and clearing: these are February's work, for they can be done in frost and cold, when the blade of the plough would fail to turn the hard, resisting earth, and the litter lies frozen to the farmyard, so that it cannot be carted into the fields.*[1]

The pollarded willows, growing beside a now frozen millstream, are gradually reduced to bulbous stumps, but they will sprout again in spring, providing another crop of poles in a few years' time. The lopped branches will be used to make hurdles for the sheepfolds, the men work steadily with their bill hooks, the sounds echoing across the frozen fields. **SM**

1. Leighton, C. (1933/2012), *The Farmer's Year: A Calendar of English Husbandry*, Little Toller Books, p. 8

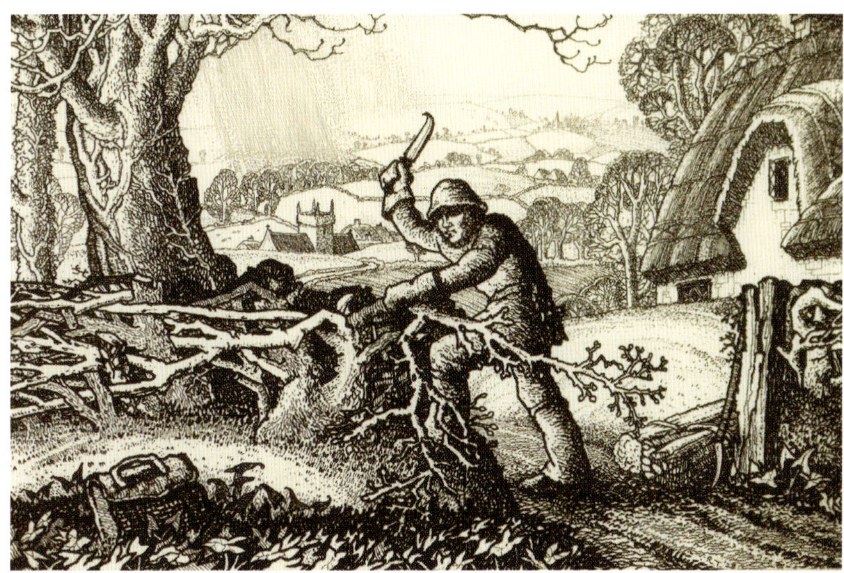

Robin Tanner (1904–1988)

Wiltshire Hedger

1928 • etching • 100 x 149 mm

Stuart Southall Collection
image © The Estate of Robin Tanner

After leaving school in Chippenham, Robin Tanner considered ways to fulfil his dual ambition of becoming an artist and a teacher. In 1922 he began a teacher training course at Goldsmiths' College in London, spending his Saturdays visiting galleries or haunting the print room at the Victoria & Albert Museum. During this time he also discovered the etchings of F.L. Griggs (1876–1938): 'the marvellous realisation of stone and water, foliage and sky, and the intense feeling for Cotswold England bowled me over'.[1] After taking up his first teaching post he started evening classes at Goldsmiths' School of Art where he studied life drawing with Clive Gardiner and etching with Stanley Anderson. His artistic development was greatly influenced by experiencing the 1926 exhibition of Samuel Palmer's work at the V&A. Palmer's idyllic vision of the Kent countryside also inspired another group of Goldsmiths' student etchers including Graham Sutherland and Paul Drury. Having absorbed these influences Tanner developed his own re-imaginings of rural Wiltshire, but one that was based on an intimate knowledge of a vanishing landscape and way of life.

Tanner produced his first etching, a barn interior, in 1926. Two years later *Wiltshire Hedger* became his seventh plate. It was intended as part of a series on rural labours along with *Wiltshire Roadmaker* (1928) and *Wiltshire Woodman* (1929). In the end only these three plates were completed. Tanner felt the first two had been rushed because of pressure from his publisher and vowed to take more time in future.[2] He based the setting on landscapes around Weavern and Slaughterford where he had watched a hedger at work.[3] Hedging was a job for winter when other tasks on the farm were impossible and here upright shoots are being partially cut with a bill hook and then woven into a stout framework from the hedge would regrow. **SM**

1. Tanner, R. (1987), *Double Harness*, Impact Books, 1990 edition, p. 31
2. Ibid., p. 46
3. Garton, R. (1988), *Robin Tanner: The Etchings*, Garton & Co., p. 25

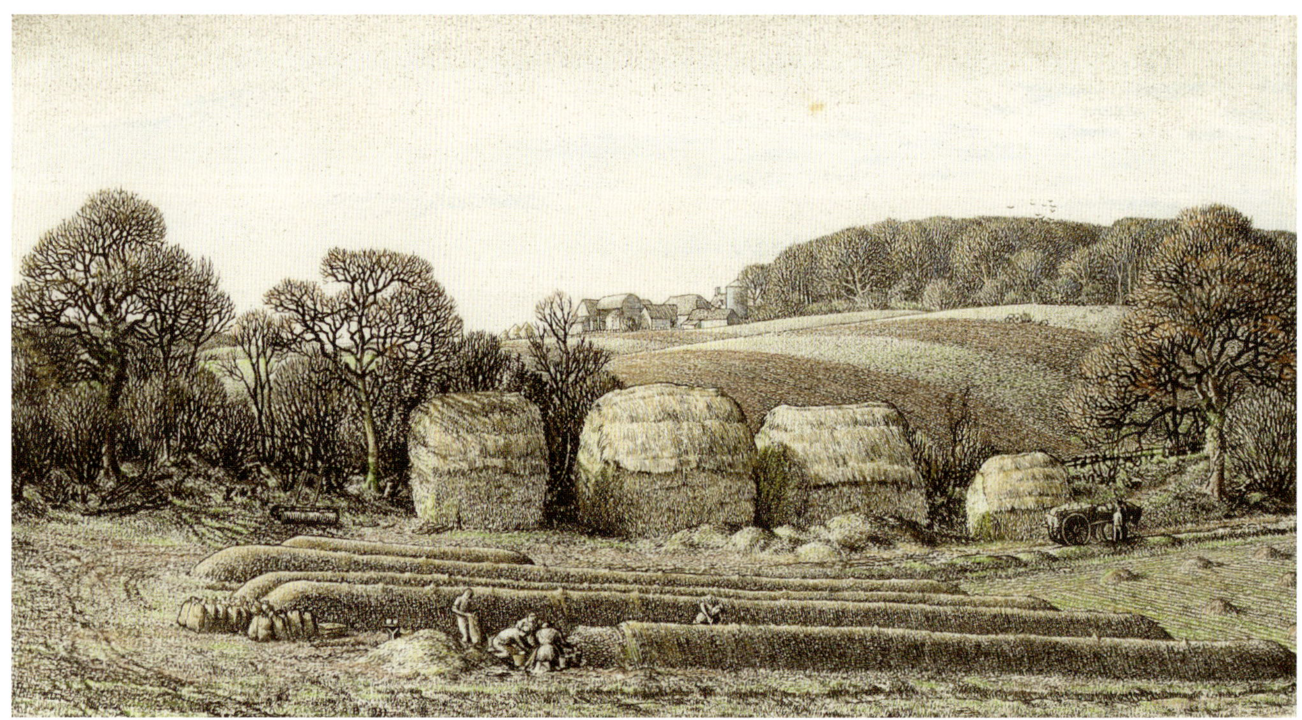

Stanley Badmin (1906–1989)

Potato Clamps

1931 · hand-coloured etching
100 x 180 mm

Stuart Southall Collection
image © The Estate of S.R. Badmin

Stanley Badmin won a scholarship to Camberwell School of Art in 1922 and in 1924 moved to the Royal College of Art. He studied drawing with Randolph Schwabe, a 'fantastic draughtsman and a wonderful illustrator'.[1] The admiration was returned, Schwabe recording in a diary entry for 1931: 'I was much struck by some of Badmin's work and assume a little credit to myself for having directed his beginnings at the Camberwell School and the RCA.'[2] On leaving education he was able to capitalise on the last years of the etchings boom and also began exhibiting at the Royal Academy and Royal Watercolour Society to good reviews. During the Second World War he contributed to the *Recording Britain* scheme, making drawings of places at risk from development, decay or enemy action in Suffolk and Northamptonshire. He was later called up and served with the RAF, making models of the French coast that were used for the Dieppe Raid and D-Day landings.[3]

Badmin reached his widest audience as a commercial artist and illustrator working on children's books such as *Village and Town* (1939), *Trees in Britain* (1942) and *Farm Crops in Britain* (1955) for Puffin and a variety of commissions from Ladybird, Odhams Press, Shell and The Reader's Digest. Many of these publications focused on the countryside, nature and farming, clearly subjects for which Badmin had a great sympathy. This coloured etching shows potatoes being retrieved from a clamp: they are sorted, sacked and then carted away. The clamp needed well-drained soil so the potatoes would not rot. The base was covered with a layer of dry straw and the potatoes piled on top forming a long ridge with a triangular section. This was covered with more straw and then soil. Badmin took great care to depict the ventilation holes appearing at intervals along the clamp: 'You can see the straw ventilation going up, covered with earth, like little chimneys'.[4] Protected from frost and damp in this way the potato harvest could last through the winter. **SM**

1. Beetles, C. (1985), *S.R. Badmin and the English Landscape*, Collins, p. 14
2. Clarke, G. (ed.) (2016), *The Diaries of Randolph Schwabe: British Art 1930–48*, Sansom & Company, p. 86
3. Beetles (1985), op. cit., p. 24
4. Beetles, C. (2015), *S.R. Badmin RWS: Paintings, Drawings and Prints*, Chris Beetles Ltd., p. 44

Charles Tunnicliffe (1901–1979)

Uncovering Mangold Roots

1959 · watercolour · 270 x 176 mm

Charles Frederick Tunnicliffe was Britain's most notable twentieth-century wildlife artist, his significance and stature reflected in his election as a Royal Academician in 1954. He was a prolific book illustrator, working on over eighty publications during a forty-year period. Tunnicliffe was also commissioned by companies such as Shell, ICI, Mackeson Stout and Harris Tweed to create artwork for products and advertising campaigns and illustrated several sets of Brooke Bond Tea collectible cards. As a result there can be few people living during the 1940s, 1950s and 1960s who did not come across his work, even if they never knew the artist responsible. For those interested in natural history or farming Tunnicliffe was a revered figure who also inspired a new generation's interest in the countryside through his work on the Ladybird *What to Look For* books, first published between 1959 and 1961.

What to Look for in Winter was the first of the series, its purpose being that:

> *Many people seem to think that there is nothing to see in the countryside during the cold, wet winter months, but this book is designed to show how very many things there are to interest you if you know what to look for – and where to look.*[1]

E.L. Grant Watson's text and Tunnicliffe's evocative watercolour illustrations celebrate the everyday wonder to be found on country walks, at the farm, by the seashore and in the garden. This illustration shows mangolds being retrieved from a clamp to feed the waiting cows but also includes carefully observed details such as the hovering kestrel and two fleeing mice in the bottom left corner. **SM**

1. Watson, G.L. (1959), *What to Look For in Winter*, Ladybird Books, frontispiece

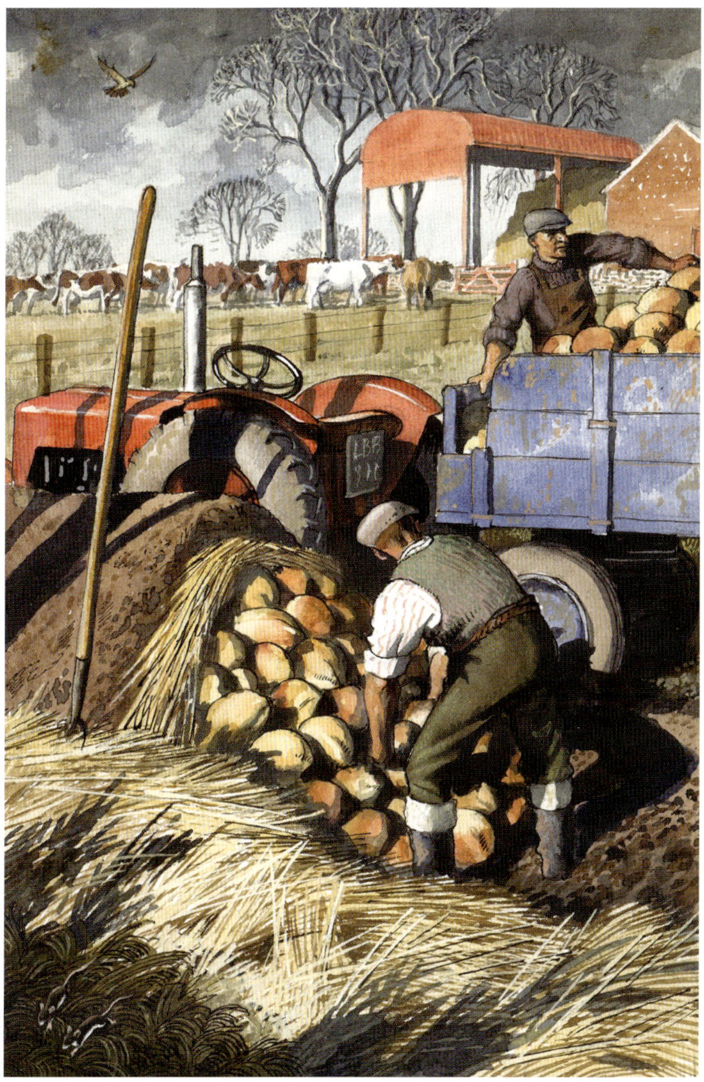

"

Gertrude Hermes (1901–1983)

Mistletoe

1930 · wood engraving · 230 x 134 mm

Stuart Southall Collection · image © The Estate of Gertrude Hermes

Gertrude Hermes was born in Bromley, Kent and from 1922 studied at Leon Underwood's Brook Green School of Painting and Sculpture in Hammersmith. There she met Blair Hughes-Stanton (1902–1981) whom she married in 1926. They were both to become key figures in the revival of British wood engraving between the wars. In January 1928 they were living in Hammersmith Terrace when the Thames burst its banks, flooding their basement flat, almost drowning Hughes-Stanton and destroying much of their work.[1] They decided to retreat to the country, moving to Hatcheston in Suffolk, where they rented a cottage with a large garden at the bottom of which flowed another river, the Ore. This was the inspiration for Hermes' wood engraving *Willows and Waterlilies* (1930) a tranquil evocation of summer on the river.[2] It was at Hatcheston during 1929 that she developed the illustrations for *A Florilege: Chosen from the Old Herbals* (written by Irene Gosse and published by the Swan Press in 1931), her most significant body of work at that time.

Mistletoe is one of twenty wood engravings Hermes created for *A Florilege*. As a group they are a remark-ably powerful set of botanical portraits, combining accurate detail with a dynamic use of abstract pattern and sharply contrasting darkness and light. Hermes' love of the natural world is reflected by the sketch-books she kept, crammed with studies of plants and animals. This first-hand knowledge underpins the deft cutting techniques used to convey the hairiness of borage, the sinuous twining of convulvulus or deli-cately drooping fritillaries. Each of these plants has its own beauty and flowering season but *Mistletoe*, which appears against a burst of light bringing all its associations of Christmas jollity and renewed fertility in the depths of winter, is perhaps the most arresting image of all. **SM**

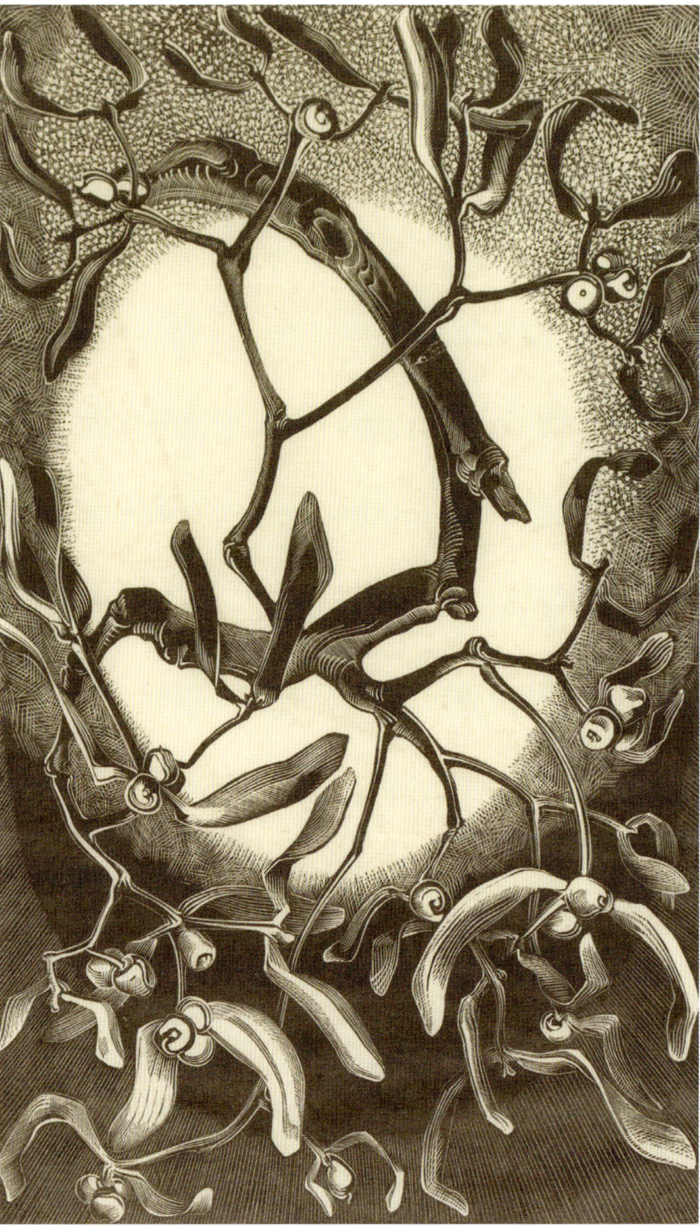

1. Katherine Eustace in *Underwood's Children* from *The Wood Engravings of Gertrude Hermes and Blair Hughes-Stanton*, Ashmolean Museum, Oxford, 1995, p. 15
2. Russell, J. (1993), *The Wood Engravings of Gertrude Hermes*, Scolar Press, p. 113

Robin Tanner (1904–1988)

Christmas

1929 · etching · 335 x 280 mm

Stuart Southall Collection · image © The Estate of Robin Tanner

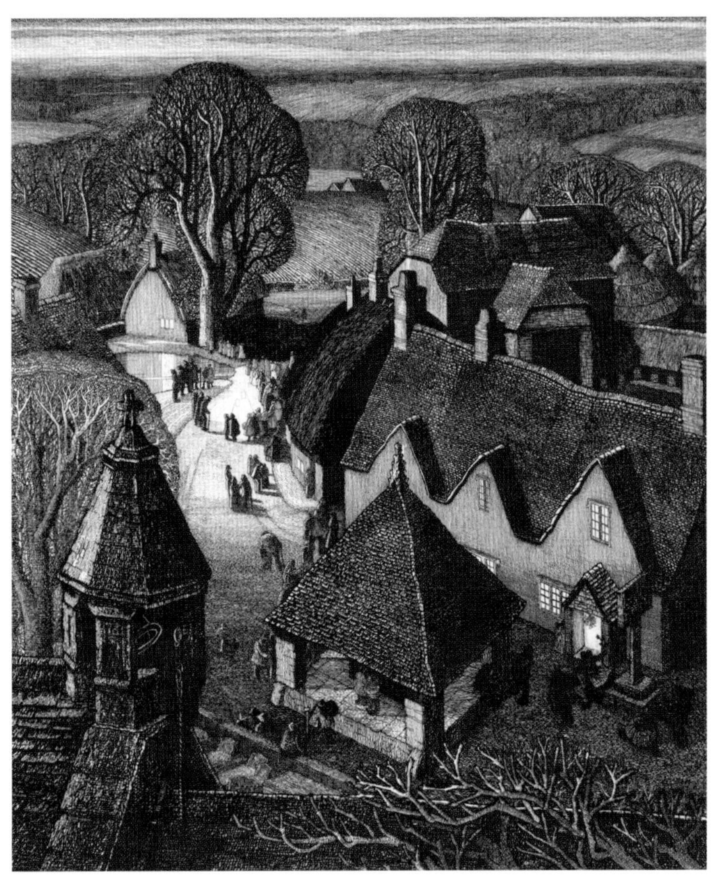

Robin Tanner's etched world was an ideal rural world in which he drew on scenes within a few miles of his home in north west Wiltshire although he had no interest in being topographically faithful. He explained in *The Etcher's Craft* (1980) that it is:

> *... a world of pastoral beauty that could be ours if we did but desire it passionately enough, instead of littering it with poles and wires, corrugated iron, pylons, and barbed wire. Worse still it is now proposed to pursue the lunatic course of poisoning it to eternity with nuclear power installations.*[1]

Christmas completed half a century earlier remains an enduring image of much that Tanner held dear throughout his life. Detailed studies were made at Biddestone of the bell turret, pond and thatched cottage, a few miles west of Chippenham where Tanner was living and where he later printed it. The tall Flemish buildings, barns, inn and market cross were sketched by moon-light, when he and Heather, whom he met when both were pupils at Chippenham Grammar School, walked to Castle Combe late one night. Tanner recalled how eerie it felt in the empty village hearing the sleeping villagers snoring and bedsprings creaking.

A sense of timelessness and anticipation of the festivities to come is evoked in *Christmas*. Children carry lanterns and gather round as the waits, who were local people who received money for their singing, commence. In *Wiltshire Village*[2] Heather Tanner commented on the old custom of waits (the sexton, teacher, mason and undertaker) singing on Christmas Eve at a market cross; one of her many astute observations of rural life in Kington Borel an imaginary community.

Christmas and *The Gamekeeper's Cottage* (1928) were Tanner's first works to be exhibited at the Royal Academy in 1929. At the so-called Varnishing Day when artists traditionally added the finishing touches to their work, Tanner met fellow etcher Frederick Griggs and was greatly encouraged by him. Griggs, a member of the hanging committee allowed him to replace his etching *Christmas* with a richer impression of it. In response to Griggs' interest Tanner explained that he was presently working on *Harvest Festival* (p. 95) and *Wiltshire Woodman*. **GC**

1. Tanner, R. (1980), *The Etcher's Craft*, Friends of Bristol Art Gallery, p. 18
2. They married in 1931, *Wiltshire Village* was first published in 1939, Robin provided sixty illustrations.

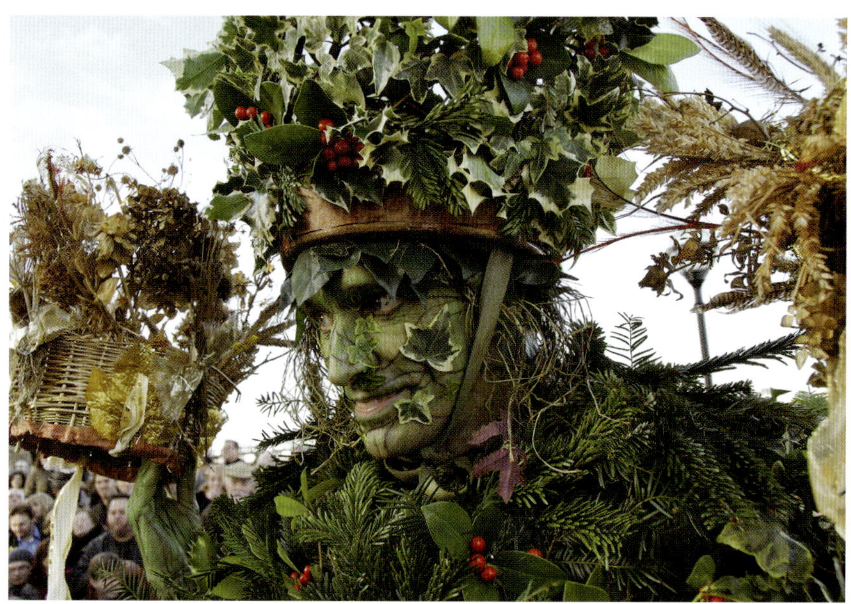

Sara Hannant (b. 1964)

The Holly Man,
Twelfth Night, Bankside

2007 · archival pigment print
280 x 400 mm

collection of the artist · image © Sara Hannant

On Twelfth Night – the end of Christmas festivities, also the day before a general return to the rigours of work known as Plough Monday – members of the The Lion's Part perform an ancient midwinter celebration with a contemporary twist. The Holly Man, who they describe as 'the Winter guise of the Green Man from our pub signs, Pagan myths and folklore', 'wassails' or toasts the people, the River Thames and Shakespeare's Globe. The Bankside Mummers then perform a St George Folk Combat play, featuring the Turkey Sniper, Clever Legs, and the Old 'Oss. At the end of the play, cakes are given to the crowd, those who find a bean and a pea hidden in their cakes are hailed King and Queen for the day and crowned with ceremony. They then lead the people through the streets culminating in drinking, dancing, singing and storytelling. **Sara Hannant**

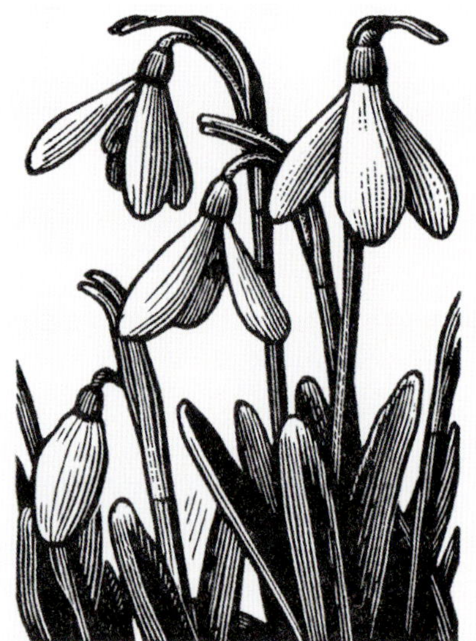

Howard Phipps (b. 1954)

Snowdrops

2004 · wood engraving · 50 x 35 mm

collection of the artist · image © the artist

In 1989 I was commissioned to engrave five vignettes as chapter headers for a book by Mirabel Osler on her Shropshire garden, including tulips – white against dark foliage. An ideal subject for the wood engraver given we start with a blackened rectangle of wood, and that each incision into the surface of the boxwood will appear as white in the final proof.

I have since then enjoyed making occasional very small vignettes such as a primrose bank, the pale flowers set against the dark of ivy and grasses. In *Snowdrops* however, despite them being white, I selected a ground level view, just simple shapes against the white of the paper, defined in the main by black line, which means carefully lowering the area all around and endeavouring not to bruise that black line.

Snowdrops are the first cheerful signs of spring, and are a common sight alongside the chalk rivers here in Wiltshire. **Howard Phipps**

SPRING

Along each hedge and sprouting bush
The singing birds are blest,
And linnet green and speckled thrush
Prepare their mossy nest;
On the warm bed thy plains supply,
The young lambs find repose,
And 'mid thy green hills basking lie
Like spots of ling'ring snows.

John Clare · The Shepherd's Calendar · 1827

The sap is rising, birds are singing, the days lengthen, the sun is warmer: it is time to throw off winter's torpor. The word 'spring' comes from the Old English 'springan' meaning to leap, spring up or grow. It is a season associated with new growth, fertility, rebirth. Astronomically speaking spring runs from the vernal equinox to the summer solstice. The equinox falls on 20 or 21 March and marks the day when hours of daylight and darkness are equal. British summertime traditionally begins at the end of March, but usually we take the spring months to be March, April and May. The timing of Easter with its focus on death and resurrection provided continuity with the pagan festival of Ēostre, which had been celebrated at the spring equinox to welcome new life emerging from the darkness of winter. Rogationtide which occurred forty days after Easter Sunday was a traditional time to bless fields, crops and livestock, this came to include beating the bounds; walking the parish boundary to perpetuate knowledge of its path and to call on divine protection. The pagan festival of Beltane fell on the first day of May and marked the beginning of summer, coming halfway between the spring equinox and the summer solstice. It involved lighting protective bonfires and decorating houses with flowers and greenery, a tradition which survived in 'maying' or 'bringing in the May'. Maypole dancing dates back to medieval times, although the interweaving ribbon dances we know today are a nineteenth-century creation (fig. 8). Both Maying and Maypole dancing were seen by Puritans as pagan rites and an excuse for lewdness and were banned during the Civil War.[1] Urban areas also developed their own May Day traditions: in London chimney sweeps dressed as Jack-in-the-Green would join in dances with milkmaids wearing elaborate headdresses made of silver plate, teapots and tankards (fig. 9). The survival or revival of such traditions was the subject for photographer Sara Hannant's project *Mummers, Maypoles and Milkmaids*.[2]

March provides the transition from winter into spring. This is reflected in the old saying 'March comes in like a lion and goes out like a lamb'. The beginning of the month can be rough and March is known for its cold winds, but temperatures rise triggering new growth of grass in pastures and lawns. A cold snap at this time was known as a blackthorn winter when the snowy blossom in the hedgerows might coincide with falls of the real thing. In her painting *Spring* (p. 41) Laura Knight tried to include all the things she loved about the season. With its rainbow, departing clouds and may blossom the work captures the optimism March can bring. The sense of renewed activity and bustling energy can also be felt in Knight's urban take on the subject *Spring in St John's Wood* (1933, Walker Art Gallery Collection). Despite its reputation for showers (perhaps due to the opening lines of Chaucer's *Canterbury Tales*) April is often the driest month of the year. Winds are light and fields become greener as crops develop. Nevertheless, spring weather can be unpredictable with wintry conditions possible even into May. The saying 'ne'er cast a clout till May be out' refers to the month and not the appearance of blackthorn blossom: switching to your 'summer wardrobe' in March in Britain would be rash.

Spring brings fresh colour to the landscape, whether it be the greening of trees coming into leaf or the flowers that begin to multiply in woodland, hedgerows and gardens. Annie Ovenden's *Lanhydrock Woods* (p. 44) vividly conveys

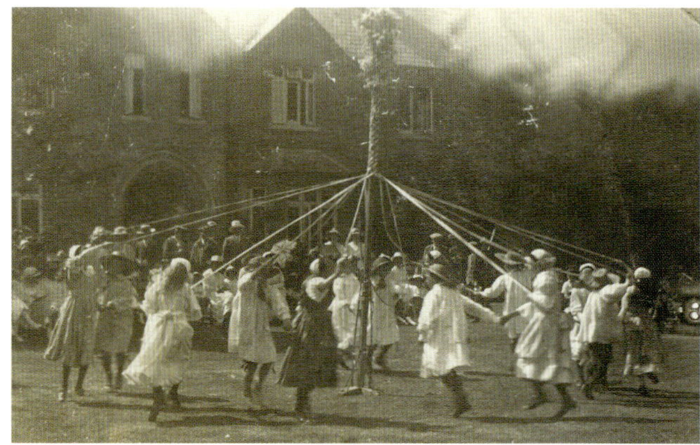

FIG. 8 • Maypole dancing near New Milton, Hampshire, 1918
St Barbe Museum and Art Gallery Collection

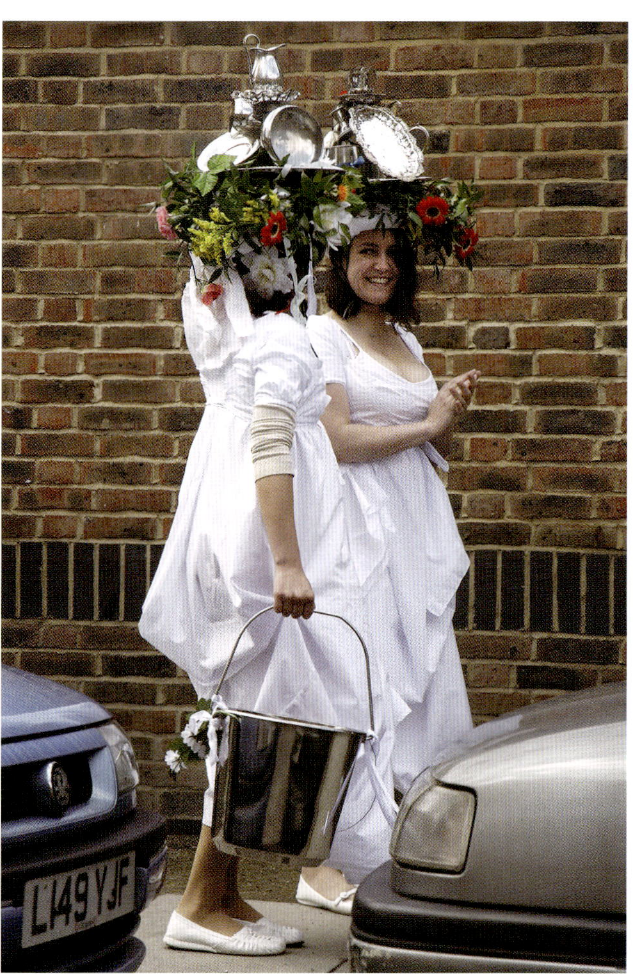

FIG. 9 • Sara Hannant
Milkmaids, Jack-in-the-Green procession, Deptford, London
2006
© the artist

sunlight filtered through fresh new leaves. Artists looking
for a symbol of spring have also been drawn to blossom,
which brings a burst of colour and a promise of fruitfulness
to come. David Inshaw's *May Blossom* (2012, private collection)
portrays a lone blackthorn bush on the Wiltshire downs with
an uncanny intensity. The pale flowers of elder, horse chestnut,
cow parsley and apple blossom are recurring motifs in his work,
their setting amid the ancient landscapes of Wessex highlight-
ing the ephemeral nature of these seasonal blooms. Frank
Sherwin's 1955 poster *Kent – The Garden of England* (p. 50)
was intended to lure railway passengers out of the city to
experience the joys of spring in the countryside. It presents
an enticing vision of fruit trees laden with blossom, while
oast houses and bare hop poles await the new seasons'
crop. The pure white blossom of the pear is among the first
to be seen, usually followed by cherry, plum and apple. In *The
Garden Path in Spring* (p. 49) Duncan Grant painted fruit trees
in blossom with bursts of red, yellow and blue flowers in the
beds below. Many gardeners aim to keep colour in their plots
throughout the year by careful planting; Grant and Vanessa
Bell planned the garden at Charleston in East Sussex to deliver
vibrant hues for their paintings. One of the more spectacular
spring flowerings is the horse chestnut tree, its candles appearing in monumental splendour in May. While preparing the
etching *Wiltshire Rickyard* (fig. 10) Robin Tanner changed the
season from autumn to spring so that he could include one.[3]
In Stanley Spencer's (1891–1959) *Wisteria at Englefield* (1954,
private collection) a magnificent candle-laden chestnut dwarfs
the house. Spencer depicted flowering plants in the gardens,
fields and allotments around his beloved Cookham with
great care, viewing them as much a part of God's miraculous
creation as the scenes from the New Testament he relocated
to this sleepy Berkshire village.

One of the first flowers to appear in the countryside is the
primrose, its pale flowers bringing gentle colour to the woodland floor (fig. 11). Anna Airy's (1882–1964) *Spring Hedgerow*
(1955, British Museum Collection) shows them clustered on
a bank with a few violets, the first signs of life in an otherwise
bare hedgerow. Later on woods will be carpeted with bluebells,
one of the great sights of spring in Britain. In *Bluebells, Cornflowers and Rhododendrons* (1945, British Council Collection)
Stanley Spencer depicted the plants faintly illuminated on
a shady woodland floor while Scottish Royal Academician
George Henry (1858–1943) painted three smartly dressed
young women bathed in spring sunshine in *Picking Bluebells*
(William Morris Gallery Collection). The vision of a mass of daffodils, which once so enchanted the poet William Wordsworth,
is a traditional sign that spring is upon us. As cut flowers they
also bring brightness into the home. In his wartime painting
Spring Day at Boscastle (1943, Arts Council Collection) Charles
Ginner (1878–1952) includes a vase of daffodils beside a window
that looks out on trees coming into fresh green leaf. During the
Coronavirus outbreak in 2020 David Hockney (b. 1937) chose
daffodils as the subject for an iPad sketch that he sent to
news outlets to cheer people up with the message 'they
can't cancel spring'. Hope springs eternal.

In the animal kingdom spring is the season of reawakening.
Hibernating mammals emerge and amphibians are active
once again. There is a 'changing of the guard' as winter
migrants such as the fieldfare return to their northern

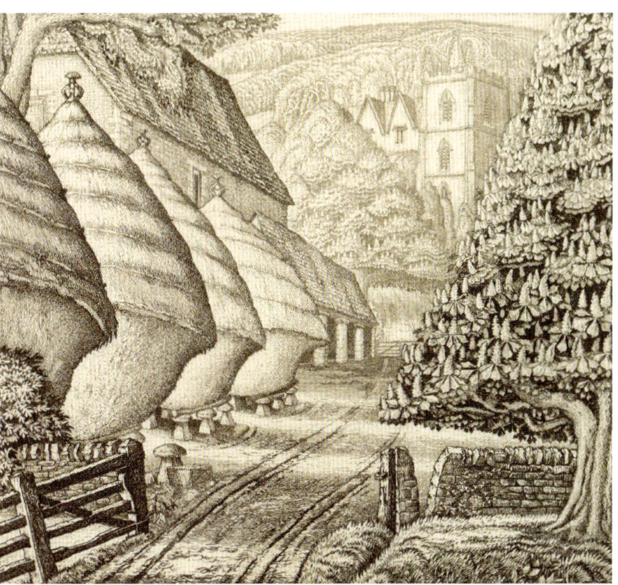

FIG. 10 · **Robin Tanner** (1904–1988) · *Wiltshire Rickyard*
1939 · etching
Stuart Southall Collection · © The Estate of Robin Tanner

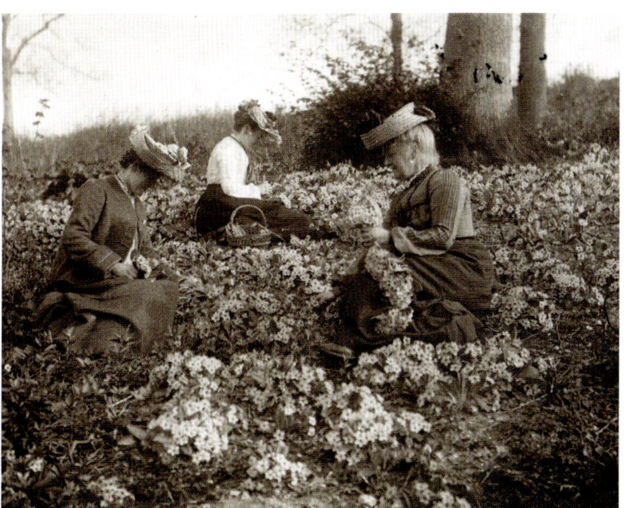

FIG. 11 · Gathering primroses
St Barbe Museum and Art Gallery Collection

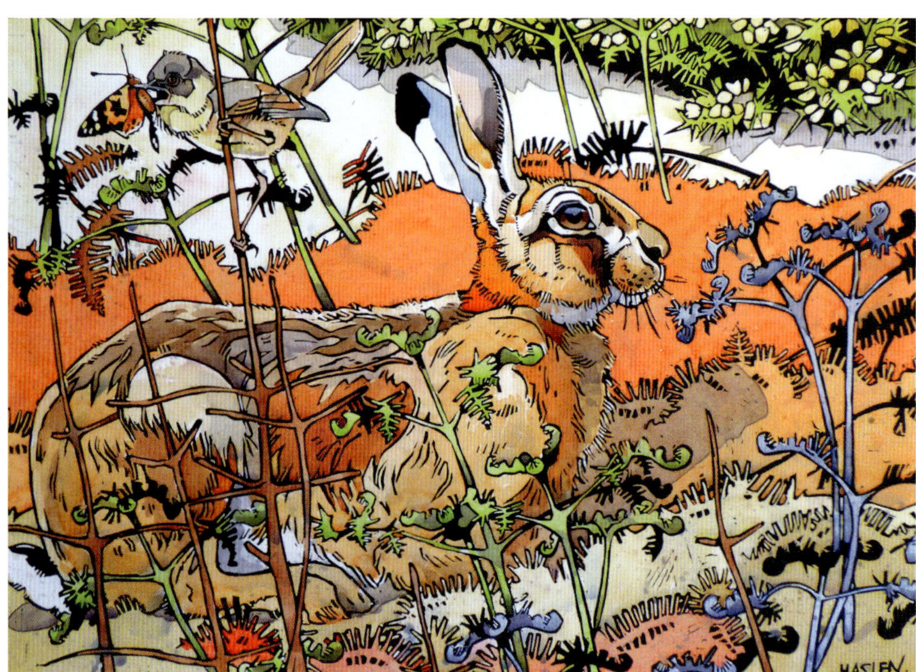

FIG. 12 · **Andrew Haslen** (b. 1953)
Spring · hand-coloured linocut
© the artist

breeding grounds while nightingales, wood warblers and swallows appear from the south. For birds it is a time for courtship, nesting and mating. C.F. Tunnicliffe's illustration for *What to Look For in Spring* (p. 51) shows rooks beginning to rebuild their nests at the beginning of March. As spring progresses the dawn chorus develops, reaching a crescendo in June as the song of resident birds is bolstered by those arriving from overseas. Birds sing to attract a mate and to mark their territory. This uses up energy so it tends to be the fittest birds that sing loudest and longest. For the female a good singer is likely to be stronger and hold a bigger territory from which to feed their young. Dawn is a good time to perform as it is difficult to find food in the half-light and the singer is hidden from predators. This springtime alarm call begins up to an hour before sunrise with the woodpigeon, robin, thrush and blackbird and gradually others join in.

The chiffchaff (fig. 13) is one of the traditional heralds of spring. Some now overwinter here but the majority arrive from warmer climes. As Carry Akroyd explains: 'Those two notes constantly chiff-chaffing from somewhere in the fresh foliage always take me by surprise and are the confirmation of spring. So the bird didn't need to be the main feature of the image, just a presence that can be heard in the surrounding woods and fields'. Swallows appear from early April onwards, having journeyed from South Africa. The adults return to the same area and even the same nest site. Robin Tanner's *The First Swallow (Alington in Wiltshire)* (p. 54) celebrates that moment when the first of these arrivals is seen flitting overhead, a signal that summer is not so far away. Recent research has shown that warmer springs driven by climate change cause leaves to open and caterpillars to emerge earlier. This has created a mismatch between the usual nesting period of woodland species such the blue tit, great tit and pied flycatcher and the peak availability of their chicks' critical food source. This climate domino effect will inevitably alter some of the key natural

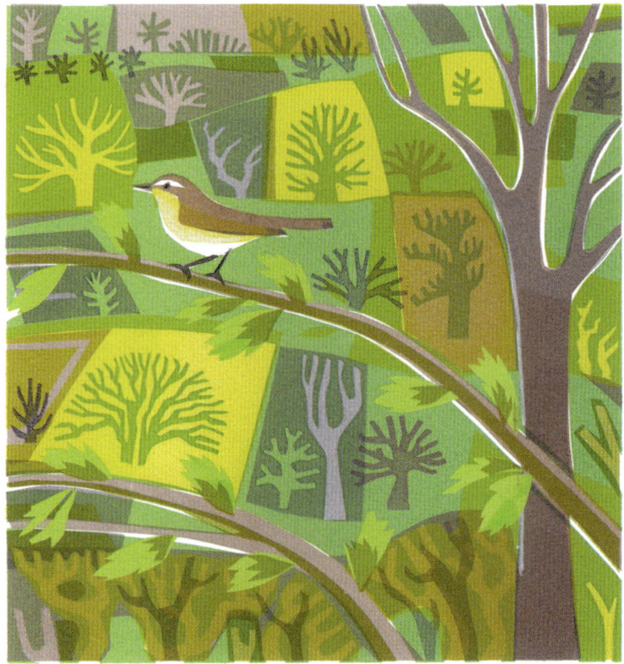

FIG. 13 · **Carry Akroyd** (b. 1953) · *Chiffchaff* · screenprint
© the artist

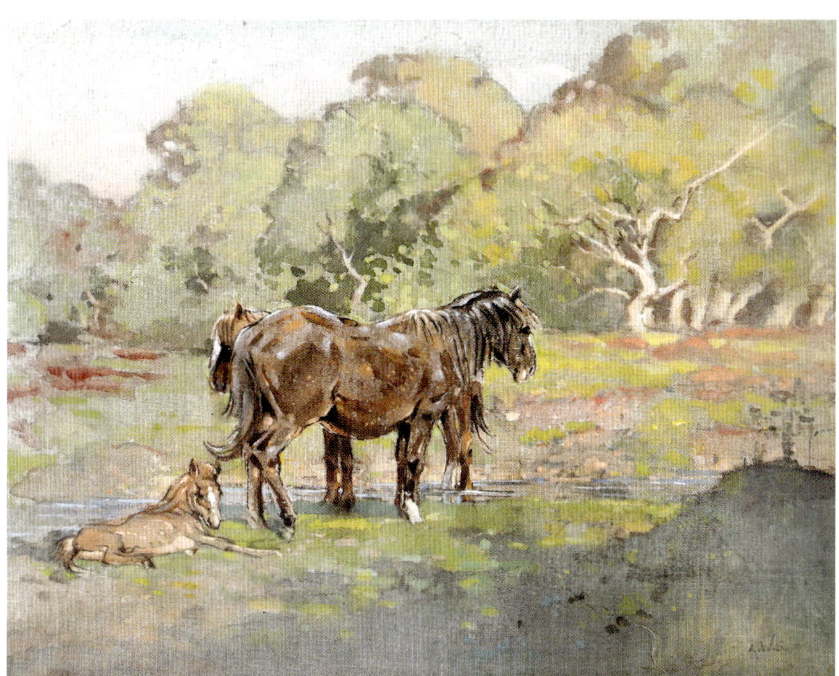

FIG. 14 • **Allen William Seaby** (1867–1953)
Head to Tail • gouache on linen
St Barbe Museum and Art Gallery Collection

signifiers of the seasons. Birds begin nesting earlier and migrants such as the blackcap arrive sooner, leading to a blurring of the familiar seasonal boundaries. It is possible that such factors are affecting the most famous harbinger of spring, the cuckoo (p. 52), which arrives from Africa in early April. Its distinctive call has been celebrated in poem and song since *Sumer is icumen in* was written in the thirteenth century. But cuckoo numbers are in steep decline – the British Trust for Ornithology calculates that numbers have dropped by 65% since the early 1980s and its voice, once a reminder to farmers to set about their spring tasks, is heard less and less.[4]

Another emblem of spring is the mad March hare, whose courtship behaviour involves frantic chases and boxing when a reluctant jill fights off an amorous jack, antics that inspired the phrase 'hare-brained'. The hare is the subject of a great deal of rural mythology. Although elusive, the 'stag of the stubble' is today a much-loved rural mammal, but it was once associated with witchcraft and seen as a creature of bad luck and ill omen. This combination of character and mystery has made it a popular subject for contemporary artists. Colin See-Paynton's startled hare in *The Merry Month of May* (p. 55) captures its eccentric appeal. Andrew Haslen has produced a wealth of paintings, drawings and linocuts based on encounters with hares near his Suffolk home. His particular understanding of their appearance and behaviour is based in part on hand-rearing orphan leverets helpfully collected by his dog.[5] *Spring* (fig. 12) shows a hare at rest among gorse and unfolding bracken with two recent arrivals from Africa, a whitethroat and its meal, a luckless painted lady butterfly. In the New Forest foals begin to appear among the pony herds. Stallions are released in May and June, so after an eleven month gestation period the foals are born in April and May when the warmer weather and new grass growth should give them a good start in life. Summer camping holidays in the Forest kindled Allen Seaby's fascination with Britain's pony breeds, resulting in a wealth of

drawings and watercolours (fig. 14). He wrote: 'At dawn, I might be awakened by the sound of their munching close by my sleeping-place. My open tent door faced the east, and early one morning, as the level rays of the rising sun fell on my face, I opened my eyes to see a little way off a mare and her foal, haloed in rosy light.'[6]

The turn of the farming year also brings dramatic changes to the rural landscape. In *Nature Through the Seasons in Colour* (1953, illustrated by Stanley Badmin, James McIntosh Patrick and others) A.G. Street noted: 'In March the farmer begins once again to paint the picture of the year. It is the same picture as the one his forebears painted a hundred years ago, but today he uses very different brushes, most of them wielded by machinery'.[7] Drying soil lightens in colour, grass in pastures becomes lush and green, ploughed fields show the first shoots of oats and barley. Fields of bright yellow oilseed rape flowers are eye-catching and are used to dramatic effect in James Lynch's *May 23 (Rape Fields, Little Knoll)* (fig. 16). Of this work Lynch says: 'I've soared over this landscape with my paraglider, and trekked through it on long hikes – making the odd drawing on the way. The rape is not to everyone's taste, but it is a visual feast. On this day the heavy late spring showers are receding'. In spring the countryside is also dotted with the mobile forms of cows and sheep returned to their pastures after being kept and fed inside over the winter. Grass is at its richest in May and June when it can be grazed in the fields or cut for silage. Horses and cattle returning to this juicy freshness and the open spaces of their fields can be seen kicking and bucking for joy. It is also the time to see lambs gambolling in the fields. Having been fed exclusively on their mothers' milk for the first four weeks of their lives, they now begin to nibble the grass. *The Valley* (p. 59) is a tranquil portrait of ewes and lambs resting at the end of the day. Charles Tunnicliffe had lived and worked on a farm until he was nineteen and here captures a cherished landscape and way of life enduring through wartime uncertainties. Clare Leighton's engraving for May in *The Farmer's Year* (p. 58) portrays the next job in the sheep farming calendar – shearing. On some farms this was a job for the summer warmth of June, particularly if the sheep had been washed to get a better price for the wool. Writing in 1936, the artist Thomas Hennell commented that: 'Sheep-shearing can only be done satisfactorily in fine weather, for to cut well the fleece must be dry'. He suggests: 'there is no pleasanter rural sight than a band of shearers at work under the shade of trees on a fine day in June'.[8] The warm spring weather causes the fleece to 'rise' from the body – a release of lanolin which separates it from the skin. With hand clippers the traditional shearer might have been expected to manage thirty sheep in a day. Today, with electrical shearing tools a sheep might be clipped in under two minutes.

The drier weather of March and April is ideal for sowing new crops: 'when blackthorn blossom's white, sow barley day and night'. First harrows and rollers would be used to break up lumps of earth to provide a fine tilth ready for planting. In Clare Leighton's illustration for April in *The Farmer's Year* (p. 57) the sower is broadcasting the seed by hand, a time-honoured and skilful activity seen in such fields for centuries. In Leighton's time sowing was more usually performed by seed drills that delivered the grain directly into the ground in neat rows. This made the process much more efficient, but the weight of the drill meant three horses were needed to pull it. A harrow would follow to bury the seed and protect it from birds. All these tasks now belong to the tractor and are completed in a fraction of the time taken a hundred years ago. Indeed, in comparison with today's machinery, even Tunnicliffe's Ladybird illustration of a tractor and seed drill from 1961 looks positively quaint.[9] Spring was also the time for planting potatoes, kale, sugar beet, mangolds and clover. There were other seasonal jobs which, while less appealing, were also important. With the animals moved out of their winter quarters it was time to thoroughly muck out farmyards and buildings, the manure being used to fertilise the fields. This work was a topic for Ralph Wightman (1901–1971) in his book *The Seasons* (1953), for which Stanley Badmin provided the

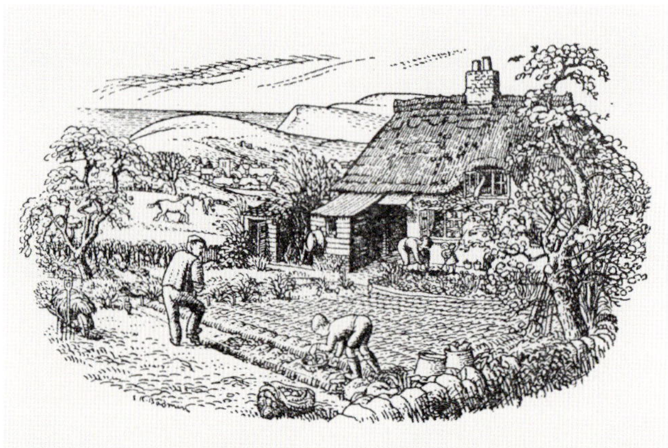

FIG. 15 · **Stanley Roy Badmin** (1906–1989) · *Spring*
headpiece decoration from *The Seasons* by Ralph Wightman, 1953

illustrations (fig. 15). Wightman, a farmer, lecturer, writer and broadcaster, brought a true countryman's insight to the changing world of agriculture after the Second World War. Of the realities of spring on the land he wryly commented: 'Poets talk of fancy turning to thoughts of love. There is wonder and amazement round every corner of every common lane. Yet we are carting manure'.[10] **SM**

1. Groom, N. (2013), *The Seasons: A Celebration of the English Year*, Atlantic Books, 2014 edition, p. 175
2. See Hannant, S. (2012), *Mummers, Maypoles and Milkmaids: A Journey Through the English Ritual Year*, Merrell
3. Tanner (1987), *Double Harness*, Impact Books, 1990 edition., p. 91
4. www.bto.org/our-science/projects/bbs/research-conservation/cuckoo (accessed 20 March 2020)
5. Haslen, A. (2010), *The Winter Hare*, Langford Press, p. 11
6. Seaby, A. (1936), *British Ponies: Running Wild and Ridden*, A & C Black, p. 4
7. Street, A.G. in *Nature Through the Seasons in Colour*, 1953, Odhams Press Ltd., p. 54
8. Hennell, T. (1936), *Change in the Farm*, republished 1977 by EP Publishing, pp. 14–16
9. Watson, G.L. (1961), *What to Look For in Spring*, Ladybird Books Ltd., p. 9
10. Wightman, R. (1953), *The Seasons*, Cassell & Co. Ltd., pp. 97–8

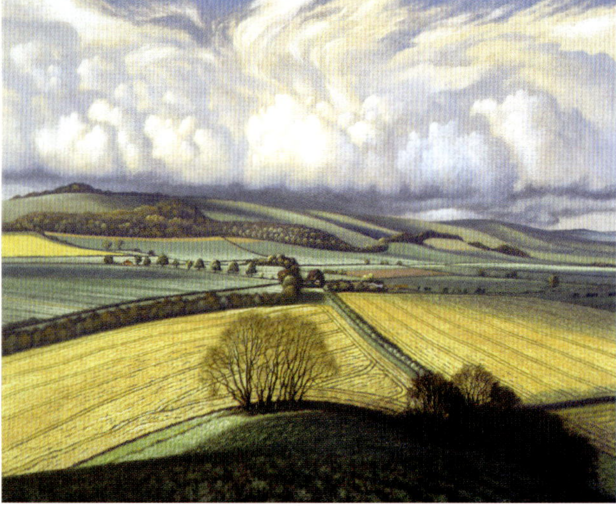

FIG. 16 · **James Lynch** (b. 1956)
May 23 (Rape Fields, Little Knoll)
egg tempera on gesso coated wood panel
© the artist

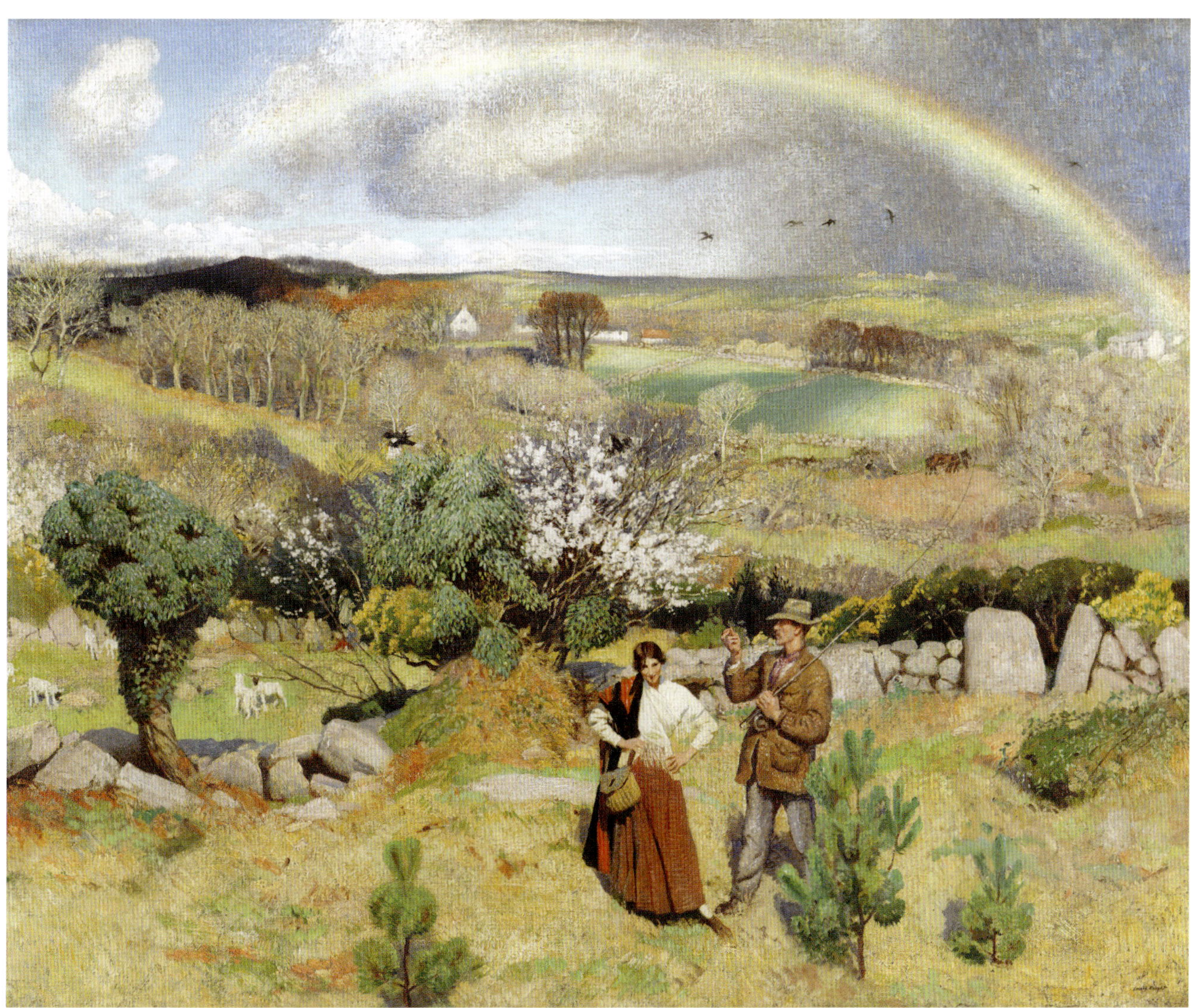

Laura Knight (1877–1970)

Spring

1916–20 · oil on canvas · 1524 x 1829 mm

Tate · photograph © Tate

Laura Knight first contemplated this painting while living at Staithes in Yorkshire. In her autobiography she recalled picking primroses in a nearby valley: 'Sheltered there, one learnt that the long winter was nearly over, in some patches of sunlight between the tracery of pale shadow it was almost warm. No one could take a step without crushing the virginal green and yellow that was springing from the black earth.'[1] She was inspired to begin work on a large canvas: 'There was going to be everything I knew of spring in that big picture'.[2] However, poor weather meant she only managed some preparatory drawings and the work did not come to fruition until she was living in Cornwall some years later.

Work on *Spring* began in 1916 when Britain was at war and painting outdoors was banned. Knight had to hide in bushes to make the preliminary sketches, fearful that she would be imprisoned if caught. The setting was the Lamorna Valley and the models Ella and Charles Naper. She later painted out the man and replaced him with a boy. When the painting was damaged while on display in America and she had to strip off the varnish the man was reinstated.[3] Knight achieved her ambition to capture the spirit of the season: bad weather departs and the couple enjoy the sunshine among the lambs, may blossom, birds and gorse flowers. However, the primroses that first inspired the painting were not included. **SM**

1. Knight, L. (1936), *Oil Paint and Grease Paint*, Ivor Nicholson & Watson, pp. 97–8
2. Ibid., p. 98
3. www.tate.org.uk/art/artworks/knight-spring-n04838 (accessed 16 April 2020)

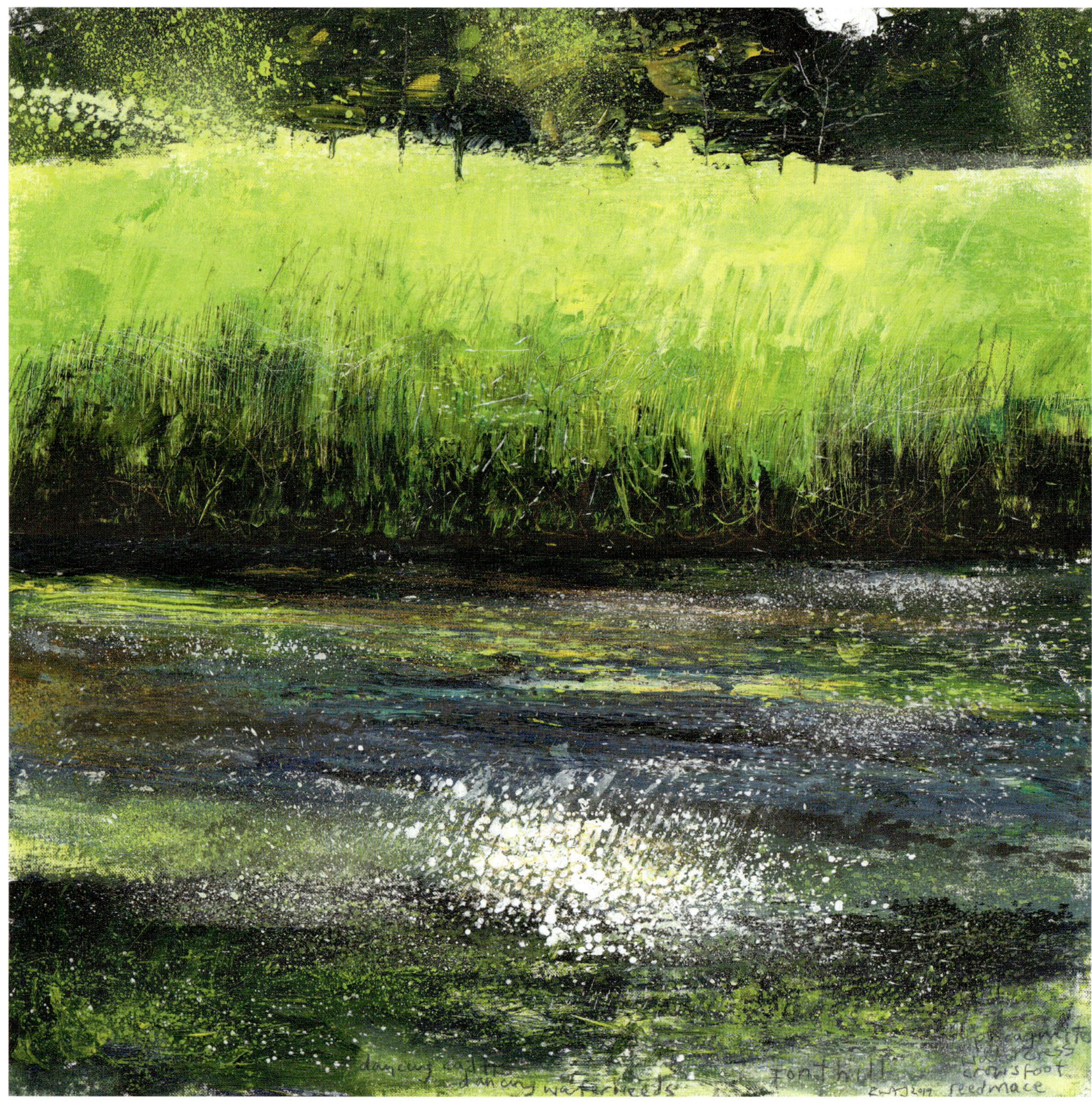

Kurt Jackson (b. 1961)

*Dancing caddis,
dancing water reeds*

2019 • mixed media on canvas board
610 x 610 mm

private collection • image © the artist

A delicate landscape, you can feel the fragility around you gently awakening. The stream threads its way through, murmuring beneath my overhanging feet and under my gaze. I use vivid greens, leaf greens, spring greens studded with golden kingcups and dandelions, blue sky blues reflected in the chalky waters, gin clear where even the trailing pond weeds are now awake; soft watercolour washes diluted by Spring water, trickle to flow to trail across the page between kingfishers and roach. **Kurt Jackson**

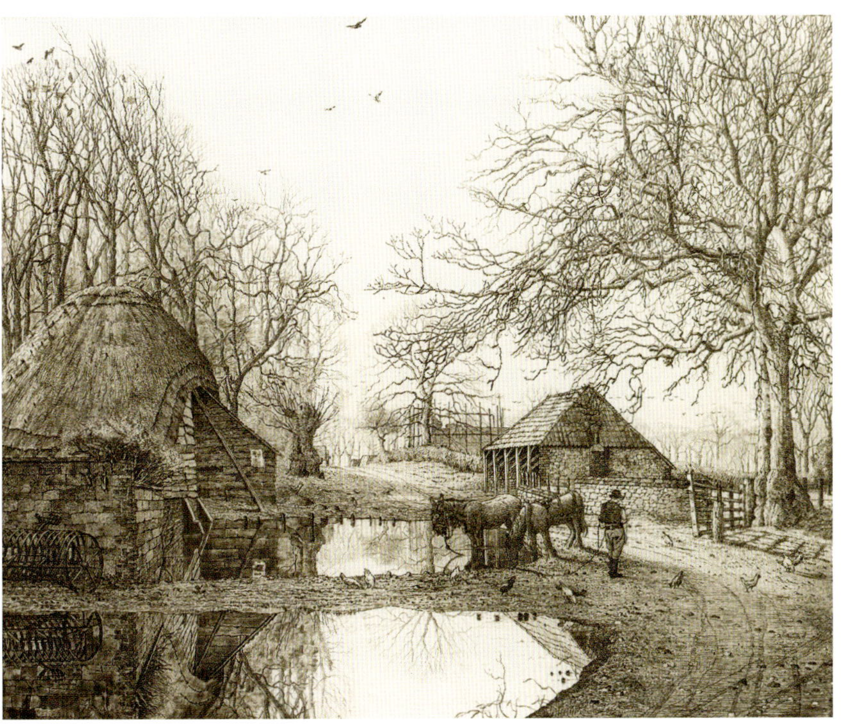

Allan Gwynne-Jones
(1892–1982)

Spring Evening, Froxfield

1928 • etching • 305 x 368 mm

Stuart Southall Collection
image © The Estate of Allan Gwynne-Jones

Spring Evening, Froxfield was one of only eleven plates Allan Gwynne-Jones produced largely between 1926–27 although there were many variants.[1] At the time he was living in a modest cottage in Froxfield, a small hamlet also known as Little Switzerland in the South Downs close to the Hampshire market town Petersfield. The cottage in Cockshott Lane, sat on high ground with views of the Hangers[2] and was built by the architect and furniture maker Geoffrey Lupton (1882–1949), who like Gwynne-Jones was educated nearby at Bedales, the progressive and first co-educational school to be established in England which moved to its present site in Steep, Petersfield in 1900.

The drawing was made in early Spring when Gwynne-Jones could observe the rooks returning home while the branches were still bare. He learnt to etch at the Saturday morning engraving classes his Royal College of Art colleague Malcolm Osborne (1880–1963) offered. From the outset Gwynne-Jones acknowledged his debt to Samuel Palmer and John Linnell, believing 'in sentiment', he explained that his 'starting point [had] always been a literary one'.[3] The closely observed barns and pond in this tranquil contemporary rural scene were a short walk from Froxfield, at the top of Stoner Hill. The oil painting of the same subject and title, dated 1922 was twice the size of the etching and purchased by Birmingham Museum and Art Gallery, the first public gallery to acquire one of Gwynne-Jones' works in 1924. **GC**

1. Ian Lowe in *Allan Gwynne-Jones: A Catalogue to a Retrospective Exhibition Organised by the National Museum of Wales in Association with the Welsh Arts Council and Royal Eisteddfod of Wales*, 1982, p. 61
2. The name 'hanger' comes from the Old English 'hangra' meaning a wooded slope
3. Gwynne-Jones, op. cit., p. 63

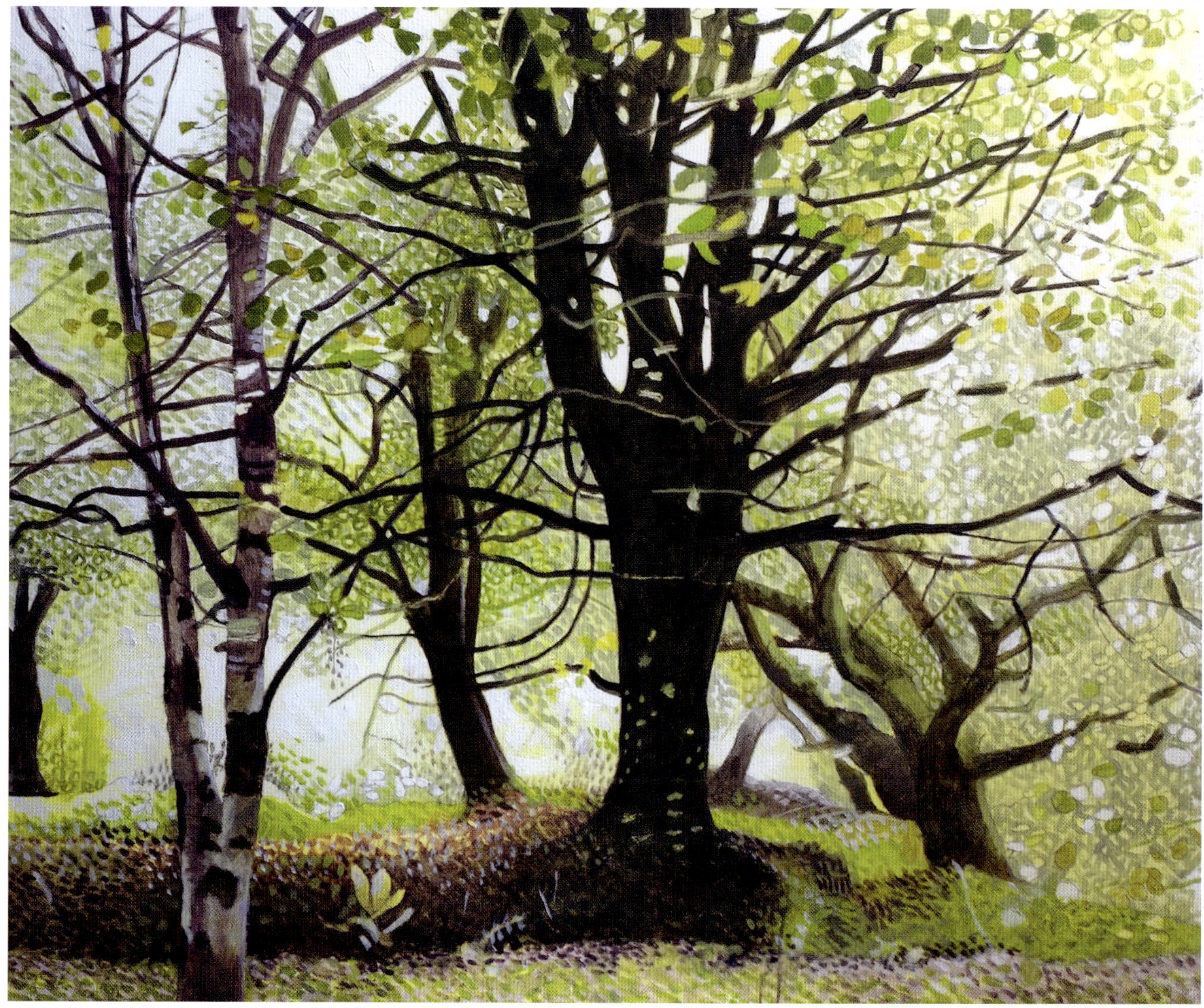

Annie Ovenden (b. 1945)

Lanhydrock Woods

oil on canvas • 254 x 305 mm

collection of the artist • image © the artist

In spring the beech leaves burst forth spreading vivid green across woodlands, needing a palette which includes light cadmium yellow, and manganese blue (the coolest range). White blossom highlights many blackthorn spikes, bluebells create mists of cobalt across woodland floors and campions magenta the hedgerows.

Summer brings more palette changes. The sun now high in the sky flattens and dries the gradually ochring landscape, it dapples the leaves which dress every tree in varying shades of phthalo, hooker and sap green, lemon cadmium and even silver pearl.

Autumn is demanding, with its riot of picture book foliage – it's easy to fall into the trap of using every colour available. The cadmiums, crimson lake and venetian red toned down with burnt sienna and Payne's grey now appear in my mix.

The four seasons – winter, spring, summer, autumn – vary significantly in characteristics. My paintings can be a reminder that time marches on and the seasons change but my ultimate goal is to portray the harmony and beauty that abounds in any season. **Annie Ovenden**

Monica Poole (1921–2003)

Spring After the Hurricane

1988 · wood engraving · 230 x 162 mm

Stuart Southall Collection
image © The Estate of Monica Poole

Monica Poole was born in Canterbury and studied
at the Thanet School of Art at Margate where she
was introduced to wood engraving by Geoffrey Wales
(1912–1990). In 1940 the family moved to Bedford
where Poole spent the war working in an aircraft
factory. In 1945 she went to London to study illustration at the Central School of Arts and Crafts, one
of her tutors being the wood engraver John Farleigh
(1900–1965). Despite the emphasis of the course Poole
only illustrated one book during her career, the volume
on Kent (1950) in Paul Elek's *Vision of England* series.
She felt that her work lacked the emotion necessary
for illustration and instead concentrated on producing
exhibition engravings on a larger scale. For a time her
somewhat unsettling portrayals of the Kent landscape
aligned her with the prevailing Neo-Romantic spirit,
but during the 1950s both this style and wood engraving fell from fashion. The 1980s ushered in a
revival of the medium and today Poole is recognised
as one of its foremost twentieth century practitioners.

Poole was inspired by the curious and intricate
structures of the natural world, her engravings tease
out the inherently strange beauty of trees, plants, rocks
and shells. An intense connection with nature meant
that she was attuned to seasonal changes such as the
flowering times of plants: magnolia, primrose, teasel,
ripe corn and the humble dandelion all feature in her
work. Figures rarely appear but in *Winter Wood* (1957)
and *Summer Evening* (1959) they give sharply contrasting seasonal moods. The first shows a woman's
impassive face hemmed in by leafless branches, while
in the second a figure contemplates a field of corn from
her garden, silhouetted against the setting sun. *Spring
after the Hurricane* or *Spring 1988* was commissioned
by the National Trust and the Society of Wood Engravers
to commemorate the Great Storm of 1987 which felled
some 15 million trees. Poole's engraving shows splinter-
ed beech trunks and yet there is hope of renewal as
despite the damage one tree is coming into leaf. **SM**

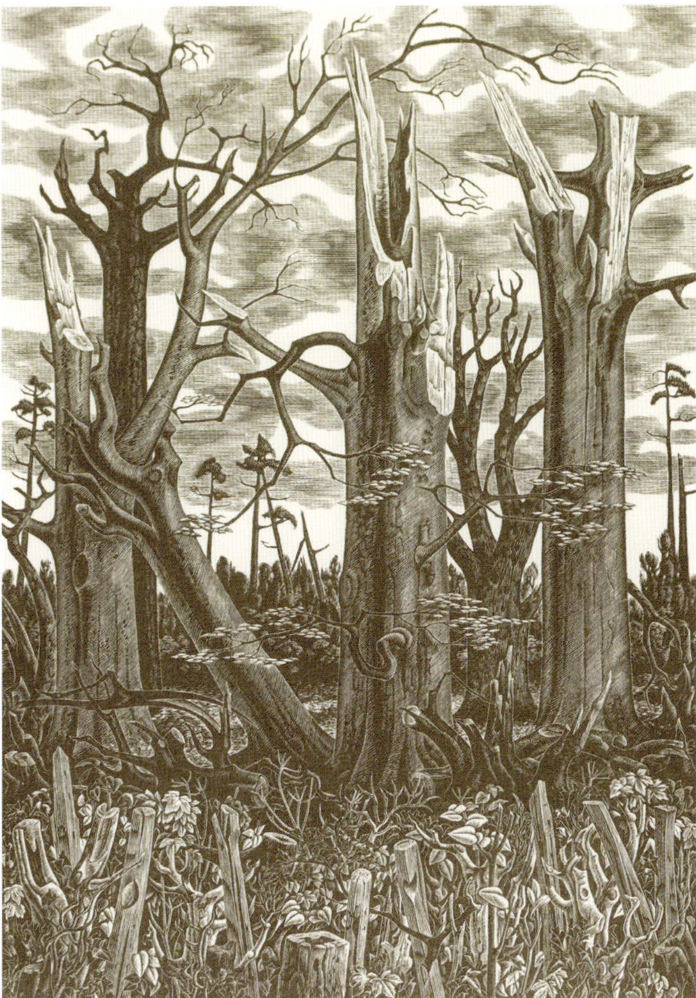

Keith Grant (b. 1930)

Early Spring, Selborne

2017 · oil on canvas · 502 x 502 mm

Chris Beetles Gallery · image © the artist

> *The parish of Selborne lies in the extreme eastern corner of the county of Hampshire, bordering on the county of Sussex, and not far from the county of Surrey; is about fifty miles south-west of London … The soils of this district are almost as various and diversified as the views and aspects. The high part to the south-west consists of a vast hill of chalk, rising three hundred feet above the village; and is divided into a sheep down, the high wood, and a long hanging wood called The Hanger.*[1]

Keith Grant first visited Selborne in the 1950s finding little had changed since Gilbert White wrote this description in a series of letters commencing initially to fellow naturalist Thomas Pennant in his literary classic *The Natural History and Antiquities of Selborne* published in 1789. Grant made a small oil study in 1959 of a frozen sheet of water under The Hanger where Gilbert and his brother John in 1753 cut the zigzag path up the slope and from where Gilbert's house 'The Wakes' could be seen. Grant's painting was purchased by eminent art historian, Kenneth Clark, confirming for him 'its significance as an icon of English landscape'.[2] It is significant too that for Grant, 'There seems no point to an art which does not have its origins in nature. Without richness of nature all themes are soon exhausted and replaced by cliché and fashion …'.[3] Given his interest in the question of conservation and how this is recorded and reflected in his paintings Grant has also written more recently of 'being cognisant of our need to respect the entire eco-system which sustains our being.'[4]

Grant completed ten oil paintings on the theme of Selborne in 2017, finding that it still retained the power to fire his imagination explaining, 'The Hanger is dominant and is depicted in six of them, whilst the remaining compositions are subjects seen "looking out" as it were, from its tree-defined slopes.'[5] Of *Early Spring, Selborne*, he wrote the following in his journal on 5 April 2017:

> *By combining geometry in the landscapes, I am simply alluding to the underlying geometry which exists hidden from immediate apprehension throughout the natural world. My task is to render this harmonising matrix visible whenever I can through a simplification of the complex forms of growth and unifying them with the demands of picture making. Sometimes it is when a form results from an analysis of a natural object or is through abstraction, formalism and simplifying that the best images are achieved. My hope is to reveal the spiritual in nature and not its already catalogued identity.*[6]

GC

1. Gilbert White (1900), *The Natural History and Antiquities of Selborne*, Macmillan and Co. Limited, p. 3, first published in 1789
2. Keith Grant (May 2017) in *Keith Grant: North by New English*, Chris Beetles Gallery, p. 50. Grant also visited Selborne in the 1970s
3. Grant's journal entry 5 April 1983, courtesy of Chris Beetles, pers. comm. to Gill Clarke
4. Grant's journal entry 12 April 2017, in *Keith Grant. North by New English*, Chris Beetles Gallery, p. 52
5. Grant (May 2017), op. cit., p. 50
6. Grant (April 2017), op. cit., p. 54. He settled in Norway in 1996, and now lives in the village of Gvarv, in Telemark, with his Norwegian wife and their daughter where he wrote this journal entry.

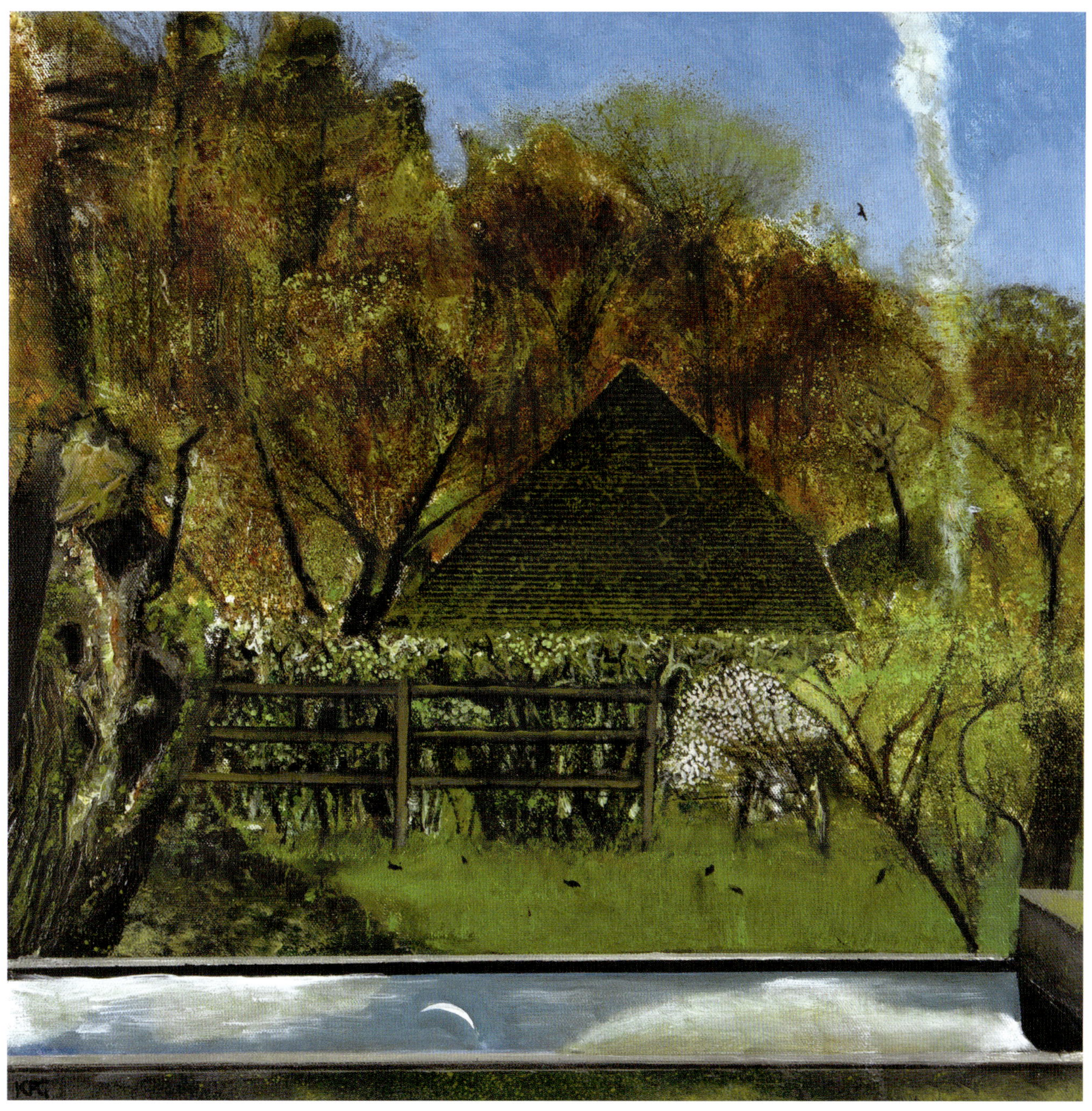

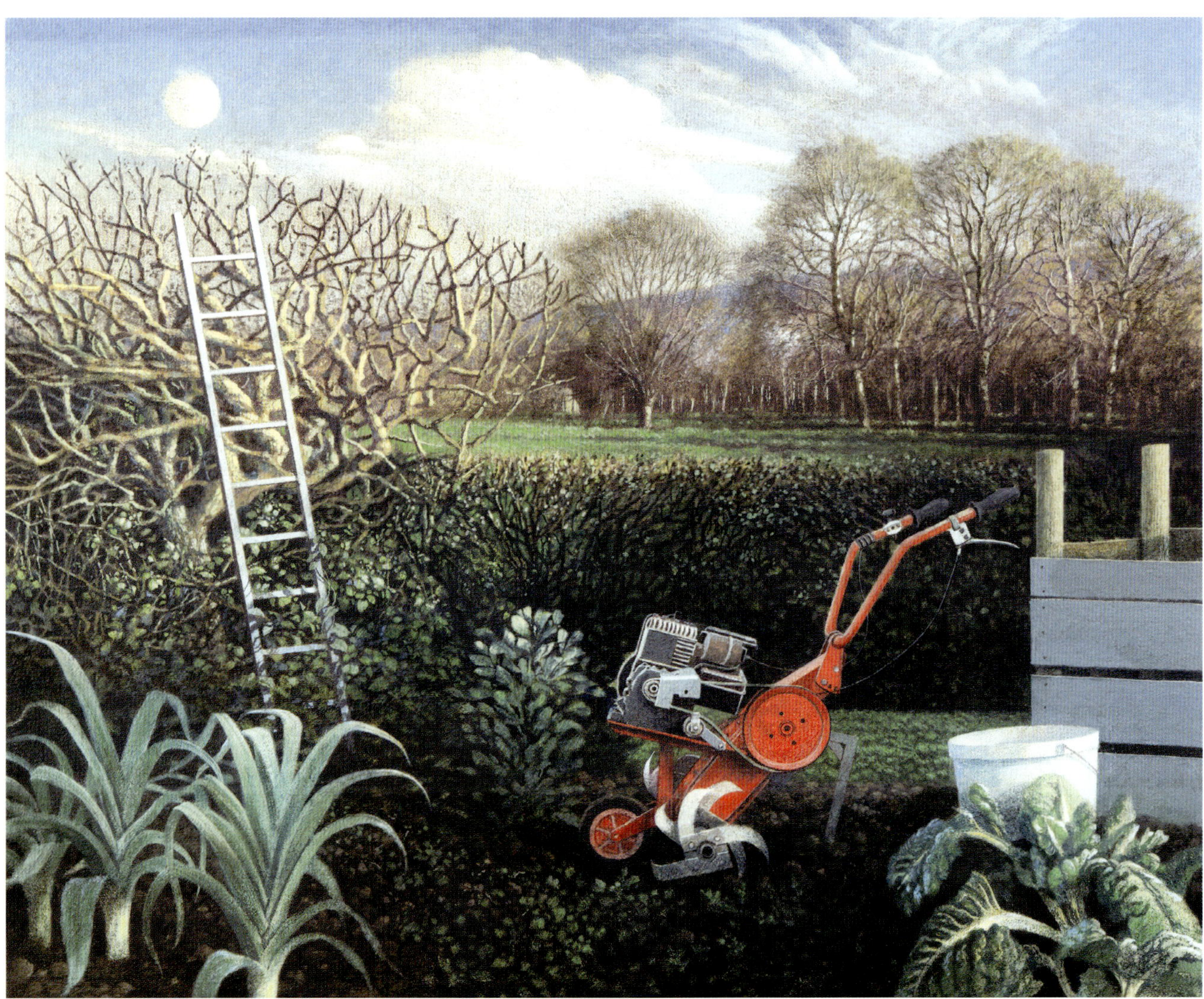

James Lynch (b. 1956)

The Ladder and the Moon, Spring Equinox

egg tempera on gesso coated wood panel
482 x 583 mm

private collection · image © the artist

I walk and cycle through the Somerset lanes and further afield over the Wiltshire Downs. Long walks and rides at the end of the day or weekends, all through the year, all seasons, all weathers. Often I will see a painting I might make in the future, or there will be just the germ of an idea. This garden is at the foot of the hill above the Somerset Levels where we live, and I pass it several times a week. Here it is late afternoon in March. The giant leeks and spinach are the tail end of winter's vegetables and about to make way for new planting. Compost bin full of rich decay. Rotavator at the ready. A ladder against the tree running up to the full moon. Endings and beginnings. Seasonal journeys. **James Lynch**

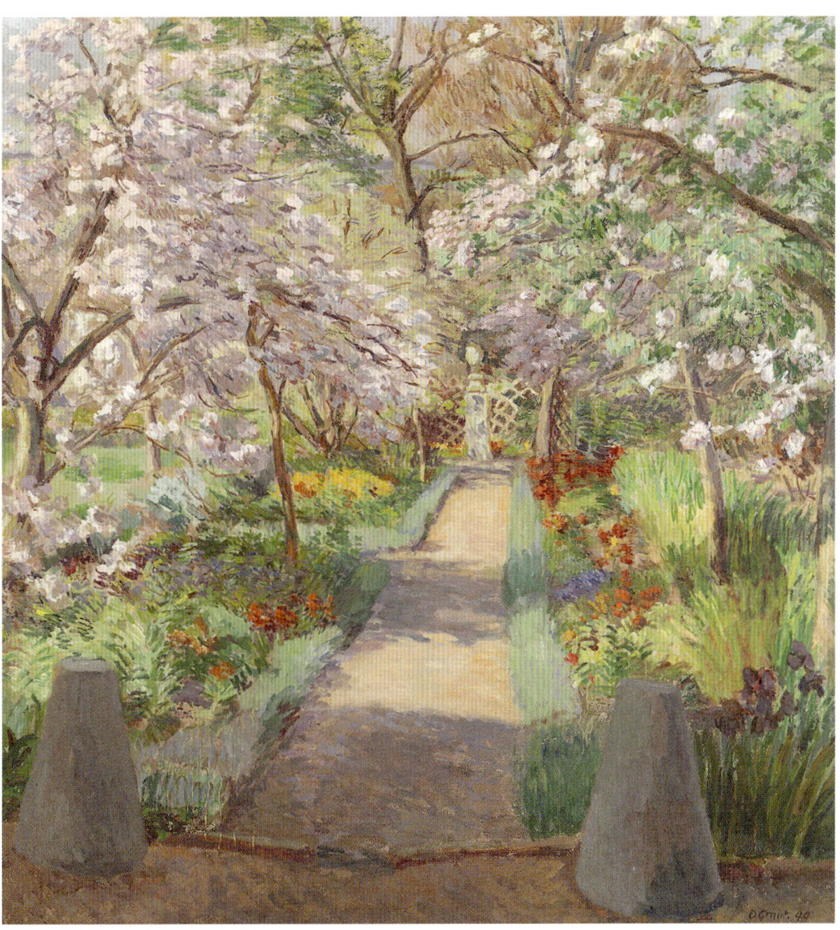

Duncan Grant (1885–1978)

The Garden Path in Spring

1944 • oil on canvas • 913 x 832 mm

The garden at Charleston farmhouse, near the village of Firle at the foot of the South Downs where *The Garden Path in Spring* was painted was described by Angelica Garnett (1918–2012), daughter of Duncan Grant and Vanessa Bell (1879–1961), who was born there, as always being an artist's garden. Grant and Bell transformed the vegetable plots and hen runs, poring over seed catalogues during the winter months selecting plants and flowers that would provide sources of interest for their paintings.

> *They favoured old-fashioned plants – German irises and single hollyhocks – as well as those that had grey, silky leaves, as they complained that England in the summer was too green.*[1]

Their dense planting avoided precision 'favouring … "sweet disorder"',[2] and combined Mediterranean influences with an English cottage garden affording impact and inspiration from varied shapes, colours and textures. *The Garden Path in Spring* with trees and plants filling the canvas makes no reference to wartime. It is an oasis of calm and harmony conveying Grant's passion for the flowers he lovingly tended and his skilful use of Impressionist colour and simplified forms. The spring garden did much to restore Grant's spirits having left his London studio for the sanctuary of rural Sussex in 1939.

Grant was little affected by fashionable tendencies and the *Manchester Guardian* art critic observed that his latest pictures in his solo show in June 1945 at the Leicester Galleries in London including *The Garden Path in Spring* showed his strong sense of design. He said they 'are quiet, penetrating, and though they look academic at first sight, they are the work of a genuinely original artist.'[3] **GC**

1. Spalding, F. (1997), *Duncan Grant*, Chatto & Windus, p. 369
2. Ibid., p. 370
3. *Manchester Guardian*, 13 July 1945, p. 4

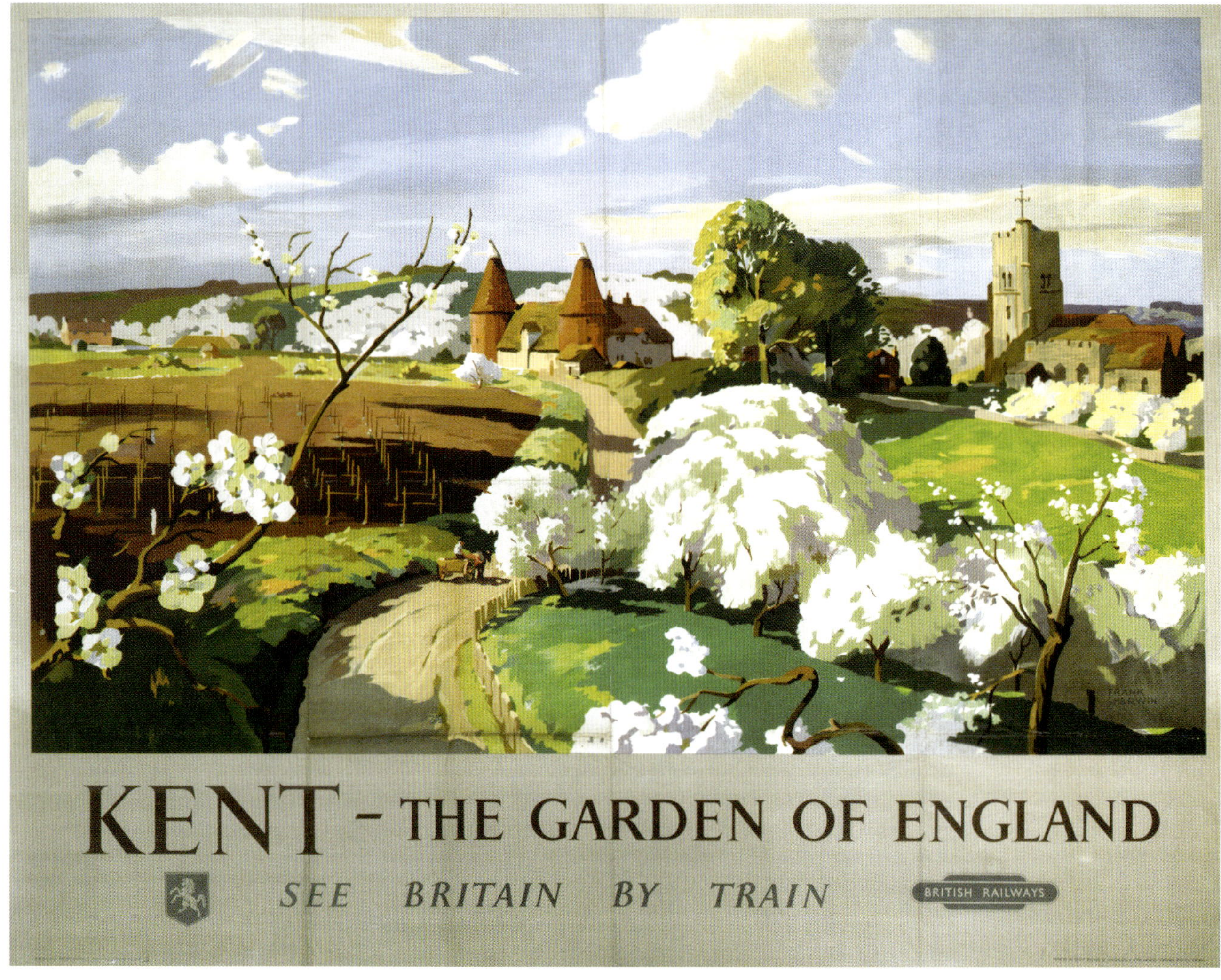

Frank Sherwin (1896–1986)

Kent – The Garden of England

1955 · poster · 1016 x 1270 mm

National Railway Museum · image © National Railway Museum/Science & Society Picture Library

Frank Sherwin was born in Derby and studied at the School of Art there before attending Heatherley School of Fine Art in London from 1920. He was primarily a watercolourist although he did also paint in oils. During the Second World War he worked on the camouflage of East Anglian airfields. Sherwin is principally remembered as a prolific poster designer who worked for Great Western Railway (GWR), London, Midland and Scottish Railway (LMS), London North Eastern Railway (LNER) and later British Railways. The period between the wars is viewed as the golden age of British travel posters when the railway companies, London Transport and Shell commissioned both commercial and fine artists to produce striking colourful imagery that encouraged people to go out and experience the beauty of the British landscape.

Sherwin would usually create his designs in gouache and these were then reproduced as lithographic posters. They play to the strengths of the printing process, using the flat, contrasting colours that made these stylised images so arresting and appealing. The design for this poster was actually made in oils and the original artwork is now in the collection of the National Railway Museum in York. It depicts a lane winding through the Kent countryside among spectacular displays of snow white blossom. The oast houses, church and solitary horse-drawn cart suggest an idealised landscape unchanged by modernisation, implying that a short train journey could transport you to this timeless pre-industrial idyll. **SM**

Charles Tunnicliffe (1901–1979)

Rooks Rebuilding their Nests

1961 · watercolour · 354 x 253 mm

Ladybird Books/University of Reading, Special Collections
image © Ladybird Books Ltd 1961 · reproduced by kind permission
of Ladybird Books Ltd

Tunnicliffe began work as a children's book illustrator on Alison Uttley's *Country Hoard* in 1943. She was delighted with the results and asked him to contribute to more than a dozen of her books in the following years. He also worked on Norman Ellison's *Nomad* series and single commissions such *The Children's Wonder Book in Colour* published by Odhams Press around 1948. His collaborator on the Ladybird *What to Look For* series was E.L. (Elliot Lovegood) Grant Watson (1885–1970), they had previously worked together on Grant Watson's books *Nature Abounding* (1941), *Walking with Fancy* (1943) and *The Leaves Return* (1947). The combination of Grant Watson's engaging text and Tunnicliffe's beautifully observed illustrations made the books a success with children and parents alike.

This illustration from *What to Look for in Spring* shows rooks at work on their nests at the beginning of March. Rooks are early nesters and the first eggs may even be laid in late February. Grant Watson explains: 'The rook sitting on the nest is displaying to her mate who is bringing an extra twig, giving him a welcome home'.[1] Tunnicliffe has carefully recreated blue-purple iridescence on the male bird's wings. In the background a heron is being mobbed: a lazy heron will sometimes take over a rook's nest for itself so these birds are chasing it away. **SM**

1. Watson, G.L. (1961), *What to Look For in Spring*, Ladybird Books Ltd., p. 10

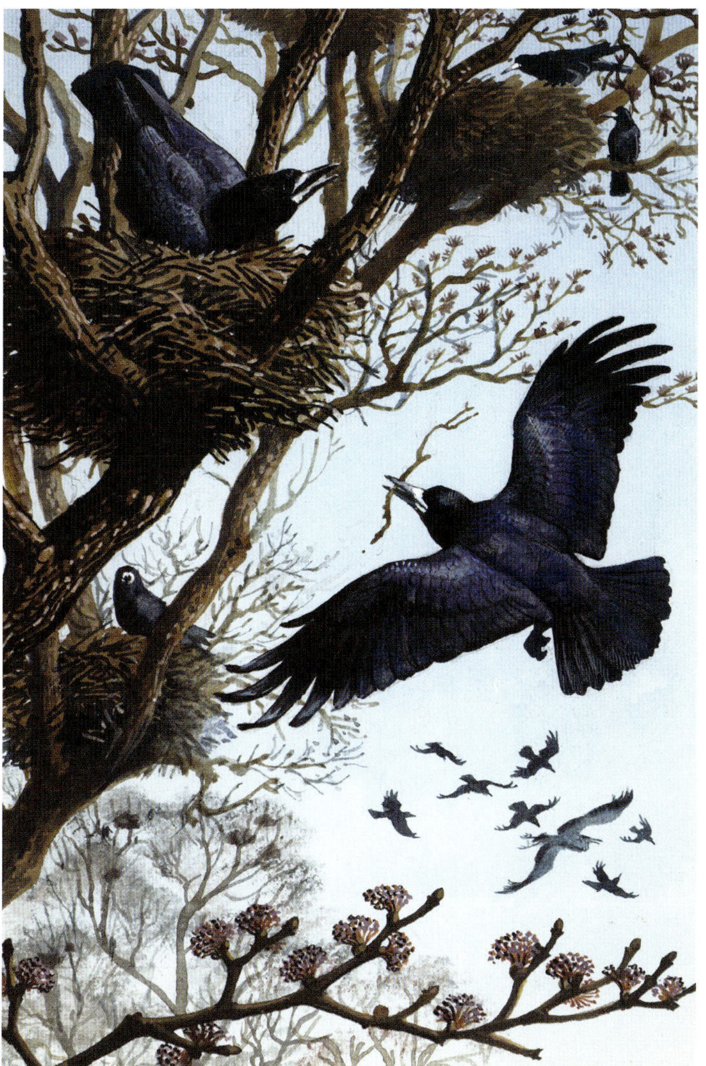

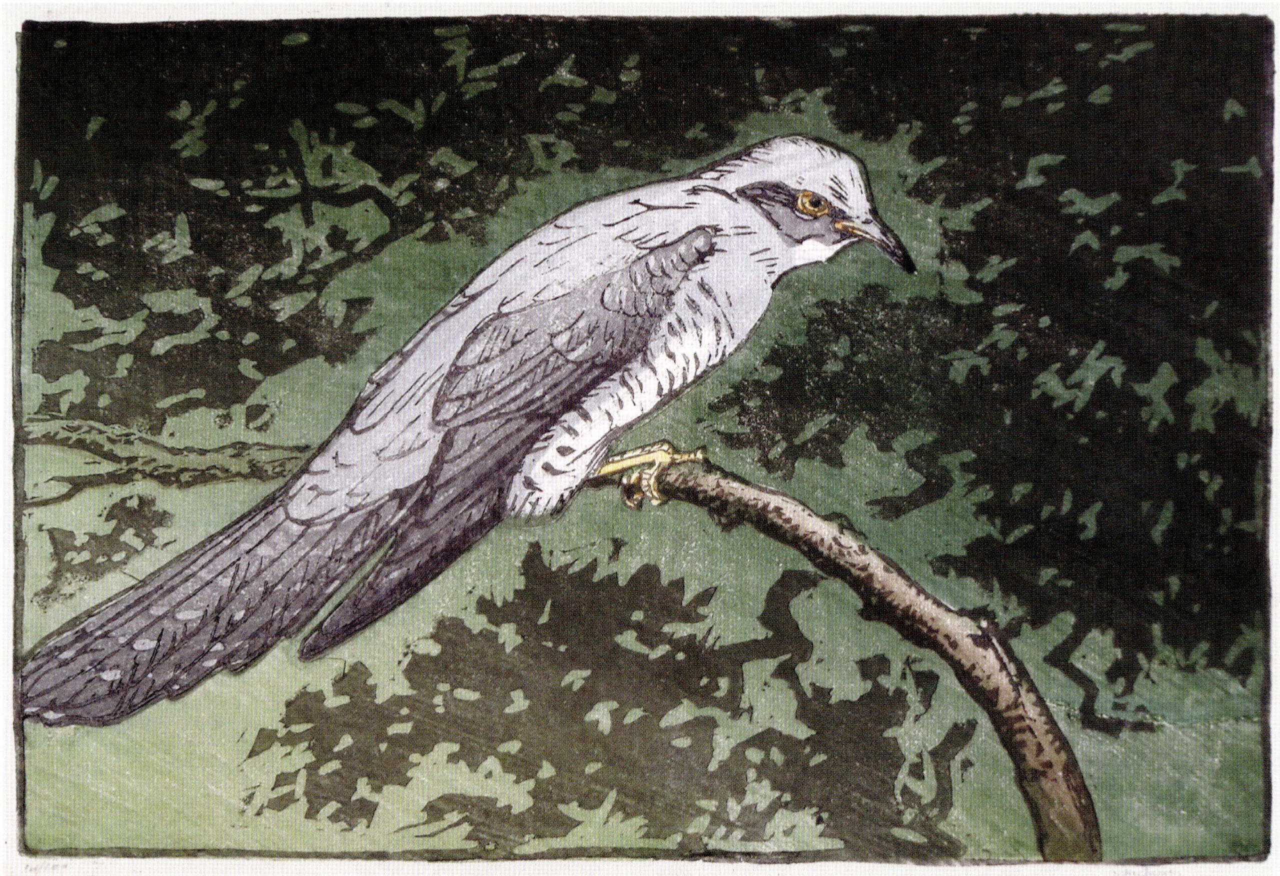

Allen William Seaby
(1867–1953)

Cuckoo

colour woodcut · 152 x 225 mm

St Barbe Museum and Art Gallery Collection
image © The Estate of Allen William Seaby

Perhaps the most celebrated indicator of spring's arrival is the call of the cuckoo being heard once again. The traditional date for its arrival was 14 April and although in recent years one has occasionally been heard as early as January the vast majority do still appear from around that date onwards.[1] Although rarely seen, the cuckoo's distinctive song has inspired a great deal of folklore and features in a number of traditional song lyrics, this perhaps being the best known:

> *The cuckoo she's a pretty bird, she sings as she flies.*
> *She brings us good tidings, she tells us no lies.*
> *She sucks little birds' eggs to make her voice clear,*
> *And when she sings cuckoo the summer draws near.*

It is actually the male that calls, usually from a high branch hidden in the leaf canopy as shown in Seaby's print. The female waits for a nearby dunnock, reed warbler or meadow pipit to lay and then adds her own eggs to the nest. Once hatched the cuckoo ejects the other eggs and takes all the food its surrogate parents can provide. The significant fall in cuckoo numbers relates in part to conditions at stopover points on its southward migration towards the Congo but also to the declining numbers of the caterpillars it eats when resident in Britain.[2] While this might be a relief to its unwitting victims, its disappearance would end a centuries long tradition of welcoming in the spring with the sound of the cuckoo's call. **SM**

1. See https://naturescalendar.woodlandtrust.org.uk/analysis/species-and-events-map/?type=5&species Id=107&eventId=12&year=2019 (accessed 28 April 2020)
2. https://www.bto.org/our-science/publications/peer-reviewed-papers/population-decline-linked-migration-route-common (accessed 28 April 2020)

Allen William Seaby (1867–1953)

Nightingale

colour woodcut, 286 x 210 mm

St Barbe Museum and Art Gallery Collection
image © The Estate of Allen William Seaby

Having spent the winter in West Africa the nightingale arrives in south east England from mid-April. These rather shy birds are not often seen but they can be heard singing by day and at night, often from an inaccessible bush or thicket. They are one of the most musical songbirds found in Britain and inspired Keats' *Ode to a Nightingale* (1819) and the popular song *A Nightingale Sang in Berkeley Square* (1939). Like the cuckoo their numbers are falling dramatically; the population has shrunk by 90% in the last fifty years.[1] This is probably due to climate change affecting their habitats in Africa and the countries along their migration route. Their preferred environments of scrub and fields left fallow are also disappearing from the British countryside.

Today Allen Seaby is chiefly remembered as a bird painter whose illustrations appeared in F.B. Kirkman's *The British Bird Book* (1910–1913) and the Ladybird series *British Birds and their Nests*. However, his greatest impact on the world of art was as a teacher and a woodcut printmaker. Seaby joined the staff at the Reading School of Art and eventually became its director in 1911. It was there he learned the technique of making colour woodcuts using the Japanese method and he went on to become one of the leading exponents of the art. Seaby's woodcut prints are marked by the subdued colours common to Japanese prints, his compositions allowing for large areas of blended colour where the brushing of the pigment onto the block is clearly visible. This view of a nightingale singing in the moonlight was made up from five blocks printed sequentially: green for the leaves, a reddish brown for the bird's body, blue for the background sky with bare paper left for the moon, yellow and brown for the moon and branches and finally the key block in dark brown providing the details of leaves, twigs and feathers. **SM**

1. https://www.bto.org/about-bto/press-releases/threatened-nightingale-site-confirmed-britains-best-new-national-survey (accessed 28 April 2020)

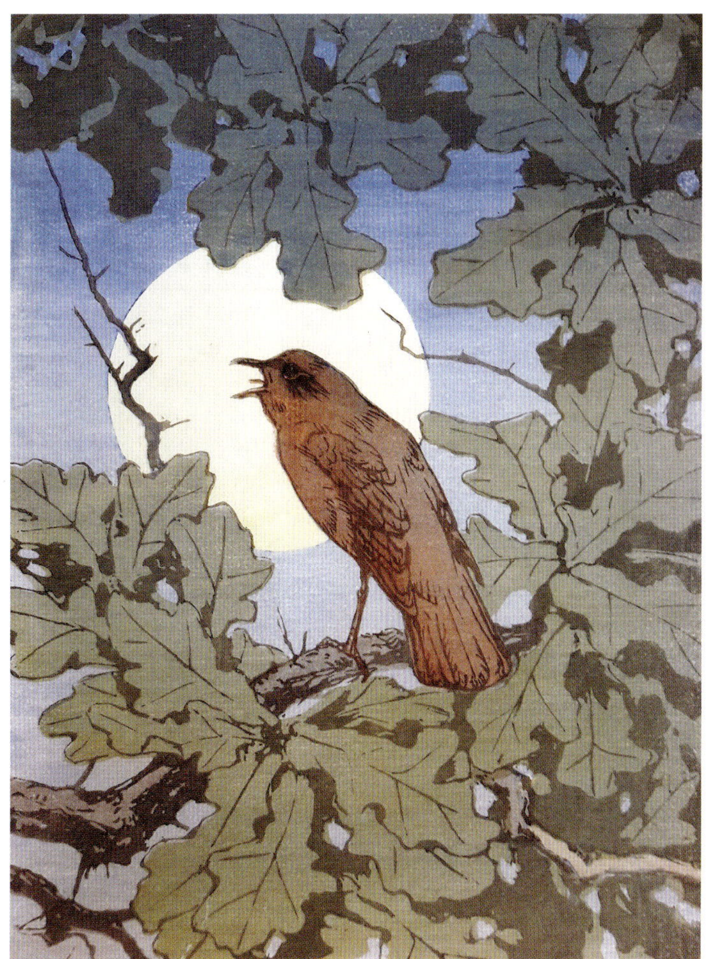

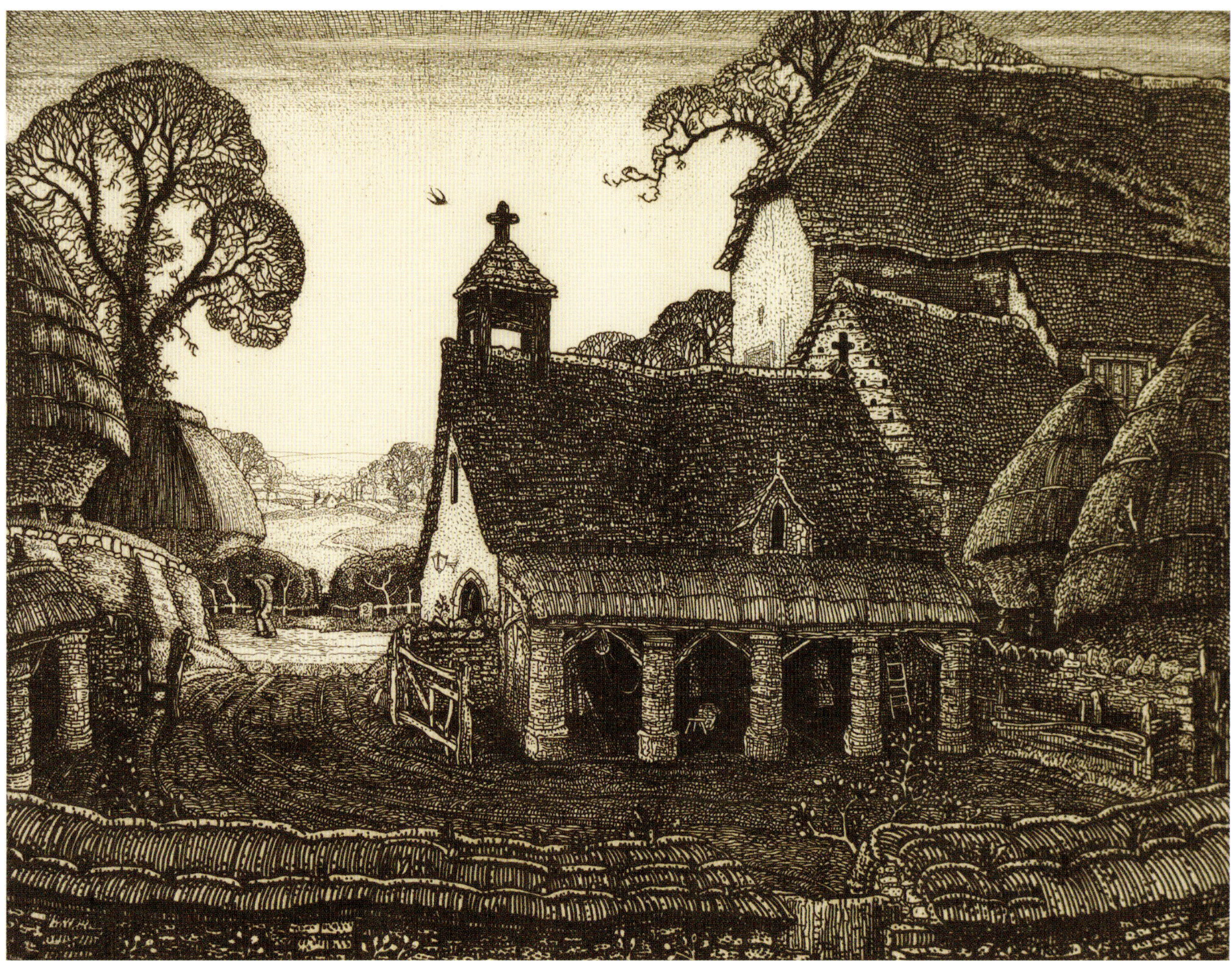

Robin Tanner (1904–1988)

The First Swallow (Alington in Wiltshire)

1927 · etching · 175 x 226 mm

Stuart Southall Collection
image © The Estate of Robin Tanner

The First Swallow was actually made when Tanner was living in London, working as a teacher in Blackheath and studying at Goldsmiths' School of Art in the evenings:

Alington in Wiltshire was a theme that was very dear to me, and I poured into it all my homesickness and love for the grey stone farms and white lanes of home. Although I used the drawings I had made of the pillared cow byre and thatched walls and mossy-roofed barns and a crude little chapel-of-ease in a hamlet of that name, I could never work with any degree of topographical accuracy. That didn't interest me at all. What I wanted to say was what I felt about my countryside, and particularly at that moment of spring when the swallows come back and the naked fans of elm trees begin to thicken.[1]

This is very much a composite image with elements of different buildings combined and the landscape beyond completely re-imagined to achieve the desired effect. Tanner even changed the spelling of the village's name to distinguish it from the real thing. This is the second state of the etching that includes the newly arrived swallow captured in the air above the chapel, but the bird was burnished out from the plate before the edition was published in 1927 as *Alington in Wiltshire*. Tanner's intense love of nature and the traditions of rural England made him a particularly seasons-conscious artist. Almost all of his etchings contain elements that tie them to particular months or times of year, often through the appearance of flowering and fruiting plants. **SM**

1. Tanner R. (1987), *Double Harness*, Impact Books, 1990 edition, p. 38

Colin See-Paynton (b. 1946)

The Merry Month of May

wood engraving · 381 x 203 mm

collection of the artist · image © the artist

It really is quite marvellous, wild brown hares are
resident in my garden! I have been living here in
the same house in mid-Wales for almost fifty years
and the hares will I am quite sure, through many
generations, have been here much, much longer.
Over time somehow these beautiful and mysterious
creatures have reconciled and familiarised themselves
with my presence here. I see them regularly and I
feel privileged to be able to observe them so closely;
through courting, mating and rearing their young, as
well as the long periods of relaxation. Hares will spend
hours grooming and dozing.

Some of the windows in my house and studio go
down to ground level, perfect for hare watching, but
still better, when I am outside sitting quietly they will
approach to within touching distance. Not that I have
ever attempted that.

Perhaps then it is not surprising that these wild
hares have been an unending source of inspiration
and continue to feature in my work. My wood engraving *The Merry Month of May*, depicting a hare together
with cockchafers (maybugs), is no more or less than
a simple expression of my ongoing enchantment.

Colin See-Paynton

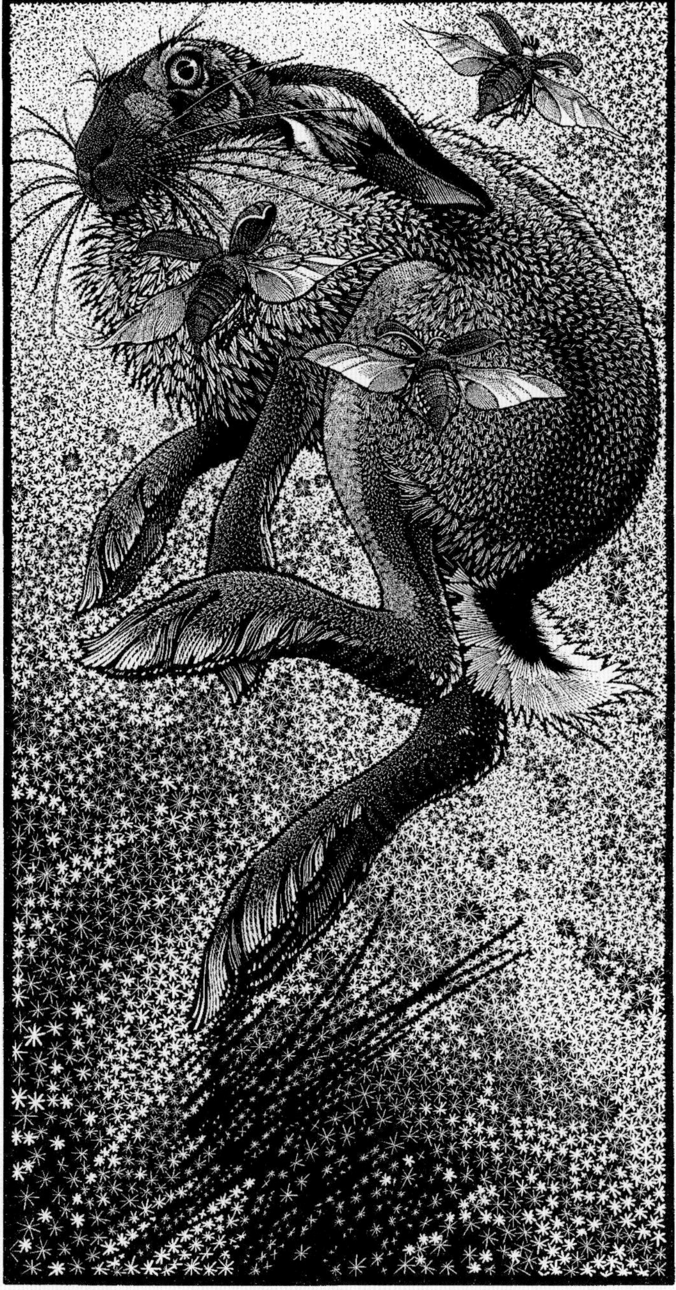

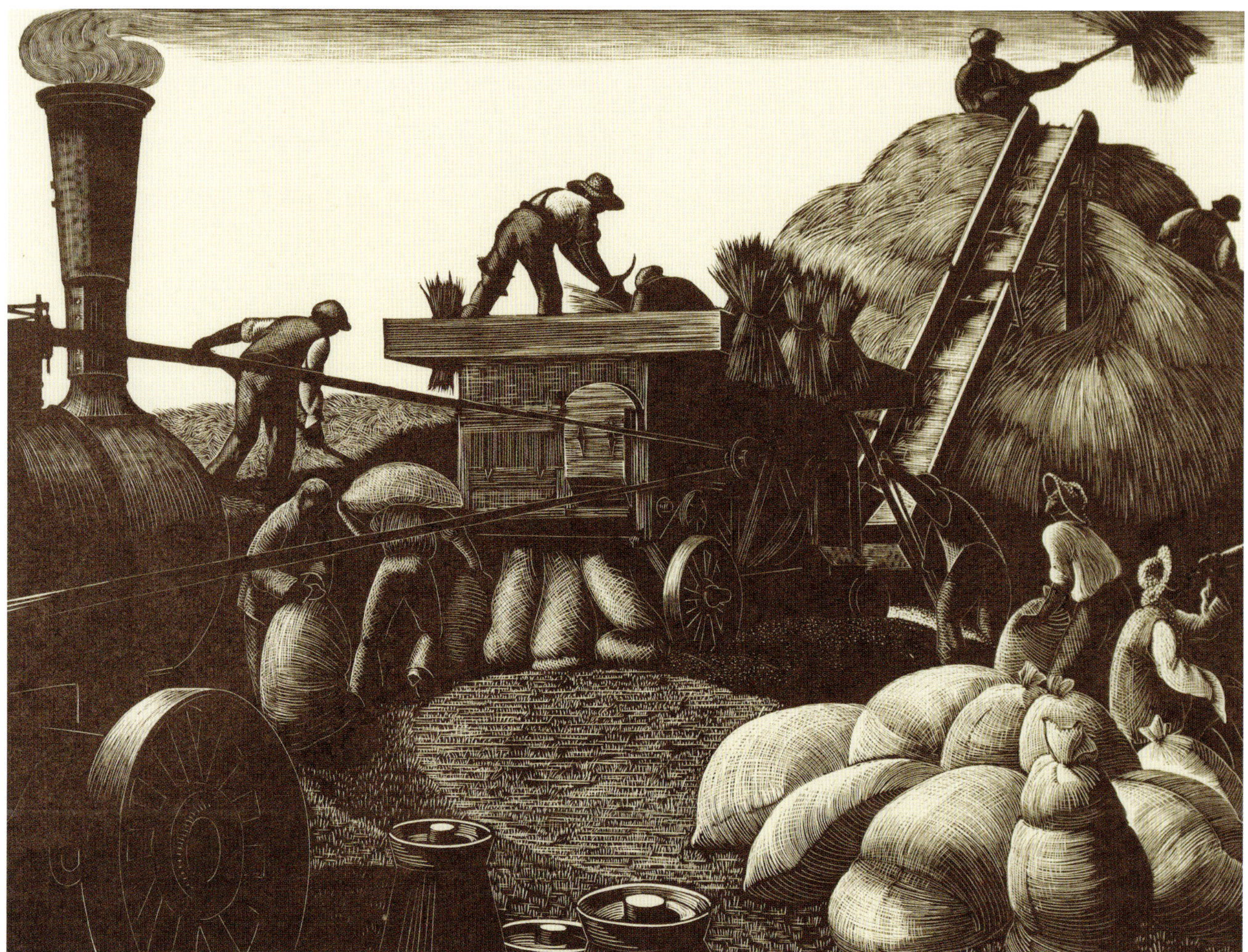

Clare Leighton (1898–1989)

March

1933 · wood engraving · 203 x 266 mm
from *The Farmer's Year*

Stuart Southall Collection · Clare Leighton's
wood engravings are reproduced courtesy
of the artist's estate

Early spring in rural communities in the 1930s would have resounded with the familiar humming of the threshing of the farmer's remaining ricks and the chug of the steam engine and clank of the elevator. Threshing was physically demanding and potentially dangerous in such noisy, dirty conditions with dust muting the colours of clothes and machinery and penetrating everything. With the light fading the workers flag further and everything grows quiet in the rickyard. Leighton writes: 'men remove and weigh the full sacks and hoist them across shoulders and take them up tiny wooden steps to the granary, like figures in the background of a Dürer print.'[1]

Leighton was well aware of and concerned by moves to replace tasks done traditionally by men and women on the land with machinery, observing:

> *There is something eternal in this sound of threshing, even though it be made by machinery; it recalls the primeval songs of the women in the small islands of the Mediterranean as they chant in their strange Lydian mode to the horses and mules trotting round and round, blindfold, on a circle of sheaves, as they tread out the grain with their hoofs. For all sounds of the labours on the land date from the beginning of time.*

GC

1. Leighton, C. (1933/2018), *The Farmer's Year: A Calendar of English Husbandry*, Little Toller Books, p. 19

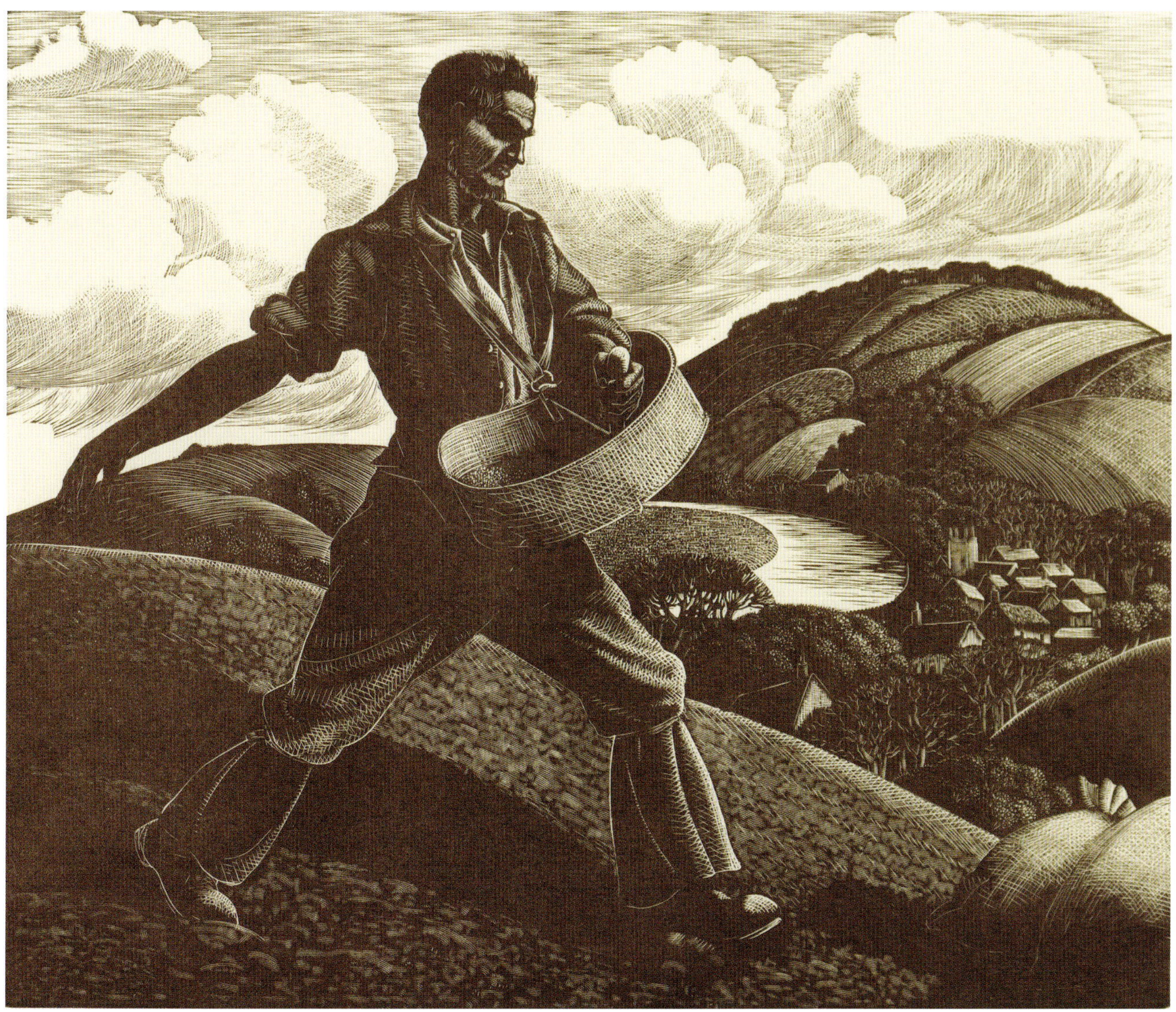

Clare Leighton (1898–1989)

April

1933 · wood engraving · 216 x 254 mm
from *The Farmer's Year*

Stuart Southall Collection · Clare Leighton's
wood engravings are reproduced courtesy
of the artist's estate

The rapid onslaught of social and economic change and the increasing use of
drillers on farmland made hand sowing a rare sight. Clare Leighton while lamenting
this loss in her eloquent and sincere text accompanying her engraving *Sowing*
recognised that it would soon pass irrevocably into history. She presents the sower
on a small hillside farm striding purposefully across the recently ploughed field
which has been harrowed of stones and weeds. Across his chest is strapped the
hopper full of seed the contents of which are flung rhythmically and evenly onto
the earth before him in order to avoid waste and ensure his crops would not grow
patchily later in the year. There is a feeling of heroic labour set against rolling hills
and billowing clouds which echoes Jean-François Millet's (1814–1875) well-known
painting *The Sower* (1850) a subject he repeated several times. Leighton's subject,
symbolic in its action is like Millet's, a profound expression of her beliefs about the
plight of rural workers. It is likely no accident that the powerful image of *The Sower*
featured on the cover of *The Farmer's Year*. **GC**

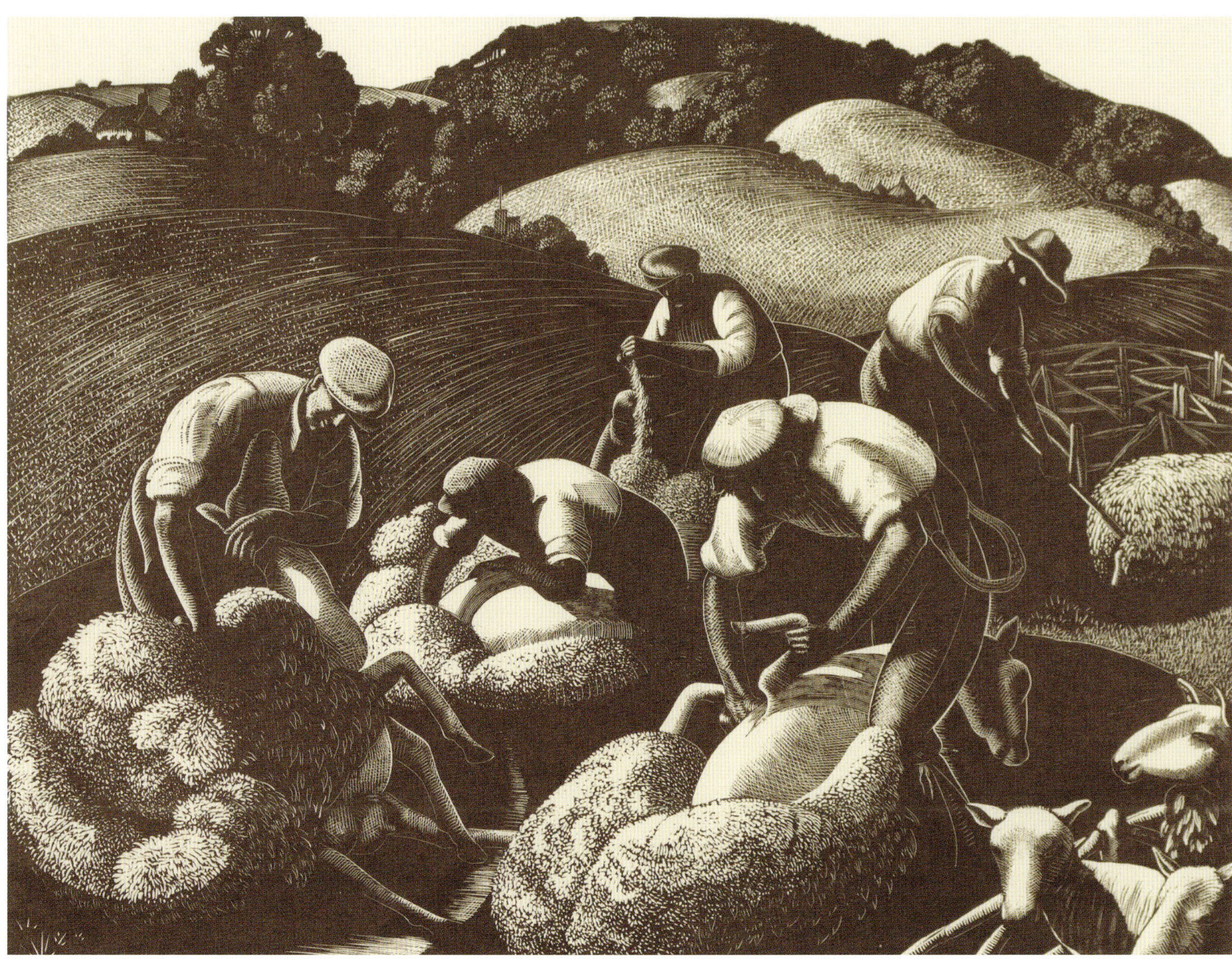

Clare Leighton (1898–1989)

May

1933 · wood engraving · 203 x 266 mm
from *The Farmer's Year*

Stuart Southall Collection · Clare Leighton's
wood engravings are reproduced courtesy
of the artist's estate

In Maytime with warmer weather meadows grow lush and high while lambs grow too, their gambolling and frisking a thing of the past. The sheep's fleece thickens and lengthens and becomes increasingly burdensome. But as Clare Leighton pithily notes through her own rediscovering of the countryside and understanding gained of the pattern of the seasons:

> *... the shepherd is wise. He knows his England. The nightingale may sing in the oaks night and day, and the buttercup fields blaze golden in the sun; but still there will be wind and cold rain and many nights to come may silver the meadows with frost. May is two-faced to poet and shepherd.*[1]

Sheep Shearing conveys the bustle of the event still done by hand on this small farm, the hurdles of the catching pen are in place ready to receive the bleating sheep. The three shearers will work from early morning to dusk for several days before all the flock is shorn. **GC**

1. Leighton, C. (1933/2018), *The Farmer's Year: A Calendar of English Husbandry*, Little Toller Books, p. 19

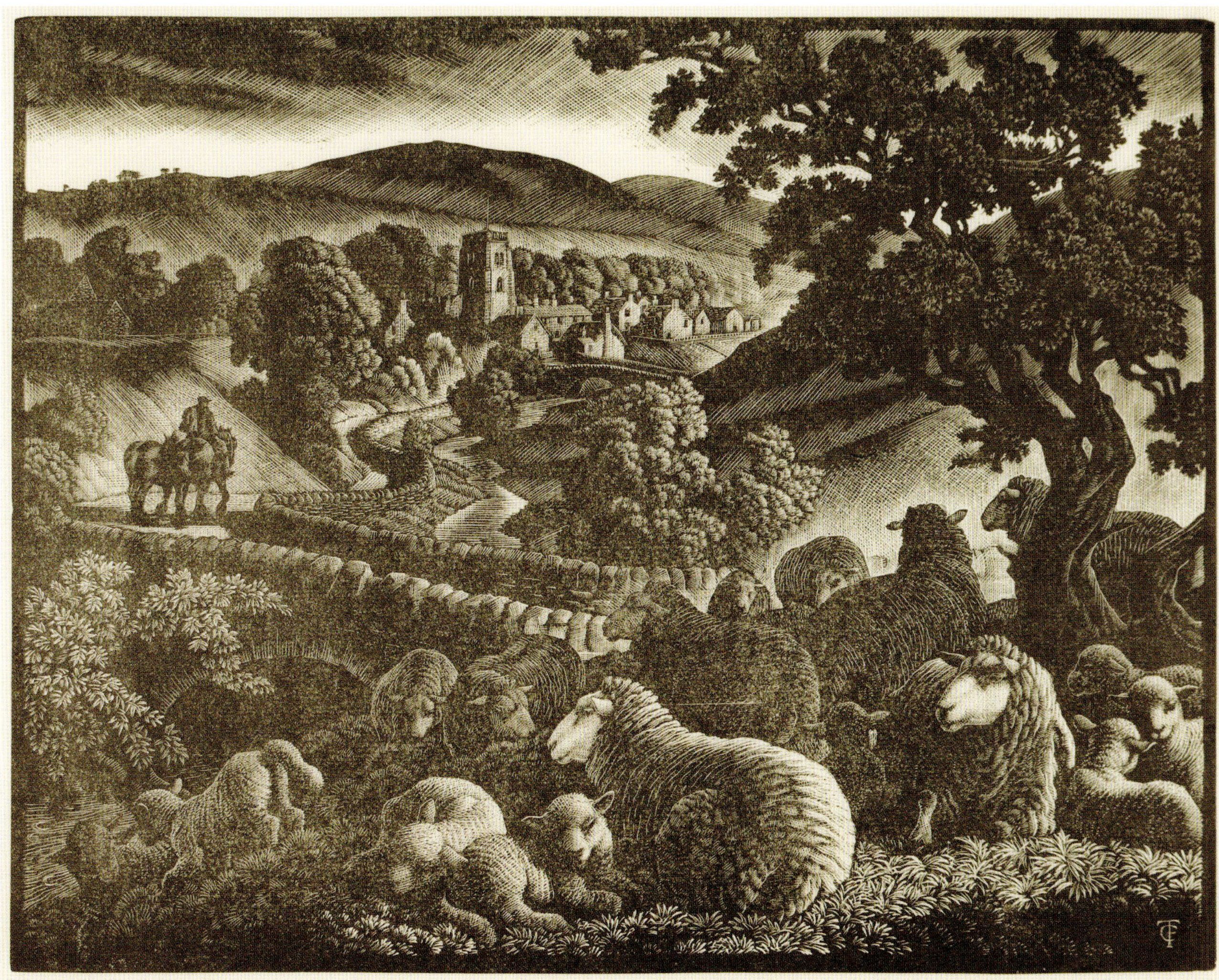

Charles Tunnicliffe
(1901–1979)

The Valley

1942 · wood engraving · 190 x 240 mm

Stuart Southall Collection · reproduced by kind
permission of The Estate of C.F. Tunnicliffe

The Valley was completed when Charles Tunnicliffe was teaching art at Manchester
Grammar School having been rejected for active service. Alongside his teaching
responsibilities he carried out fire watching duties and served as an air raid warden
in Macclesfield where he lived. Despite these demands Tunnicliffe produced illustrations for the 'Dig for Victory' campaign and other Ministry of Food promotions;
managing to acquire large pieces of boxwood for his engravings while materials
for artists were scarce and expensive.

Tunnicliffe's mastery of the medium of wood engraving is much in evidence in
The Valley despite his two-year hiatus from printmaking.[1] Nonetheless, it differs
markedly in sentiment from his earlier etchings of milking, mucking out and pig
slaughtering. The peaceful bucolic scene with village church nestled snugly in
the valley and weary labourer returning home while sheep and lambs are in the
meadow is redolent of the posters designed by graphic artist Frank Newbould
(1887–1951) for the series *Your Britain Fight for it Now*. The posters were issued in
1942 to arouse patriotic feelings and nostalgia for the British countryside and the
'worth' of fighting for your country and preserving the unspoiled rural landscape.
Tunnicliffe often spoke of his love for the countryside and in his autobiographical
and lavishly illustrated *My Country Book* (1942) describes 'a country which is full
of variety, and surprises, and which never palls.'[2] **GC**

1. Meyrick, R. and Heuser, H. (2017), *Charles Tunnicliffe Prints: A Catalogue Raisonné*,
Royal Academy of Arts, p. 185
2. Tunnicliffe, C.F. (1942), *My Country Book*, The Studio, p. 7

Cedric Morris (1889–1982)

Landscape of Shame

c. 1960 · oil on canvas · 756 x 1002 mm

Tate · image © The Cedric Morris Foundation/Bridgeman Images

Cedric Morris had a great love of and engagement with the natural world, spending most of his days out of doors, much preferring the country to town, becoming not only an accomplished painter but a prominent expert and breeder of irises. From the 1920s he produced some remarkable paintings of birds, an ability singled out by *The Times*' art critic:

> *… he evidently has something special to say … particularly about birds. 'Wading Birds', 'Cormorants' and 'Great Crested Grebes' are excellent performances boldly formalized and yet intensely real – as if the artist had some secret understanding with the kind …*[1]

Morris's understanding was based on studying living birds in varied conditions and rather than seeking precision like Tunnicliffe (p. 51) he sought to capture their essence. His intention was: 'to provoke a lively sympathy with the mood of the birds which ornithological exactitude may tend to destroy.'[2] This sympathy embraced an early concern for birds' habitats as conveyed in *Shags* (1938, National Museum Wales, National Museum Cardiff). The three sea birds perched on the cliff edge appear to have a personality of their own; Morris told fellow artist John Bensusan-Butt (1911–1997) and art critic for the *Essex County Standard* that they were angry at the threat of pollution as represented by the oil tanker steaming across the horizon.

Landscape of Shame with its stark depiction of scores of dead and dying birds including a rook, moorhen, partridge and sparrow hawks littering a barren landscape personifies the depth of Morris's environmental concerns. He had become a vociferous opponent of the damaging impact on birdlife of the use of pesticides and the intensification of agricultural practices.[3] During the late 1950s and early 1960s he had often picked up dead or dying birds in fields around his home at Benton End, near Hadleigh, Suffolk where with his partner Arthur Lett-Haines (1894–1978) they had established the East Anglian School of Painting and Drawing. In the spring of 1960 reports of the death of birds were widespread and Morris wanted to title the painting "Homage to [named manufacturer of pesticides]" but was eventually persuaded by Lett-Haines that it might result in a lawsuit.'[4] *Landscape of Shame* was likely completed between 1958 and 1963. It was in 1963 that American scientist and ecologist Rachel Carson's *Silent Spring* was published in Britain and drew attention to the deleterious impact of indiscriminate application of agricultural chemicals and pesticides on animal and human populations. In her chapter 'And No Birds Sing' she commented at some length on the bird deaths in Britain in the 1950s and 60s.[5] While Morris may not have read it, he was according to friends aware of its contents. **GC**

1. Art Exhibitions, *The Times*, 5 February 1926, p. 12
2. Morris (1936) cited in *Cedric Morris* (1984) by R. Morphet, The Tate Gallery, p. 86
3. Morris bequeathed £5000 to the Suffolk Wildlife Trust
4. Painter Glyn Morgan regularly visited Benton End during this period, see https://www.tate.org.uk/art/artworks/morris-landscape-of-shame-t04996 (accessed 27 April 2020)
5. See http://library.uniteddiversity.coop/More_Books_and_Reports/Silent_Spring-Rachel_Carson-1962.pdf (accessed 27 April 2020) and also Morphet (1984), Op cit., p. 118

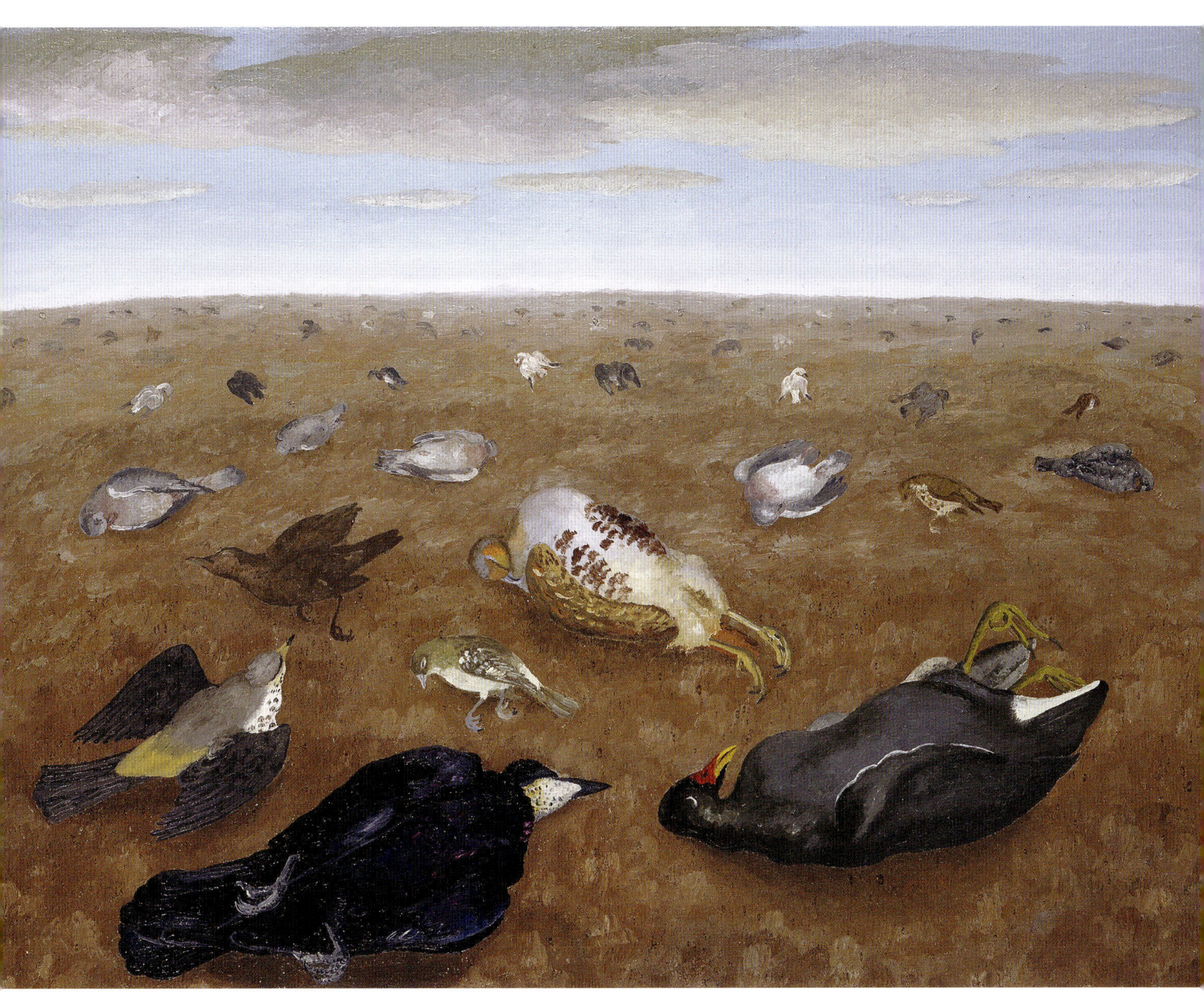

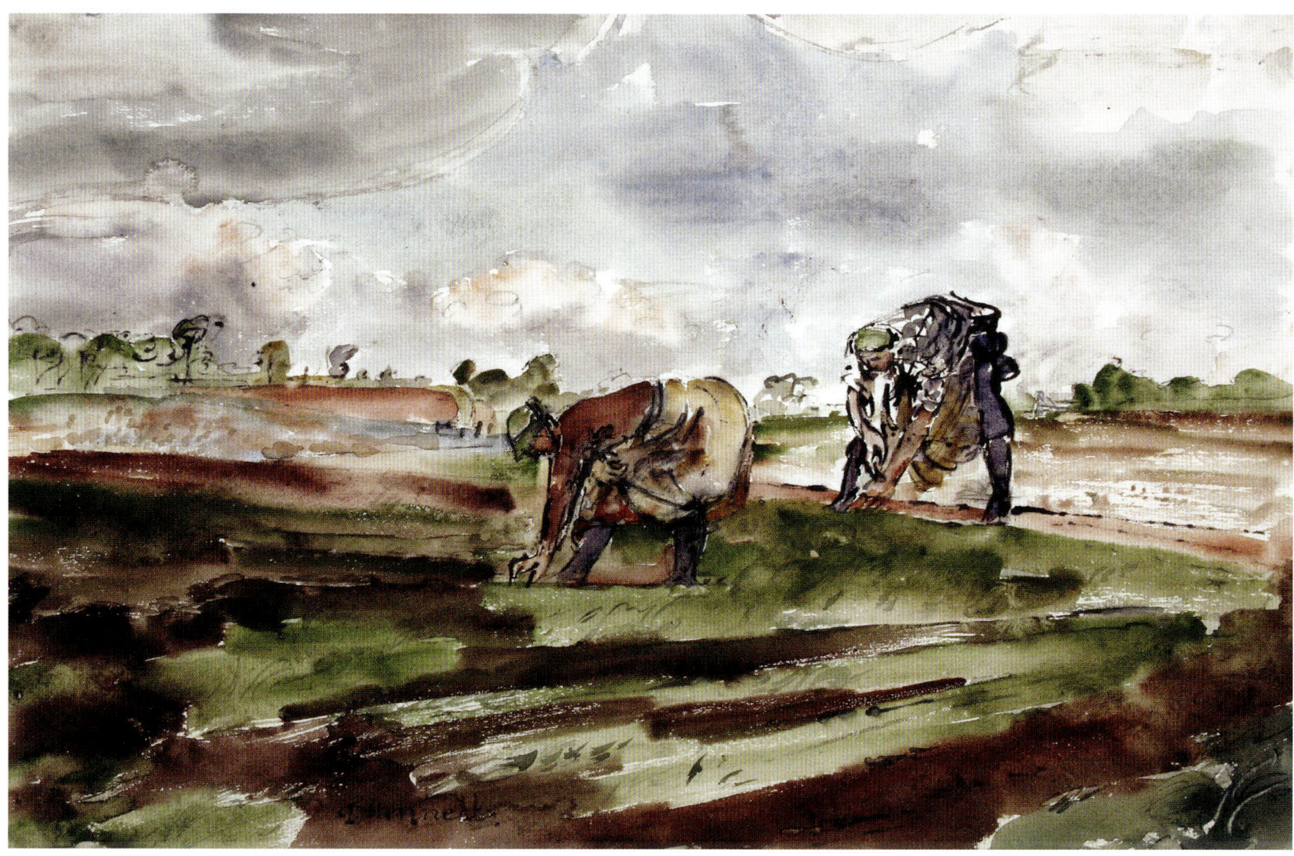

Thomas Hennell (1903–1945)

Weeding Onions

1943 • watercolour with pencil
317 x 477 mm

Chris Beetles Gallery
image courtesy of Chris Beetles Gallery

Wartime for Thomas Hennell meant there was 'heaps to paint, especially interesting jobs on the land.'[1] He was admirably suited to these jobs given his deep-seated knowledge of husbandry and rural crafts having recorded many of the latter for books he wrote and/or illustrated on agricultural matters. These included *British Craftsmen* (1943), part of the Britain in Pictures series published by Collins as a part of Britain's wartime propaganda efforts. Hennell drew on this rural understanding in 1940 for his work on the *Recording Britain* project contributing eleven watercolours of his native Kent, Hampshire, Dorset and the Cotswolds.

In June 1943 Hennell was invited by the War Artists' Advisory Committee (WAAC) to replace his friend Eric Ravilious (reported missing off Iceland in September 1942) for a three-month commission with the honorary rank of Lieutenant, Royal Naval Volunteer Reserve. *Weeding Onions* was completed a few weeks before he was sent by troopship to Reykjavik. The watercolour is of one of Hennell's sensitive yet 'rapid, rurally well-informed notations, often worked up on the spot … refreshingly free from nostalgia or idealisation.'[2] It was probably executed near his home in Ridley, a small secluded village not far from Shoreham. The women weeding may be Land Girls, albeit not wearing their iconic baggy brown breeches and green jerseys. In 1941 Hennell also recorded the harvest in Kent for the WAAC including threshing, stooking wheat and baling straw; the following year the Committee purchased his delicate and evocative watercolour of *Land Army Girls Resting at Lunch-time* for five guineas.[3] **GC**

1. Letter from Hennell to John ('Jack') Ensor, n.d. *c.* 1942, in MacLeod, M. (1988), *Thomas Hennell: Countryman, Artist and Writer*, Cambridge University Press, p. 188
2. MacLeod (1988), Ibid, p. xi
3. See Clarke, G. (2008), *The Women's Land Army: A Portrait*, Sansom & Company

SUMMER

Now Summer is in flower, and Nature's hum
Is never silent round her bounteous bloom;
Insects, as small as dust, have never done
With glitt'ring dance, and reeling in the sun:
And green wood-fly, and blossom-haunting bee,
Are never weary of their melody.
Round field and hedge, flowers in full glory twine,
Large bind-weed bells, wild hop, and streak'd woodbine
That life athirst their slender flowers,
Agape for dew-falls, and for honey showers;

John Clare · The Shepherd's Calendar · 1827

When summer comes in nature is literally humming with life as insects proliferate. Hedgerows are frothy with cow parsley while the meadows are mapped with con-stellations of buttercups. After the feverish energy of spring, there now comes a more restful season: growth is slowing down and bird song lessens. The sun is high in the sky and it is time to be outdoors, enjoying the warmth and appreci-ating the countryside at its best: it is the season for picnics, outings and fetes. Colourful railway posters once enticed holidaymakers to seaside resorts with a promise of family fun, leisurely promenades and guar-anteed sunshine. London Transport's posters promoted bus trips to the country or the chance to cool off at the bathing pond (p. 79). Summer was the busiest season of the year for the farming community; with the hay and corn harvests to be gathered there was no time to think about holidays. Long school vacations were originally timed to ensure there was enough labour available for all the tasks associated with harvest time. Fruit, berries, and nuts swell as summer passes and by August, when the reapers are busy in the fields and the days are shortening, thoughts are turning to autumn and the need to ensure there is sufficient food and fodder for the winter to come.

The summer solstice usually falls on 21 June. It marks the longest day and the moment when the sun reaches its zenith. It has become the focus for latter day pagan rituals at Stonehenge but in the past the more traditional date for celebration was Midsummer's Day on 24 June (also the feast of St John the Baptist) when bonfires were lit to bless the fields and drive away evil spirits. Another important date was Lammas, which falls on 1 August, halfway between the summer solstice and the autumn equinox. The word Lammas was derived from Old English words meaning 'loaf mass' – it was customary for a loaf made from newly harvested corn to be blessed in church. There is also a connection with the Celtic festival of Lughnasadh which marked the beginning of the harvest. Lammas is one of the main festivals celebrated by the modern pagan movement

(fig. 17). Another tradition related to the harvest was the making of corn or kirn dolls to bring luck to the household and its livestock and ensure fertility for the next year. The last cut corn would be made into the figure of a child. This was saved, perhaps to preserve the spirit of the corn, until the spring when it would be returned to the soil by being ploughed into the first furrow of the new season.

June is generally the sunniest month of the year and perhaps the time to see the countryside at its finest under clear blue skies and without the oppressive heat of late summer. This is certainly the atmosphere conveyed in James Bateman's *Haytime in the Cotswolds* (p. 78). July tends to be warmer and wetter and is known for storms: strong air currents rising from the land may climb high enough to create cumulonimbus clouds, the towering bringers of heavy rain and thunder. The so called 'dog days' from July to mid-August are associated with hot sultry weather and are named after Sirius, the Dog Star, which rises and sets with the sun at this time of year. Cloudy and wet conditions are more likely in August as west-erly depressions bring dull rainy skies especially in the north and west. Rain before the corn harvest could spell disaster so there is a wealth of weather lore relating to this time of year. Rain on St Swithin's Day, 15 July, was thought to foretell forty days of wet weather to follow. Country folk would also look to the behaviour of animals as a meteorological forecast. The sight of rooks remaining by their nests was thought to indicate rain to come, but swallows flying high on fine evenings (chasing insects carried up on warm air rising from ground) promised warm settled weather. The saying 'dew at night, the day will be bright' reflects the fact that dew forms when skies are clear and so foretells another fine day. For the farmer plenty of rain in May and early June and a drought from July to September would be ideal. Even today heavy rain in July can flatten crops and make them more difficult to harvest mechanically.

Summer also brings changes to the landscape. Heath and moor turn purple as heather comes into bloom. This is subtly

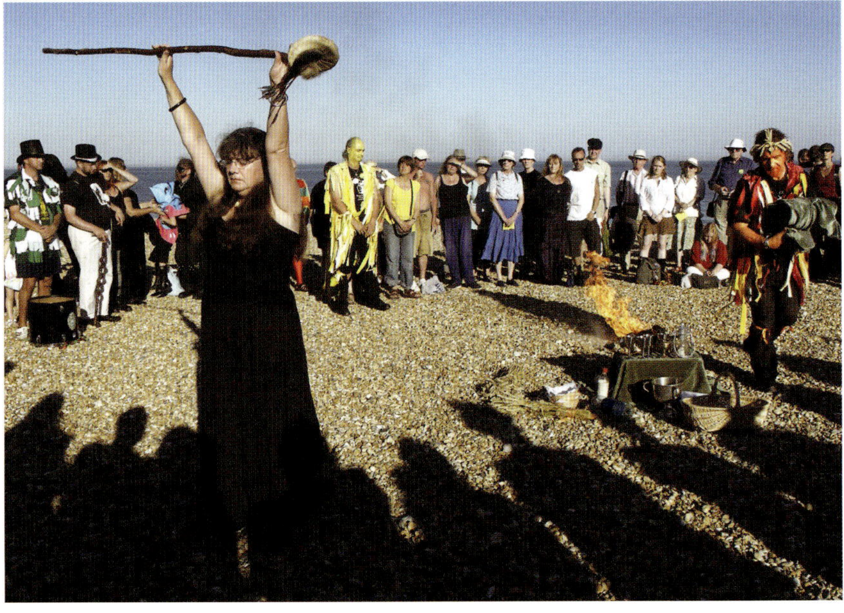

suggested in Frederick Golden Short's *Beaulieu Road, New Forest* (1900, Southampton City Art Gallery Collection) where the colours are muted as the sun sets over Lyndhurst church. Carry Akroyd's screenprint *Heath* (p. 73) shows that, however dominant the heather, its blooms are only one part of a New Forest habitat that comprises masses of gorse, grassy lawns and clumps of woodland. As the months draw on, the foliage of wood and hedgerow takes on the deeper green of summer. Cornfields change from fresh green to gold indicating that harvest time is near. This gentle transformation was captured by Rex Whistler (1905–1944) in the painting *The Vale of Aylesbury* (1933, National Trust Collection), which was also the basis for a Shell poster. The fields are bleaching to an ivory colour contrasted against the darker tones of trees and hedges that recede in ranks towards the distant hills. The artist can be seen seated, book in hand, in the shade of a tree contemplating this peaceful scene. By August summer is on the wane and in dry years trees may already be showing autumnal colours, the horse chestnut often in the vanguard. After the harvest, vistas of waving golden corn such as that depicted by Alan Reynolds in *Summer: Young September's Cornfield* (p. 76) are reduced to stubble.

Fields of wheat and barley and the activity of harvesting have long been popular subjects for artists. John Constable (1776–1837) painted *The Cornfield* in 1826 (National Gallery Collection) and in perhaps his most celebrated work *The Haywain* (1821, National Gallery) the titular cart is making its way across a stream towards a distant line of reapers. Cornfields have attracted a surprisingly wide range of artists including John Linnell (1792–1882), W.H. Allen, Joan Eardley (1921–1963) and Euston Road School founder Claude Rogers (1907–1979). Perhaps the most influential was Samuel Palmer (1805–1881), whose paintings of Shoreham transformed the Kent countryside into a paradise on earth. The ink drawing *The Valley Thick with Corn* (1825, Ashmolean Museum Collection) identifies the corn harvest with the bountiful plenty of God's creation: a man lies reading among uncut corn, stooks stand drying nearby, a shepherd and his flock rest in the shade of a tree while in the distance a church tower rises above the quiet valley. Paintings such as *The Gleaning Field* (c. 1833, Tate Collection) depict a pastoral idyll that was more a creation of Palmer's visionary imagination than a portrayal of the often harsh reality of agricultural life at the time. Yet these works have an irresistible power and cast their spell over a new generation of artists in the early twentieth century. Graham Sutherland's etching *Cray Fields* (p. 75) with its hop poles, cornfield and weary labourers seems to pick up where Palmer left off a hundred years earlier. Palmer also inspired the younger generation of Neo-Romantic artists, although anxiety induced by the threat and outbreak of war gave their drawings a darker edge. John Minton's *Landscape with Harvester Resting* (c. 1944, private collection/Pallant House Gallery) shows a young man reclining beside a line of corn stooks and in John Craxton's *Poet in Landscape* (1941, estate of the artist) there is a distant view of haycocks but the plant life surrounding the figure seems unnaturally alive and threatening.

Before the advent of pesticides, cornfields were speckled with the bright colours of poppies, cornflowers, corncockles and corn marigolds, a phenomenon that Edward McKnight Kauffer's poster *Flowers o' the Corn* (1920, London Transport

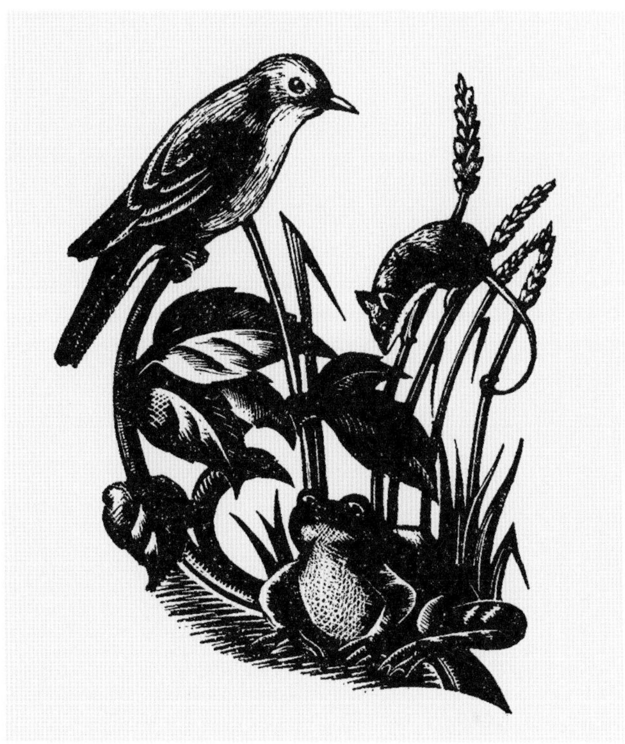

FIG. 18 · **Clare Leighton** (1898–1989)
illustration from *The Natural History of Selborne*
Penguin Books, 1941

Museum Collection) encouraged Londoners to go and experience for themselves. C.F. Tunnicliffe's illustration for *What to Look For in Summer* shows poppies mixed in with the corn as well as thistles and ragwort.[1] Spear thistles flower from July to October and are a valuable source of nectar for bees and butterflies. Ragwort provides food for the caterpillars of the cinnabar moth but is also highly toxic to horses and cattle and must be removed from paddocks and pasture and from the roadsides of the New Forest. One of the joys of summer is the fragrance of honeysuckle or woodbine which fills the air around hedgerows and gardens on still, warm evenings. Wild rose and elderflower are in bloom in June (p. 74), indeed the English summer is said to begin with elderflower and end with elderberries, which ripen in August and September. From mid-May until August wild orchids can be seen, particularly in woods and open grassland. The lupins, peonies and poppies of James Lynch's tempera painting *Ted's Greenhouse, Summer* (p. 69) are just some of the blooms that can create a riot of colour in June gardens. As the season wears on plants put their energy into seed and berry. By August hazelnuts, blackberries and the fruits of the orchard are almost ready for picking, a sure sign that autumn is coming.

The young of small mammals like hedgehogs, dormice, harvest mice and bats are born and reared during the summer months. The sight of bats acrobatically catching insects on the wing at dusk is another of the wonders of the season. Gertrude Hermes compared the hanging bat with the spider waiting in its web in an illustration for the 1932 Gregynog Press edition of Gilbert White's (1720–1793) *The Natural History of Selborne*.[2] White was a pioneering naturalist, his writings based on first hand observation of the wildlife around his home in Hampshire. He was the first to identify the noctule bat and the harvest mouse and distinguish the chiffchaff, willow warbler and wood warbler as three separate species. His *Natural History* is still viewed as a seminal work and has been regularly re-published, attracting such notable illustrators as Eric Ravilious, John Nash and Clare Leighton (fig. 18). Summer is the time to appreciate butterflies with almost all the British species on the wing between June and August. The painted lady arrives in June, occasionally in vast numbers, part of an incredible 7,500-mile round trip that takes it from tropical Africa to the Arctic Circle. Dragonflies and damselflies with their colourful bodies and gossamer wings are busy patrolling riverbanks and hedgerows. Summer has always been marked by the buzz and hum of insects. Moths would mob lit windows at night while flies were plastered on car windscreens, but this is less and less the case. Populations of bees, butterflies, ladybirds and moths seem to be in freefall under the pressures of pollution, pesticides, habitat change and climate change. This decline could have a catastrophic impact because insects have a vital role as pollinators and are the foundation of a food chain that stretches all the way up to humans. Their plight inspired Kurt Jackson's exhibition *Bees (and the odd wasp) in my Bonnet*, held at Oxford University Museum of Natural History in 2016, which explored a longstanding interest in insects stemming from his time as a student of zoology and more recently as a beekeeper at his home in Cornwall.

Summer is a quieter time for birds, as they no longer need to sing to attract a mate or establish territory. Once they have finished breeding they also moult to replace worn feathers, a process which takes several weeks. At this time they are more vulnerable to predators so avoiding attention is a use-ful survival mechanism. The resulting silence can add to the oppressive atmosphere on still, humid days. Birds are also less obvious in gardens as they seek out new food sources, perhaps on farmland where there might be spilt grain or among the berries and seeds of the hedgerow. However, these pickings are becoming increasingly thin. The Department for Environ-ment Food & Rural Affairs has found that farmland bird pop-ulations have dropped by 55% since the 1970s and for species such as the corn bunting, turtle dove, grey partridge and tree sparrow the decline is over 90%.[3] While the steep falls of the 1970s and 1980s have slowed and many farmers are taking positive steps to conserve wildlife the trend remains down-ward. These changes are attributed to the decline in mixed farming, the tendency to sow in autumn rather than spring and cut grass for silage rather than hay, the increased use of pesticides and artificial fertilisers and the stripping out of hedgerows. The latter has significantly changed the rural landscape, the historic patchwork of fields with their natural boundaries and margins giving way to huge open areas suited to the massive machinery of industrial scale farming. These vast tracts with their precise tractor patterns feature in some of James Lynch's Wessex landscapes (fig. 16, p. 40).

In the south June is the month for haymaking. Hay was once the most important food for livestock and its harvest was a critical event in the agricultural calendar. The work of the hay harvest has been popular with British artists since Constable and David Cox (1783–1859) were painting in the

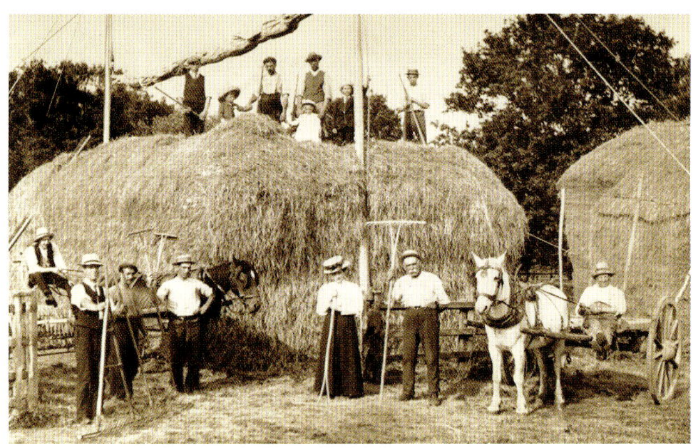

FIG. 19 · Haymaking with an elaborate rick cloth frame at Clayhill near Lyndhurst
St Barbe Museum and Art Gallery Collection

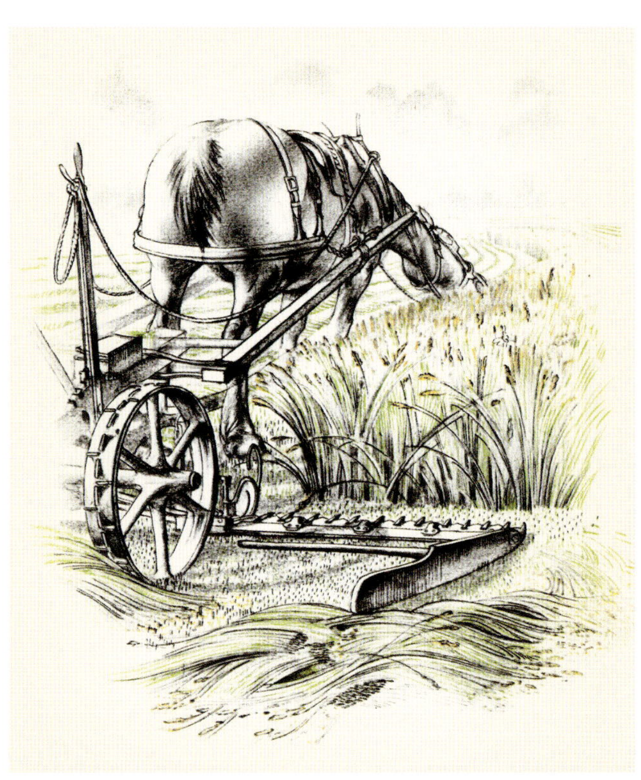

FIG. 20 · **C.F. Tunnicliffe** (1901–1979)
The Business End of a Mowing Machine
from *My Country Book*, 1942

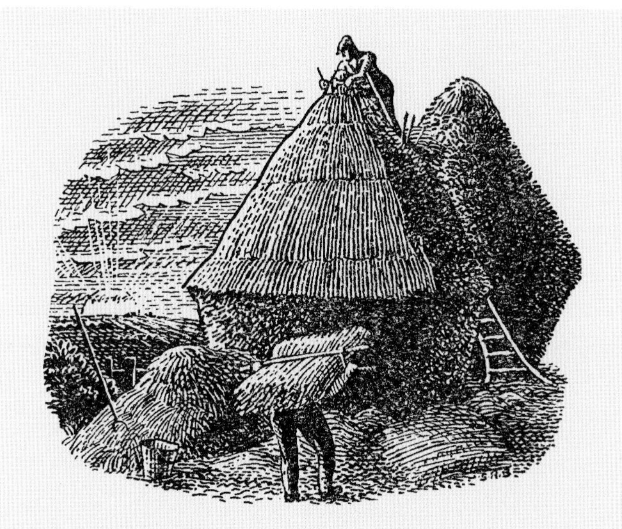

FIG. 21 · **Stanley Roy Badmin** (1906–1989)
Thatching the Rick
tailpiece decoration from *The Seasons* by Ralph Wightman, 1953

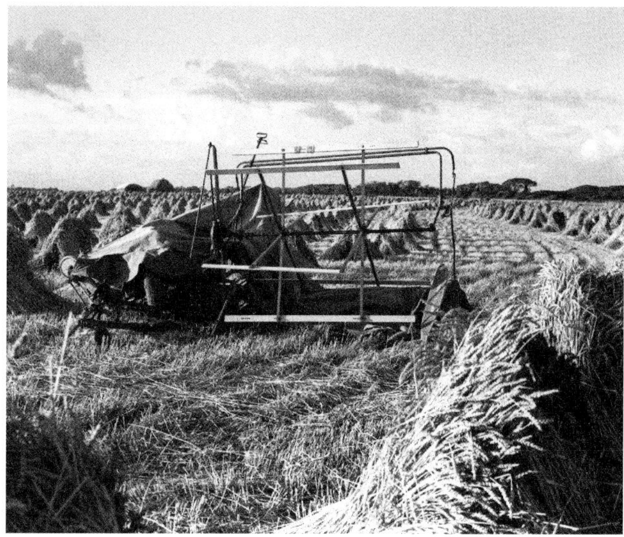

FIG. 22 · A binder among the corn stooks at the end of the working day
St Barbe Museum and Art Gallery Collection

early nineteenth century. Clare Leighton chose it as her subject for June in *The Farmer's Year* (p. 80). An unusual and typically surreal approach can be seen in Tristram Hillier's (1905–1983) *Haymaking* (1943, York Art Gallery Collection). Brightly coloured carts, harness, tools and clothing have been suddenly abandoned, not a soul remains. Perhaps they have stopped work to cool off in the shade, but somehow the empty scene and circling birds suggests something altogether more sinister. Once haymaking was characterised by lines of men with scythes moving slowly across the field with regular stops to sharpen their blades. Each man was expected to cut an acre in a day. By the second half of the nineteenth century many larger farms had horse-drawn mowers whose teams might cut twelve acres in the same time. In *My Country Book* C.F. Tunnicliffe remembered using one on his father's farm (fig. 20): 'when the machine is in position for the cutting of the first swathe, the cutter bar is dropped and with a "suss-a-russ" the grass falls to the flashing knife and is turned by the arm of the grass-boards into even swathes. Down they go, grasses, daisies, sorrels, and a few thistles (curse them! for they prick when loading with bare arms)'.[4] The job was no longer as labour-intensive but the timing was just as important, the problem being that when the grass is at its best before it puts its energy into making seeds, the weather cannot be relied on, hence the old adage 'make hay while the sun shines'. Once cut, hay was left for a day or two and then turned so that it dried evenly. Once this was done by men and women with hay forks or a horse-drawn swath turner. Thomas Hennell recorded the varying regional methods of harvesting in *Change in the Farm* (1936), an elegy for the disappearing techniques and equipment of traditional farming, written just as mechanisation and wartime necessity would change the face of agriculture for good.[5] If rain threatened the hay could be gathered into rolls and heaped up in haycocks. Water would run off these and not penetrate. Once dry enough to store, hay was carefully built into a rick (fig. 19). There was a real art to this work that included thatching a roof to keep the rain off as seen

in Tunnicliffe's etching *The New Rick* (p. 84) and Stanley Badmin's tailpiece for Ralph Wightman's book *The Seasons* (fig. 21). Today tractors leave the hay in neat rows, returning later to turn it and then again to bale it in plastic-covered rolls, now a familiar part of the summer landscape, as seen in James Lynch's tempera painting *Pink Bales, Mere Down* (2018).

Summer was also a time for hoeing root vegetable fields, sheep dipping and maintaining meadows by weeding, cutting and harrowing. But thoughts would soon be turning to the corn harvest. Barley must be dry enough to store or it will rot. Farmers would look at the colour and crunch grains between their teeth. If soft and juicy it was not fully ripe, but if too hard it could be overripe and the grain would fall from heads during harvesting and be wasted on the ground. Today a moisture meter allows such decisions to be made with certainty. Once the whole community was involved in the harvest. The corn was cut with sickles or scythes and bundled into sheaves which were loosely stacked to finish drying. Orderly lines of stooks had an obvious visual appeal: stooked corn in the rosy light of sunset was a favourite subject for W.H. Allen and took on an even deeper resonance in Adrian Allinson's wartime *Harvesting Scene* (National Archives Collection). Over time the business of harvesting was mechanised: a horse-drawn clipper simply cut the corn but a reaper binder (fig. 22) seen working in the background of Tunncliffe's etching *The Wheat Field* (p. 83), combined cutting and tying up the sheaf, leaving tidy rows ready to be stacked. The binder can also be seen gradually clearing the field in John Nash's School Print *Harvesting* (1946).[6] However, if rough weather flattened the corn there might still be a need to revert to time-honoured methods, as seen in Stanley Anderson's engraving *Windswept Corn* (fig. 23). Once dry, the corn had to be threshed or built into ricks (ears inward to keep the birds and mice off), a process illustrated by Stanley Badmin in *Nature Through the Seasons in Colour*.[7] Rats also had to be kept at bay and in some areas ricks were raised off the ground on staddle stones as seen in Robin Tanner's etching

Wiltshire Rickyard (fig. 10, p. 37). In *Nature Through the Seasons in Colour* (1953) A.G. Street noted the significance of these structures to the agricultural community: 'Fifty years ago the wealth of a farmer in arable country could be judged by the number of his corn stacks'.[8]

Modern farm machinery has rendered most of these traditional tasks redundant. The combine harvester cuts the corn, the grain is shaken loose inside and funnelled to an accompanying trailer, the chaff blows away and the straw is left in rows for the baler. One of the consequences of such progress was the loss of a sense of shared purpose among rural communities. In *Ask the Fellows who Cut the Hay* (1956) the author and oral history recording pioneer George Ewart Evans (1909–1988) commented:

> *At harvest-time … there were crowds of reapers in the field, crowds also of women and children tying up the sheaves of corn and doing other light but necessary jobs … Everybody was involved … and the ritual of the harvest made it a truly communal occasion … Where twenty men formerly spent three weeks with scythes or binders harvesting the corn, today a couple of men with a combine-harvester will do the same work in a few afternoons.*[9]

SM

1. Watson, G.L. (1960), *What to Look For in Summer*, Ladybird Books Ltd., p. 45
2. Russell, J. (1993), *The Wood Engravings of Gertrude Hermes*, Scolar Press, p. 74
3. *Wild Bird Populations in the UK, 1970 to 2018*, Department for Environment Food & Rural Affairs, 2019, p. 10
4. Tunnicliffe, C.F. (1942), *My Country Book*, The Studio, pp. 36–8
5. Hennell T. (1936), *Change in the Farm*, republished 1977 by EP Publishing, pp. 106–11
6. Artmonsky, R. (2010), *The School Prints: A Romantic Project*, Antique Collectors' Club, pp. 80–1
7. *When Farmer's Work is Hardest: The Storing of the Grain Harvest* in *Nature Through the Seasons in Colour*, Odhams Press Ltd., 1953, between pp. 152–3
8. Street, A.G. in *Nature Through the Seasons in Colour*, 1953, Odhams Press Ltd., p. 116
9. Evans, G.E. (1956), *Ask the Fellows who Cut the Hay*, Faber and Faber, pp. 237–8

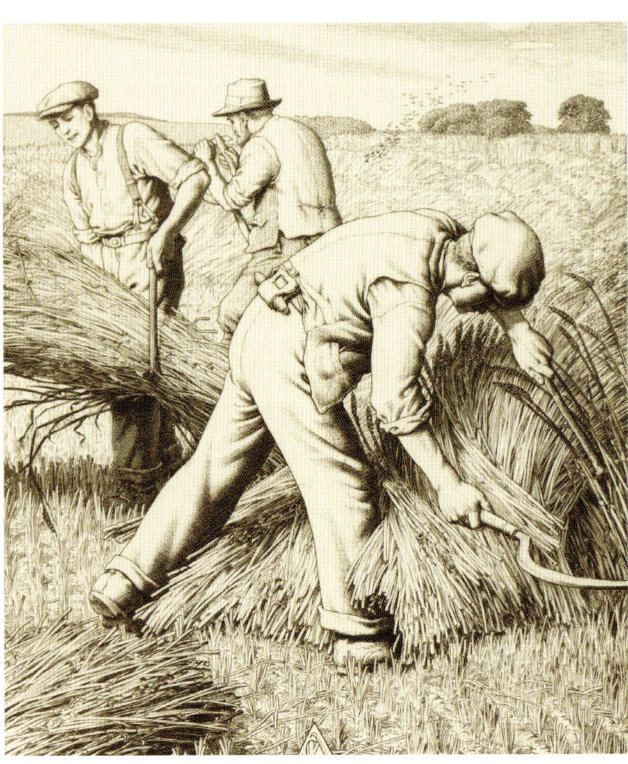

FIG. 23 · **Stanley Anderson** (1884–1966) · *Windswept Corn* 1938 · line engraving

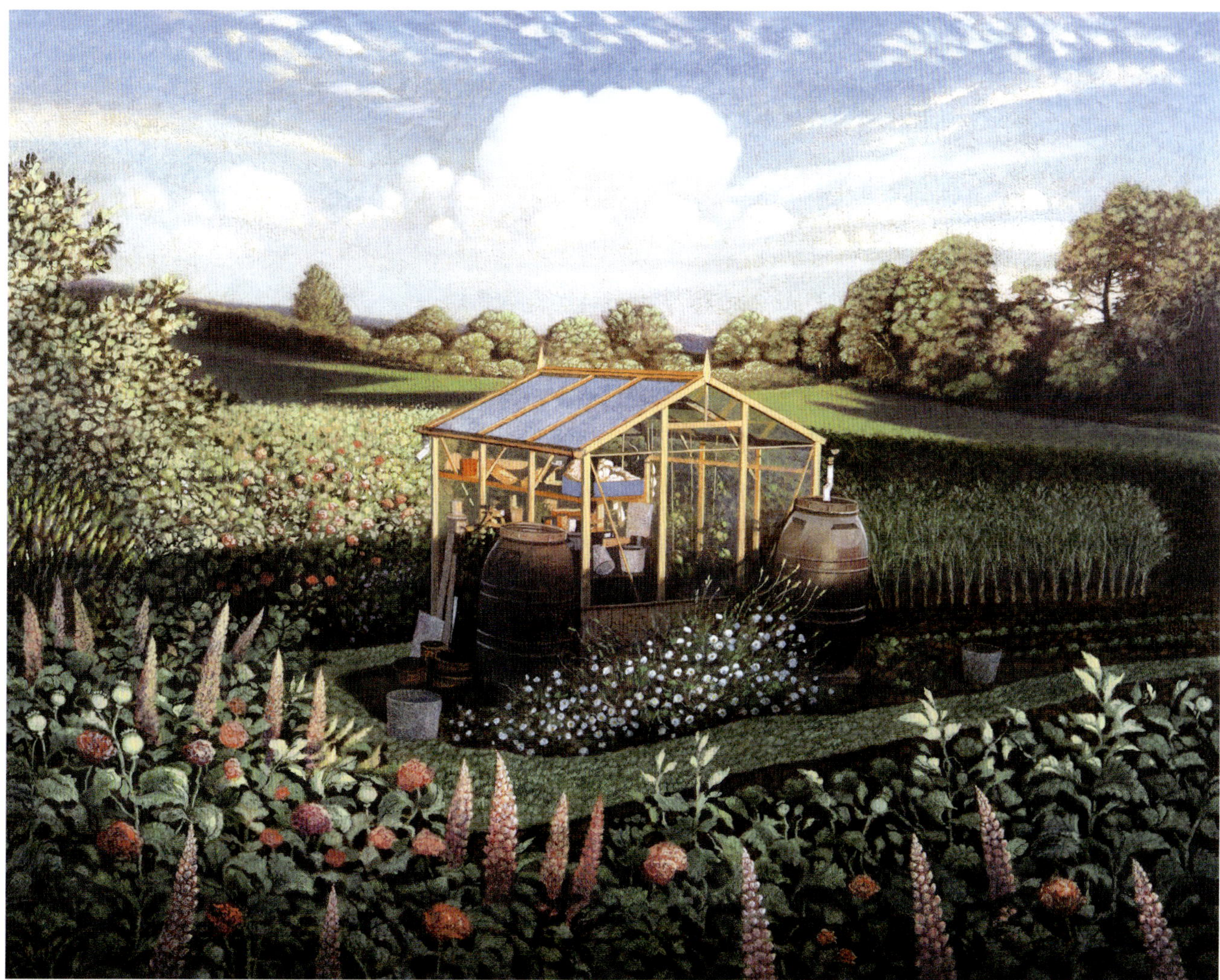

James Lynch (b. 1956)

Ted's Greenhouse, Summer

egg tempera on gesso coated wood panel
482 x 610 mm

private collection · image © the artist

A greenhouse in a garden harnessing the sun. There's the reflection of the blue infinity of the sky in the glass roof and a blue plastic box on the shelf which I painted with pure lapis lazuli – a rather exotic pigment for such common-or-garden plastic. I buy my raw pigments by weight, mixing them with water and egg yolks from my chickens and the lapis makes a radiant blue glaze.

I've always loved the interplay of sun, sky and land. The visual connections as sky bounces off puddles and glass. The sun heating the earth and the heat from the land creating thermals – currents of warm air forming clouds. My parents were obsessive glider pilots and from a very young age we were always weather-watching. I fly with a paraglider, so the relationship between land and sky is central to my life, both as a painter and for my free flying using the rising air currents, which are particularly good in the summer. **James Lynch**

Eric Ravilious (1903–1942)

Wedgwood Garden and *Garden Implements*

1938 and 1939 · ceramics

Julian Francis Collection

Eric Ravilious was not only a talented 'watercolourist of the highest order', but also 'an outstanding decorative designer'.[1] His wide-ranging interests made him well suited to producing designs for Wedgwood for transfer-printing onto ceramics. Ravilious's commissions spanned the years from 1936–41, his first was for a mug to commemorate Edward VIII's coronation but it was withdrawn on the King's abdication and subsequently adapted for the coronation of George VI and Queen Elizabeth in 1937.

Ravilious would work up his designs with the undecorated vessel in front of him: the vase in *Garden Flowers on a Cottage Table* (*c.* 1937–38),[2] was subsequently decorated with his 'Boat Race Day' design. In 1938 he also embarked on 10 elaborate vignettes (and many smaller details from these)[3] for *Garden*. The tableware included a coffee pot which featured a gardener pushing a laden wheelbarrow, behind him a wooden ladder lay propped on logs to the side of the tree. The lid of the coffee pot was decorated with reduced elements from larger vignettes in Ravilious's characteristic style: a woman gardener bending down to pick up apples; a basket of apples; a wheelbarrow filled with logs; and a ladder resting on logs. The main vignette on one of the plates is closely related to his watercolour *Two Women in a Garden* (1932, Fry Art Gallery) which depicts potter Charlotte Epton (who married Edward Bawden in 1932) reading, while artist and engraver Tirzah Garwood (who married Ravilious in 1930) shells peas in Brick House's extensive kitchen garden in Great Bardfield, where the two couples lived until the Ravilious's moved to Bank House in nearby Castle Hedingham, Essex. The plate portrays only the seated Epton. The other pieces in the series feature a range of vignettes of timeless gardening activities decorating the centre with a highlighted curvilinear repeating pattern on the borders.

Garden Implements produced in 1939 comprised of a lemonade set with 'Liverpool' jug and beakers. The front of the jug featured the motif of a wooden barrel surrounded by ivy leaves developed from the barrel on one of the *Garden* plates, 1938. On the reverse were nine small idyllic vignettes related to the garden including a cat asleep on a wall, bees buzzing around a hive, a cut sunflower in a jug, an empty wheelbarrow and a bell-shaped rhubarb forcer and plant. Owing to wartime conditions many of Ravilious's designs were not put into production in any quantity until the 1950s.[4] **GC**

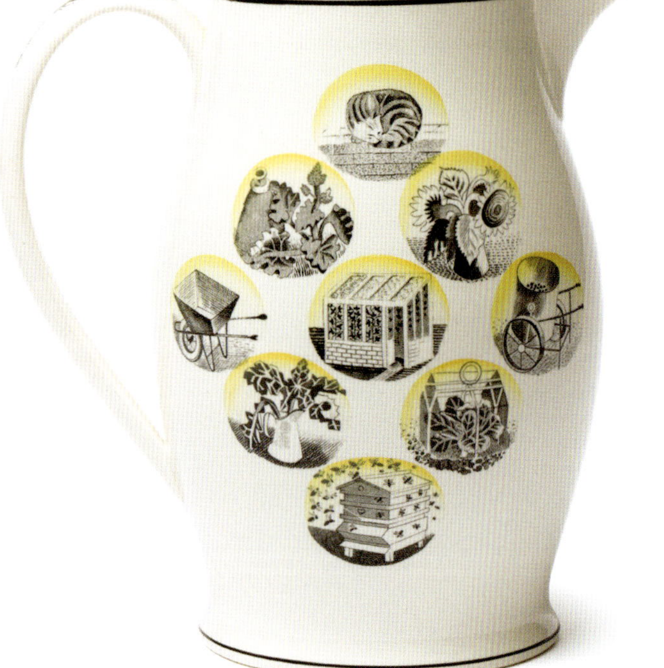

1. Robert Harling (1986), 'Eric Ravilious: A Memoir' in Dennis, R. (1995), *Ravilious and Wedgwood: The Complete Wedgwood Designs of Eric Ravilious*, this edition published by Richard Dennis, p. 9 and p. 8 respectively
2. Sold at Christie's, November 2001
3. See the catalogue complied by M. Batkin & R. Dalrymple, in Dennis (1995), op. cit., p. 50
4. See http://www.wedgwoodmuseum.org.uk/collections/search-the-collection/search/ravilious_garden (accessed 4 March 2020)

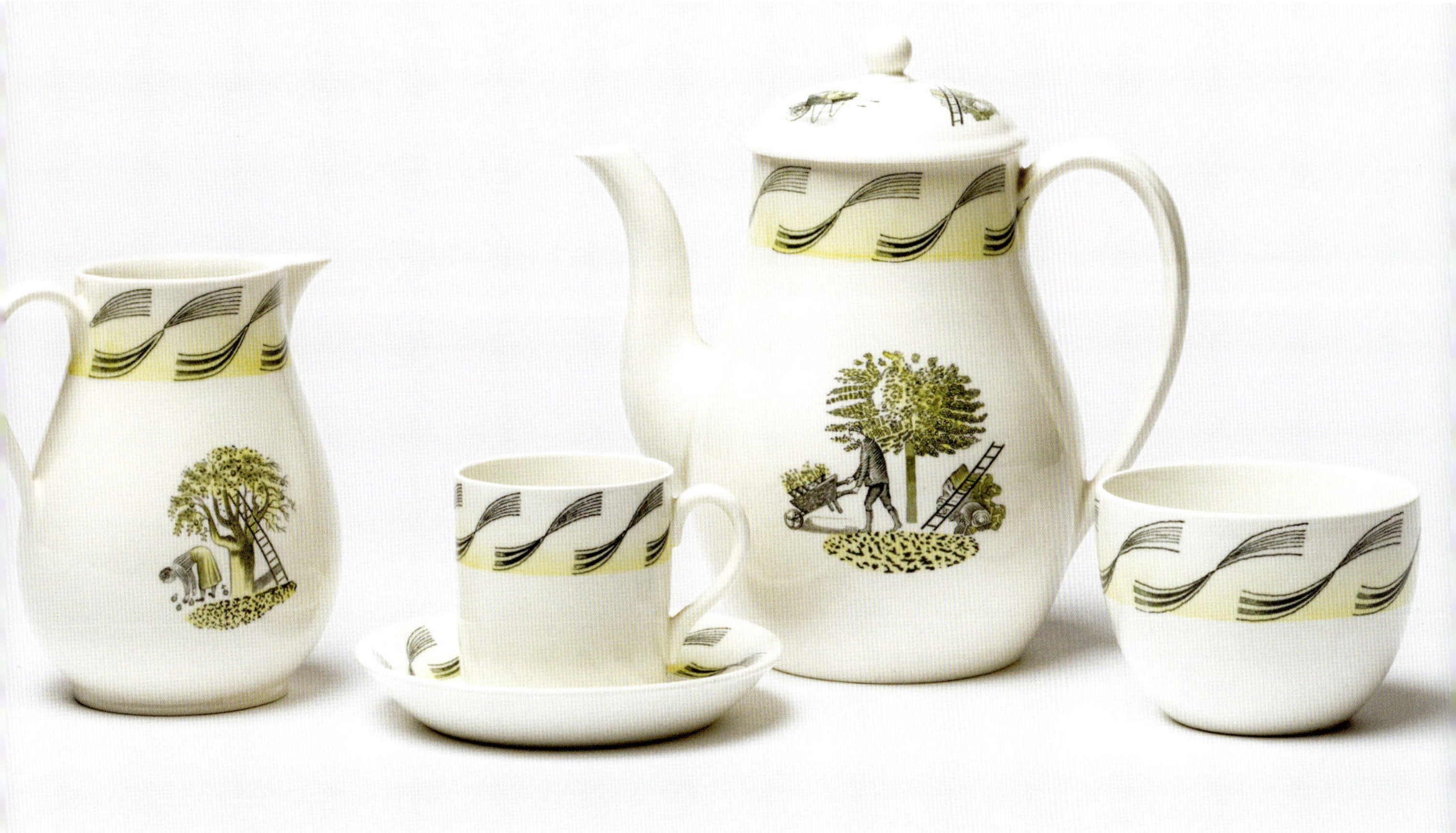

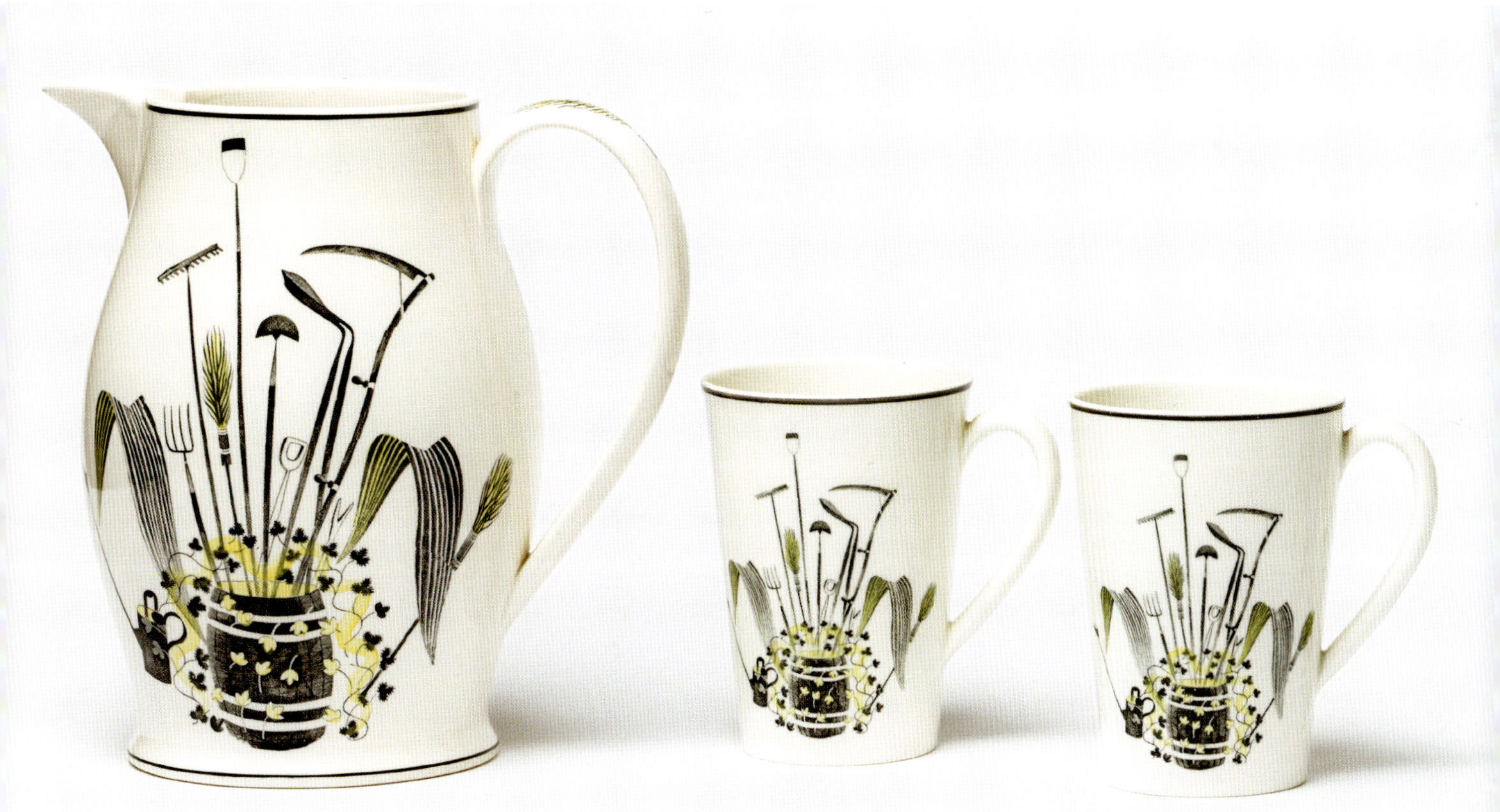

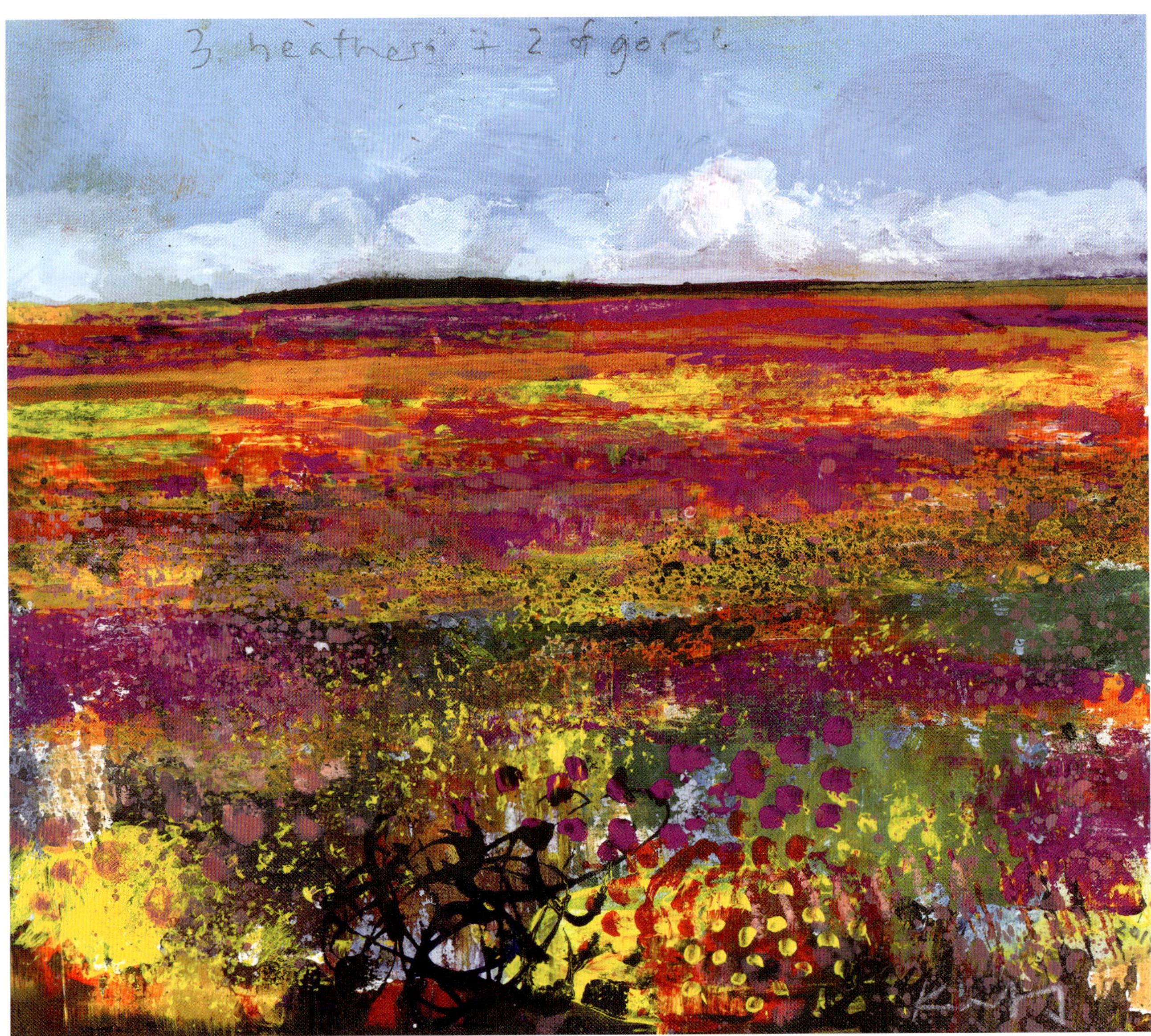

Kurt Jackson (b. 1961)

Three of heather and two of gorse

2019 · mixed media on museum board
205 x 230mm

collection of the artist · image © the artist

A plain of sloping gorse and heather moorland almost psychedelic under its coat of mauve, purple, and golden yellow. All sensations are catered for here with the blinding spread of brightness, the bee buzz under soaring skylark song, the prickly almost natural acupuncture and the intoxicating honeyed heather perfume. I cushion myself tentatively into the three species of heather and two of gorse to join in with the celebration, this spectacle of summer – intense colour saturated gouache and oil pastel smears and dabs on my lap, my pad, on me.

Kurt Jackson

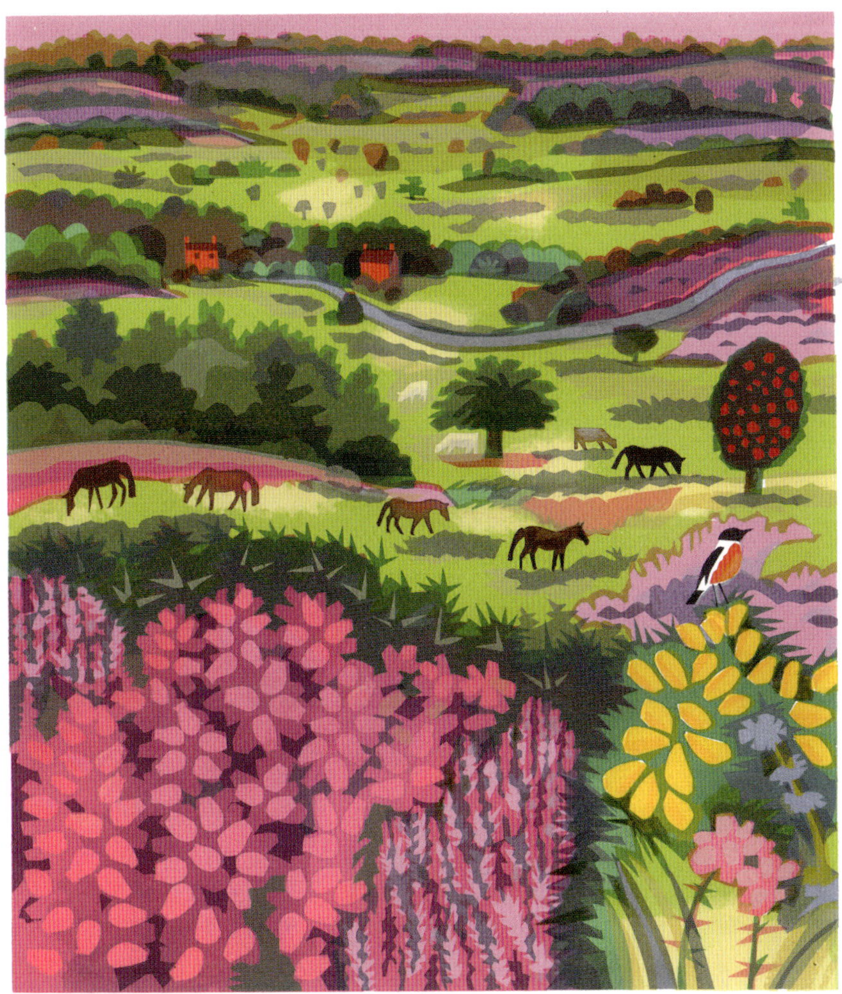

Carry Akroyd (b. 1953)

Heath

2020 · screenprint · 400 x 350 mm

for the cover of *Heathland* by Clive Chatters,
published by Bloomsbury · collection of the artist
image © the artist

A heath in high summer conceals its riches beneath a cloak of purple. Carry challenges the caricature of blooming heather and weaves other hues between the low bushes. Much of the wildlife gets along in cryptic modesty but even in the heat of the day there are flamboyant individuals to be found with the 'chak-chak' of the high-perched stonechat asserting its presence. This is a living heath, it is somewhere that people live and work, their homesteads and livestock are indivisible parts of the landscape.

Heaths and heathers are synonymous, but a heathland is a great deal more than is implied by the limits of language. In the New Forest we know this to be true as diverse heathland landscapes are part of our daily lives. Elsewhere in Britain our heaths are in crisis, the fine-grain of their habitats is becoming lost beneath the coarseness of heather, birch and bracken. The distracting dominance of heather is reflected in Thomas Hardy's *Return of the Native* (1878). The beautifully sophisticated Eustacia Vye complains to the 'native' Clym Yeobright that 'I cannot endure the heath, except in its purple season'; Carry invites us to look with the eyes of a native and to see beyond the superficial carpet of colour. **Clive Chatters**

Charles Tunnicliffe (1901–1979)

Wild Rose, Briar Rose and Elderflower on a stone wall

1960 · watercolour · 270 x 180 mm

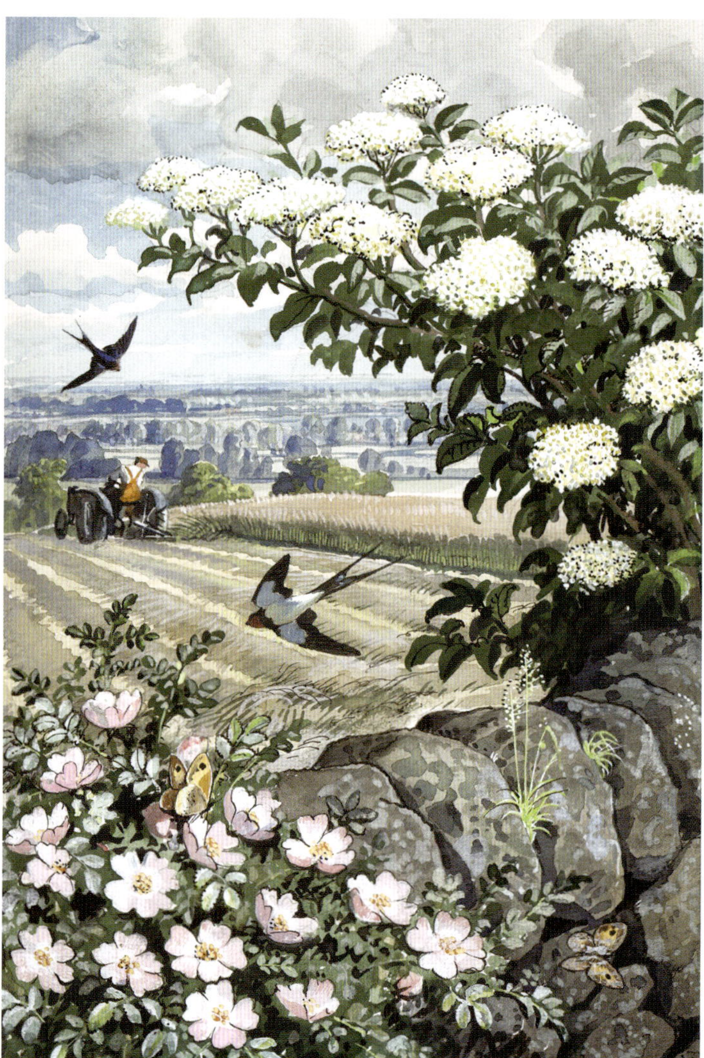

This illustration was also chosen as the cover image
for *What to Look for in Summer* as a depiction of
some of the quintessential joys of summertime. In
the foreground elder and roses are flowering and two
meadow brown butterflies flit from bloom to bloom
while swallows dart overhead. Tunnicliffe recalled in
My Country Book that as a teenager he loved to climb
the hills above his father's farm and 'look upon this
little domain of mine' for 'within a radius of three or
four miles round the farm I had an intimate knowledge
of nearly every yard of ground, and with it I was well
content, for it was a full and beautiful countryside'.[1]
Perhaps he was thinking back to that country where
'walls of dark, rough-hewn stone divided the fields
which, in spring and summer, were favourite nesting
grounds for lapwings and skylarks, and feeding places
for the curlews'.[2]

In the accompanying text E.L. Grant Watson mentions
that the swathes of hay cut by the tractor will also
be full of many different types of wildflower that 'all
contribute to the sweet scent'.[3] Compare this with the
experiences of John Lewis-Stempel in *The Running Hare:
The Secret Life of Farmland* (2016) as he attempts to
grow and harvest a field of wheat by traditional methods, a plan which is met with horror by his farming
neighbours who fear they will be overrun by weeds.
He contrasts his own modest plot, where native wild
flowers, birds and mammals quickly re-establish
themselves, with the arid monoculture of a nearby
industrial-scale farming operation. There liberal doses
of pesticides ensure that nothing but wheat can grow,
the soil is so compacted by huge machinery and the
planting so dense that no wildlife can flourish either.[4]

SM

1. Tunnicliffe, C.F. (1942), *My Country Book*, The Studio, p. 28
2. Ibid., p. 29
3. Watson, G.L. (1960) *What to Look For in Summer*,
Ladybird Books Ltd., p. 16
4. Lewis-Stempel, J. (2016), *The Running Hare: The Secret Life
of Farmland*, Black Swan edition 2017, pp. 150–4

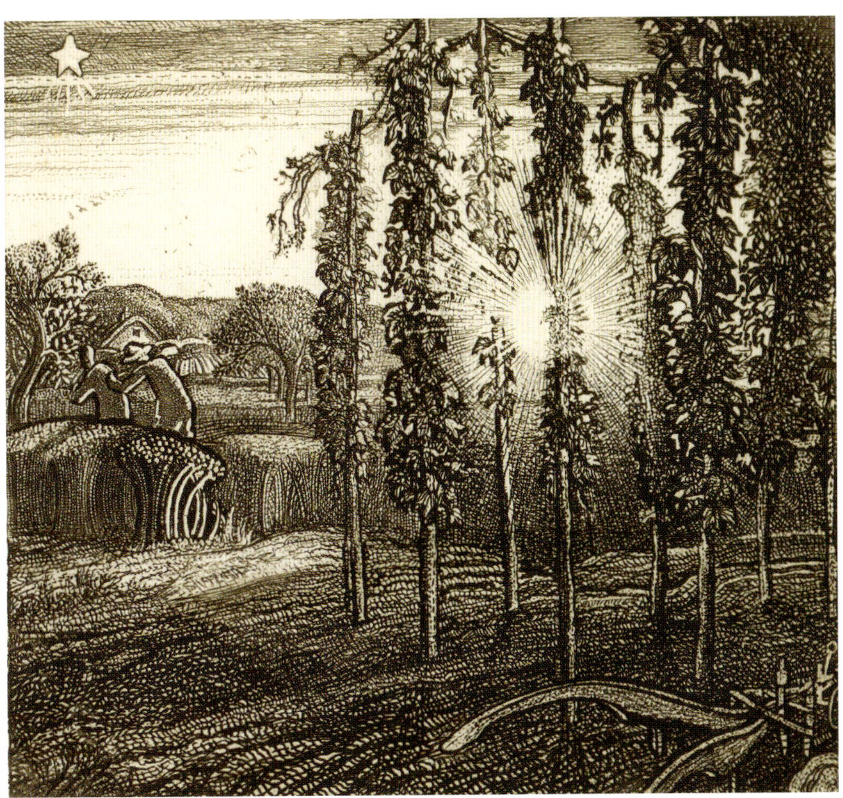

Graham Sutherland
(1903–1980)

Cray Fields

1925 · etching · 117 x 125 mm

Stuart Southall Collection
image © The Estate of Graham Sutherland

The River Cray is the largest tributary of the River Darent; the villages through which it flows are collectively known as 'The Crays'. It rises at St Mary Cray approximately seven miles from Farningham in Kent where Sutherland moved in 1927; from source to mouth it once powered fourteen watermills.

Sutherland's focus is on the hop-poles and the rich agriculture of *Cray Fields*. The romantic idealised vision was executed when he was a student in London at Goldsmiths College where alongside contemporaries Paul Drury, William Larkins and Edward Bouverie Hoyton he learned the skill of etching from Malcom Osborne and Stanley Anderson. This talented group became known as The Goldsmiths' Etchers and were forerunners of the Neo-Romantic movement. This impression was actually printed by Griggs and bears the stamp of his Dover House press.

Cray Fields is densely worked and celebrates the changing seasons and the centuries old practice of labourers cutting the ripe corn. The setting sun behind the hop-poles and the solitary evening star creates a feeling of religious intensity and time stood still as these two heavenly bodies draw the viewer into the carefully constructed pastoral scene just as in the ethereal Kentish landscapes detailed by Samuel Palmer (1805–1881) over one hundred years earlier. Sutherland greatly admired their emotional and technical completeness and also the drawings of the visionary printmaker Frederick Griggs (1876–1938) who was also influenced by Palmer. He was introduced to Griggs at the Royal Academy by Paul Drury's father in summer 1925. The following year he and Paul Drury visited Griggs' workshop in Chipping Campden in the Cotswolds taking some plates with them which he printed. Sutherland later recalled the debt he owed Griggs in terms of learning about the printing of plates and in particular the thickness of the ink and how to use the hand in wiping it off. **GC**

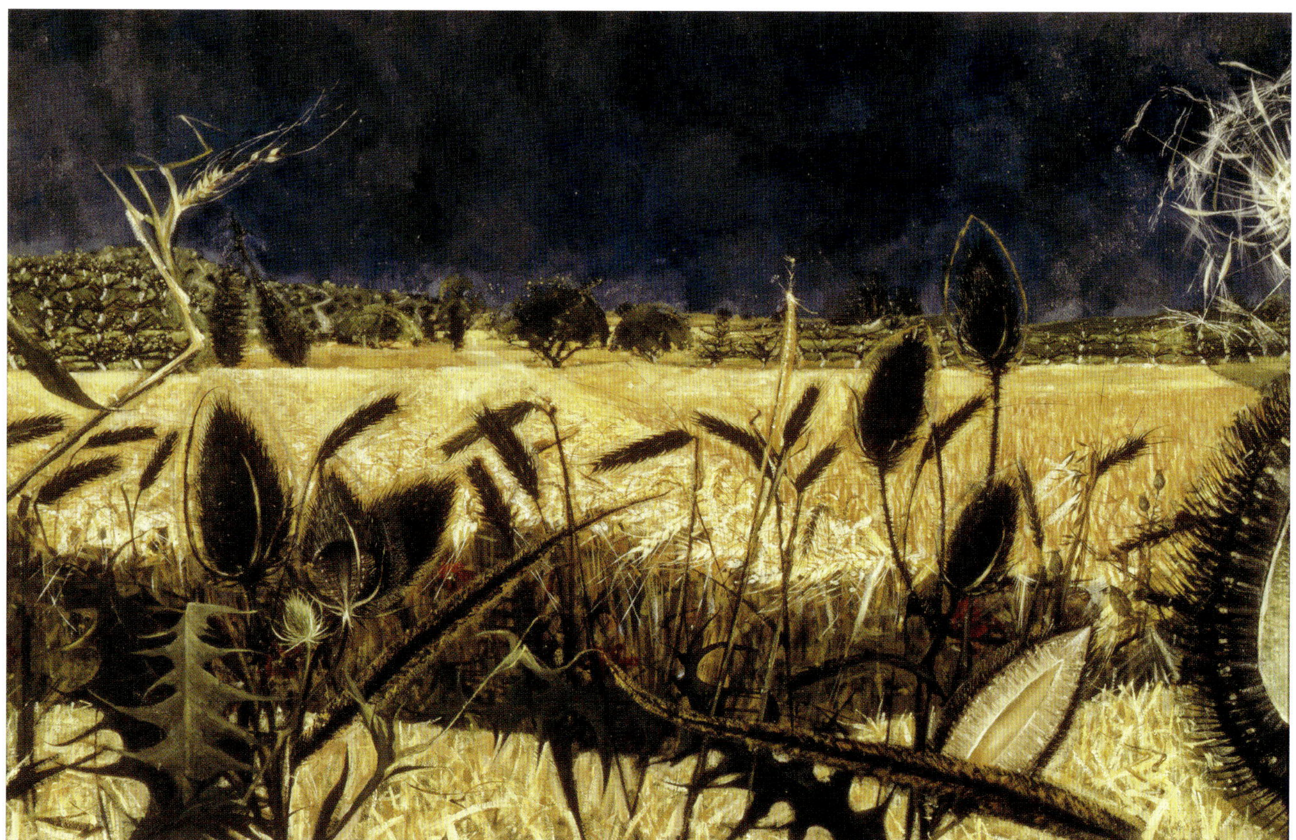

Alan Reynolds (1926–2014)

Summer: Young September's Cornfield

1954 · oil on hardboard · 1022 x 1549 mm

Tate · photograph © Tate/Kettle's Yard, University of Cambridge

Alan Reynolds' work in the early stages of his career was influenced by his love of nature including the 'forms of leaves and … the fruiting inflorescences of plants'[1] together with an interest in the shapes and forms of the landscape particularly fields and hills. Although he grew up in the flat Suffolk countryside of John Constable and loved Constable's little sketches, his neo-romantic landscapes of the 1950s with their finely observed plant life owing more to Samuel Palmer's Kent with its cornfields, orchards and rows of hop-poles.

Demobilized from the Army in 1947, Reynolds studied from 1948 at Woolwich Polytechnic School spending a year at the Royal College of Art in 1952. He immersed himself in the work of Palmer, together with Turner (1775–1851) and Blake (1757–1827), examining in depth the English watercolour collection at the Victoria and Albert Museum. While a student at the RCA his talent was recognised with shows at the prestigious Redfern Gallery in London. *The Times*' critic praised his graceful and elegant handling and his feeling for space and recession. These qualities are much in evidence in *Summer: Young September's Cornfield*, one of his quartet of large seasonal works in oil shown alongside some hundred paintings and drawings at the critically and commercially successful exhibition 'The Four Seasons' at the Redfern Gallery in 1956. Notably, *Summer* was acquired by John Rothenstein for the Tate; *Spring* by the National Gallery of Victoria, Australia; *Winter* entered The Fleischman Collection, Pittsburgh, USA and *Autumn Legend* The Richard Attenborough Collection in Britain.[2]

Painted between the end of August and last week of September 1954 the harsh, dark, large scale shapes of teasel heads and ears of corn on tall, grass-like stalks dominate the foreground under a broad expanse of deep blue sky which increases in density and is in sharp contrast to the rich golden cornfield behind. These 'elements' combine to create an eerie intensity to the unpeopled landscape. **GC**

1. 'A Poet in Paint', *The Times*, 6 March 1956, p. 3
2. Sold at Sotheby's, November 2016

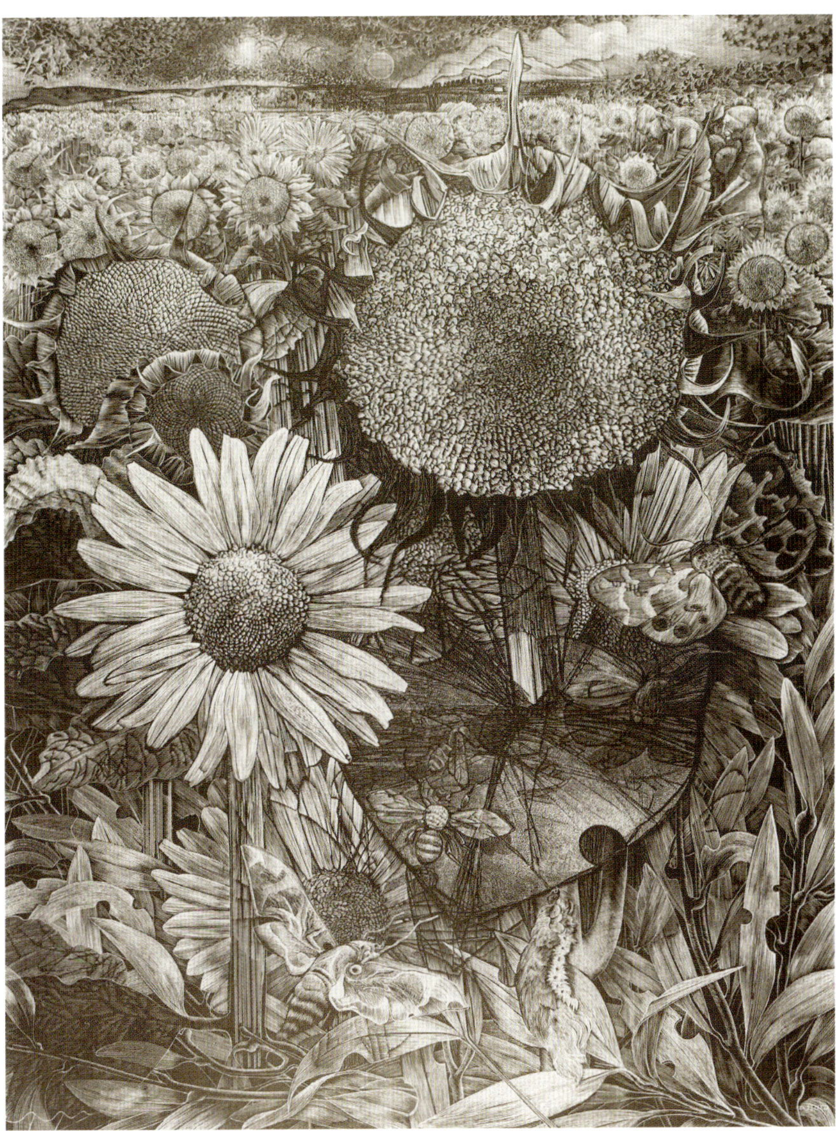

George Tute (b. 1933)

Sunflower Field

1971 · wood engraving · 402 x 303 mm

Stuart Southall Collection · image © George Tute

Fields of sunflowers were once experienced only on holidays in warmer parts of Europe but they are an increasingly common sight here as climate change makes them a viable crop across greater areas of Britain. Sunflowers are heliotropic, slowly turning so they continually face the sun. Here, the artist explains the unlikely origins of this print:

This engraving had rather a strange beginning in that it was due to a letter I received in 1956 from an art student called Marie who lived in Budapest at the time when the Russians were suppressing the Hungarian uprising and she was desperate to obtain medicine for her father who suffered from a heart problem. Marie had the novel idea to write to 'William Hogarth' care of the Royal Academy Schools and the Curator passed the letter on to me to deal with as he knew I was interested in print making and Hogarth. The long and the short of this story is that later in the '70s my wife and I met Marie and her family in Budapest and one memorable event was driving around the Puszta and fields of sunflowers that were growing, stretching to the horizon and it was there that the 'seeds' of the engraving you might say took root! The wood block has had an itinerant history being started in Bristol, worked on in Düsseldorf and Lake Garda before returning to Bristol for the finishing touches and a reference to the Chew Valley Lake! It took a period of well over a year to engrave the block. It is boxwood and a great example of craftsmanship by Lawrence's of Bleeding Heart Yard, Hatton Garden and is still in perfect condition. **George Tute**

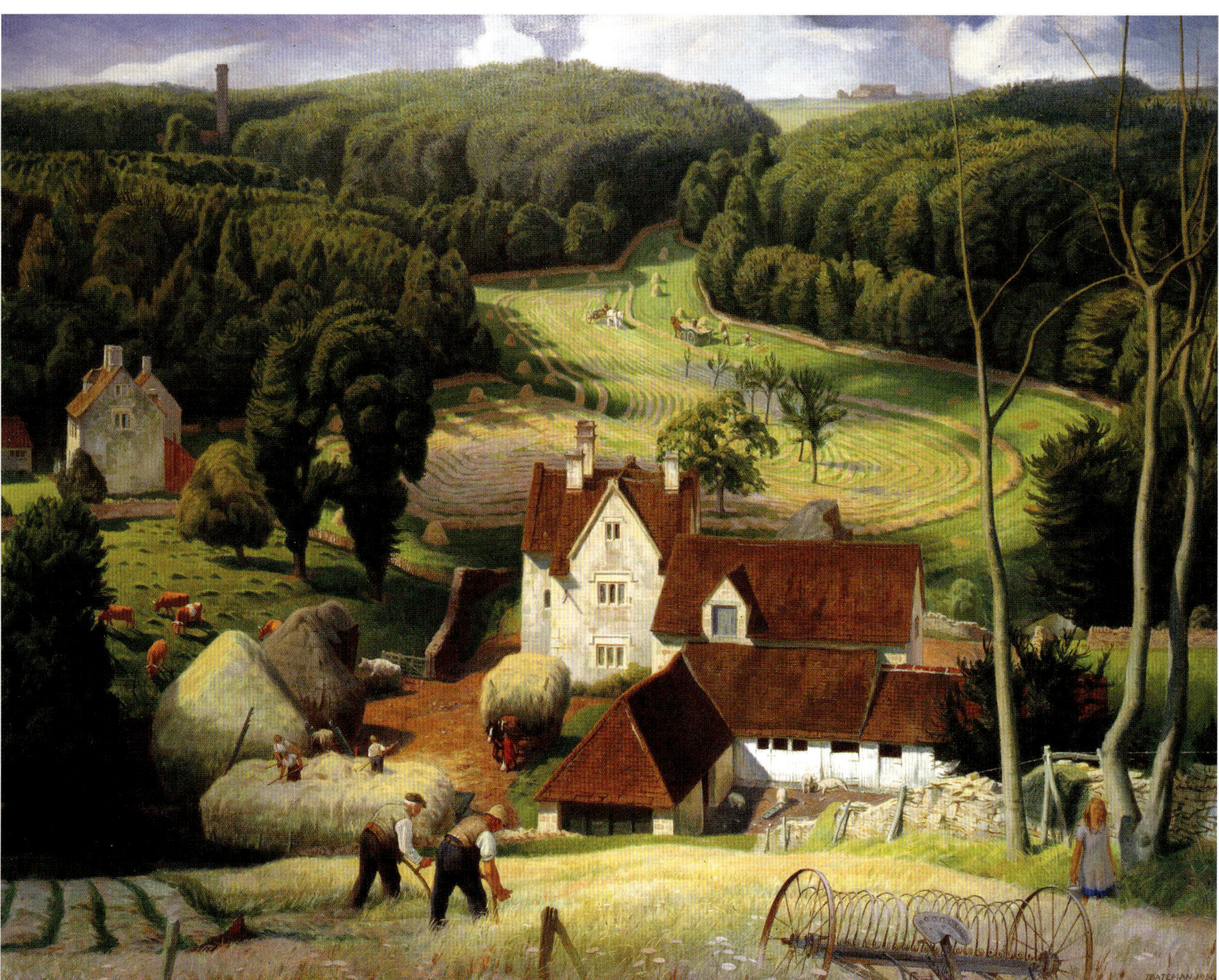

James Bateman (1893–1959)

Haytime in the Cotswolds

c. 1939 • oil on canvas • 1068 x 1338 mm

Southampton City Art Gallery • image
© Southampton City Art Gallery/Bridgeman Images

Pastoral landscapes and farmyard scenes of horses and cattle auctions in the 1930s were the subject matter on which James Bateman made his reputation. Born in Kendal in the Lake District he came from a Westmorland farming family and was well versed in farming practices. He was also familiar with the rural landscape of the Cotswolds where on many occasions he observed haytime. Bateman taught in Cheltenham at the School of Art and Crafts from 1922–28 and would regularly cycle into the countryside in search of material to work up for exhibiting.

Haytime in the Cotswolds was exhibited at the Royal Academy summer exhibition. The respected and longstanding journal *Nature* believed that 'Agriculture is fortunate in being depicted in two of the finest works in the Academy' – *Haytime in the Cotswolds* being 'one of the pleasantest landscapes of the year'. (*Harvest*, by Laura Knight, Adelaide Art Gallery, 'with its sun-chequered scene',[1] was the other.)

In *Haytime in the Cotswolds* Bateman uses an elevated viewpoint to advantage to show the 'pleasant' timeless landscape. It is both a celebration of English country life and a testament to his careful planning and skill as a colourist. The rural scene seems far removed from the ominous war clouds gathering over Europe and the declaration of war on Germany just a few months later on 3 September. In March 1940 Bateman was commissioned by the War Artists' Advisory Committee to undertake four pictures, for a fee of £100, on land work subjects: silage, the Women's Land Army, mechanical milking and haytime.[2] **GC**

1. Swinton, W.E. (1939), 'Science at the Royal Academy', *Nature*, 6 May, vol. 143, pp. 750–1
2. See Clarke (2008), *The Women's Land Army: A Portrait*, Sansom & Company, pp. 156–7

Laura Knight (1877–1970)

Summer's Joy

1921 · poster · 1016 x 635 mm

London Transport Museum
image © TfL from the London Transport Museum collection

Laura Knight's first poster design for London Underground was *Rugby at Twickenham* in 1921, she had by then left the warmth and light of Cornwall (p. 41) for London which gave her access to other subject matter, although she kept a studio in the west country for many years. Knight was one of a number of women artists (including Dora Batty, p. 94), designers and illustrators commissioned by Frank Pick (1878–1941) to design posters in the 1920s and 30s. Pick 'had a wide interest in the visual arts and fervently believed in the importance of good design in everyday things'[1] which contributed to him employing more women than rival companies.

Knight's natural feel for whatever medium she employed would no doubt have been recognised by Pick. In *Summer's Joy* she depicted a young family enjoying a day's bathing outdoors. The poster was published in the summer of 1922 to promote travel to London's green spaces by bus. The quote at the bottom of the poster, 'The cool silver shock of the plunge in a pool's living water', reinforces the joy of summer and came from the popular poem *David Singing before Saul* by Robert Browning (1812–1889).

Knight continued intermittently to design posters for the Underground Group and London Transport until 1957 when she produced *Winter Walks* which encouraged Londoners to partake of a brisk walk and purchase the 'reliable and helpful guide' *Country Walks* from Underground bookstalls and Ticket Offices priced 2/6d, the covers of which featured engravings by Eric Ravilious from the 1930s. **GC**

1. *Oxford Dictionary for National Biography*, entry for Frank Pick

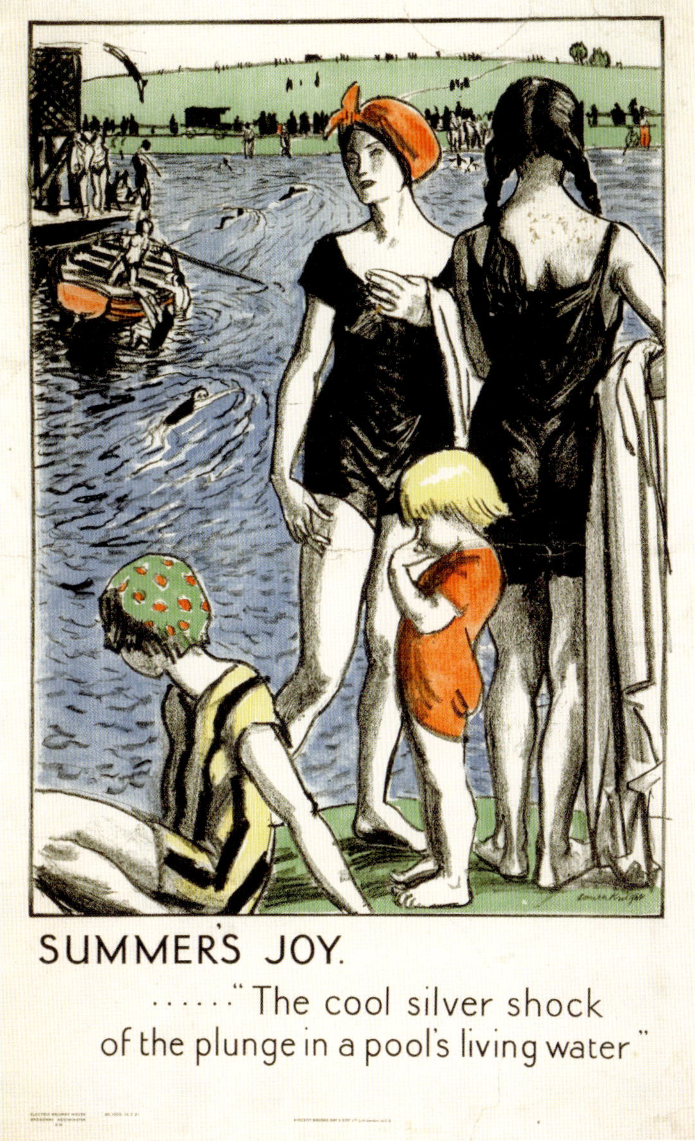

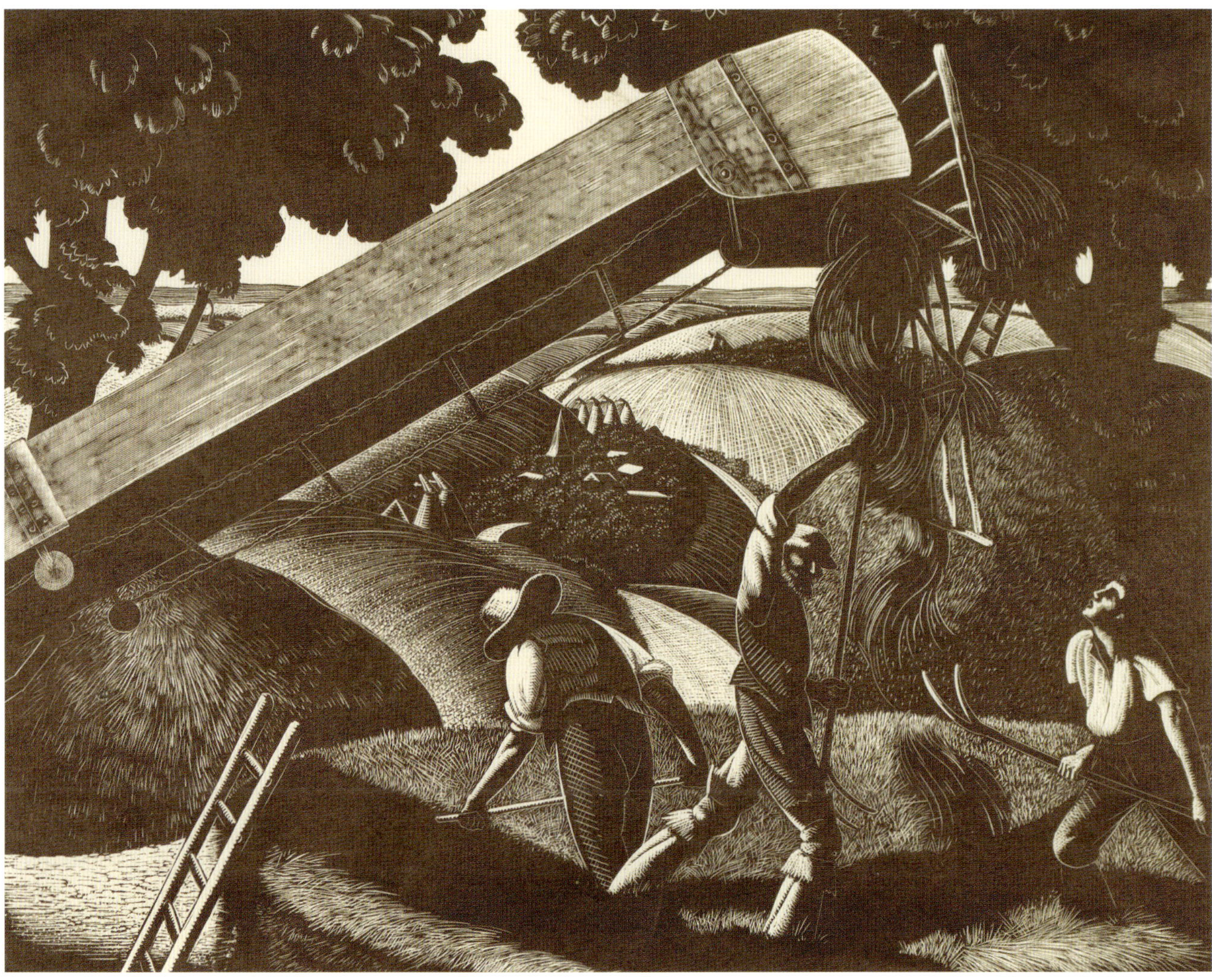

Clare Leighton (1898–1989)

June

1933 · wood engraving · 204 x 254 mm
from *The Farmer's Year*

Stuart Southall Collection · Clare Leighton's
wood engravings are reproduced courtesy
of the artist's estate

The advent of fine weather leads to the start of the hay harvest, field upon field of solid, thick waist-high, multi-coloured grass awaits the cutter. The oast houses with steep pitched roofs and cowls pivoting stand on the ridge looking down across the rapidly changing landscape. *Haymaking* captures the ensuing activity in complementary image and text which are far from superficial:

> *The first field that was cut is now dotted with an all-over design of large silver-green dumplings; for the hay there has been tossed and turned, ridged and cocked … Above the voices in the hayfield sounds the endless purr of the elevator in the rickyard; down the lane the crunching haywains pass and repass.*[1]

Clare Leighton worked repeatedly on her drawings until satisfied 'that the rhythms, the values and the spaces were right and the design [which was the exact size of the book] was "doing something".'[2] Only then would she transfer it to the boxwood block and begin the lengthy and exacting process of cutting fine lines with her graver and using large dark areas to convey the rhythms and tonal variations she sought. Leighton worked for some two to three years on *The Farmer's Year* never forgetting the words of her tutor Noel Rooke (1881–1953) at the Central School of Arts and Crafts who thought that the line made by a wood engraving was often the most beautiful thing in the world. **GC**

1. Leighton, C. (1933/2018), *The Farmer's Year: A Calendar of English Husbandry*, Little Toller Books, p. 34
2. Lindsay, G. (1991), referring to *The Farmer's Year* in the 'Introduction' to Clare Leighton's *Four Hedges. A Gardener's Chronicle*, The Sumach Press, 1935

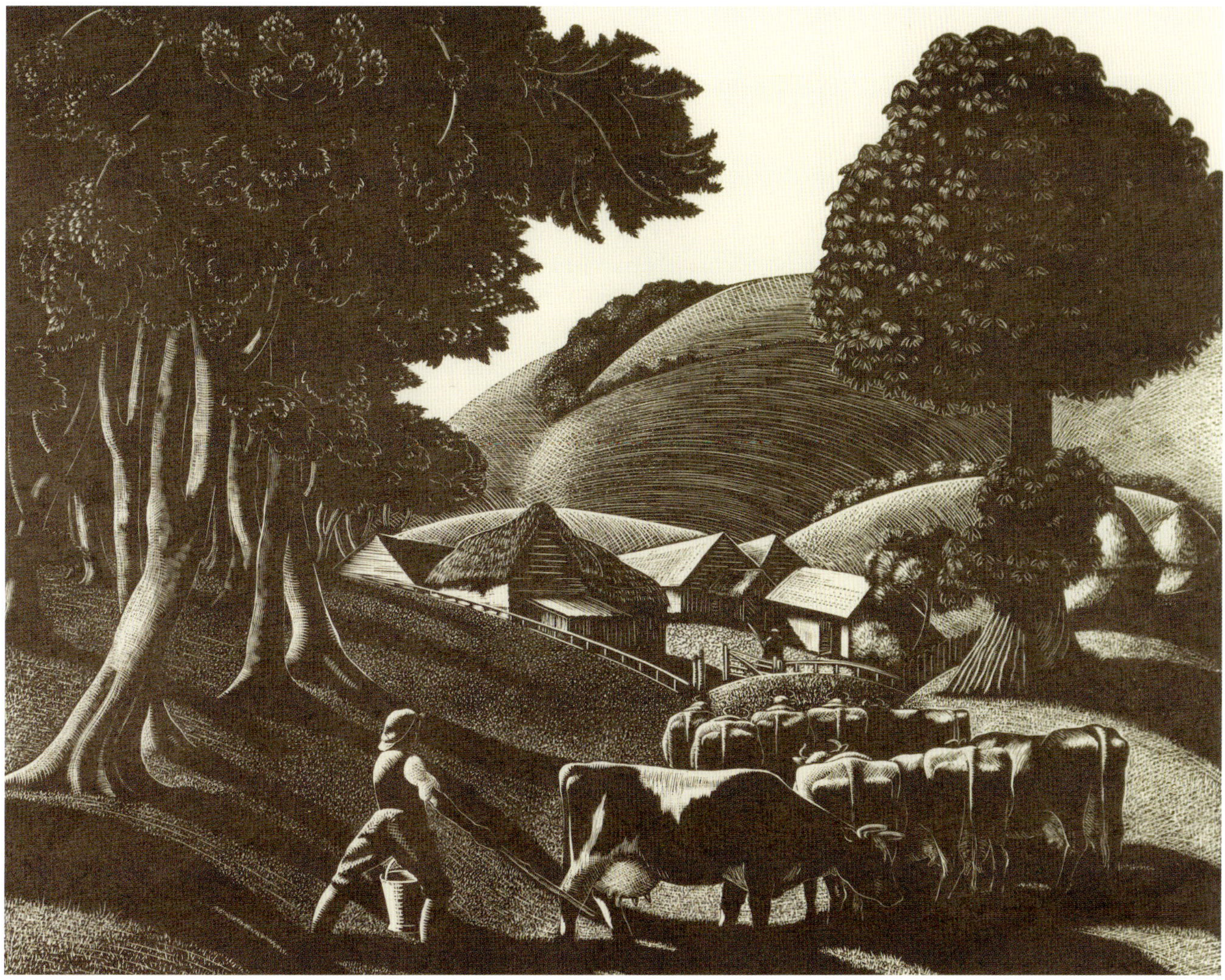

Clare Leighton (1898–1989)

July

1933 · wood engraving · 202 x 253 mm
from *The Farmer's Year*

Stuart Southall Collection · Clare Leighton's
wood engravings are reproduced courtesy
of the artist's estate

'July is a time of little events, many and intimate, hidden under the quiet routine of village days' wrote Clare Leighton. A number of these 'little events' are vividly described including the 'most essentially English thing of our country-side'[1] cottage gardens with their fragrant blooms and rainbow colours attracting bees, roses rambling round porches and darkening casement windows. Leighton explains how in the long evenings the village women tend the fruit bushes and pick baskets of shining fruit while the men are watering, hoeing and weeding the vegetables.

Although the chapter was titled *Cottage Gardens*, the engraving for July was known as *To the Milking*, the actual subject of Leighton's illustration which depicts cows with udders full and heavy languidly returning across the sloping meadow to the cowshed. The cowman has lifted the latch of the gate for them to file through in orderly fashion to take up their appointed place in the cowshed where the milkers on their three-legged stools will gently but firmly start their work. **GC**

1. Leighton, C. (1933/2018), *The Farmer's Year: A Calendar of English Husbandry*, Little Toller Books, p. 39

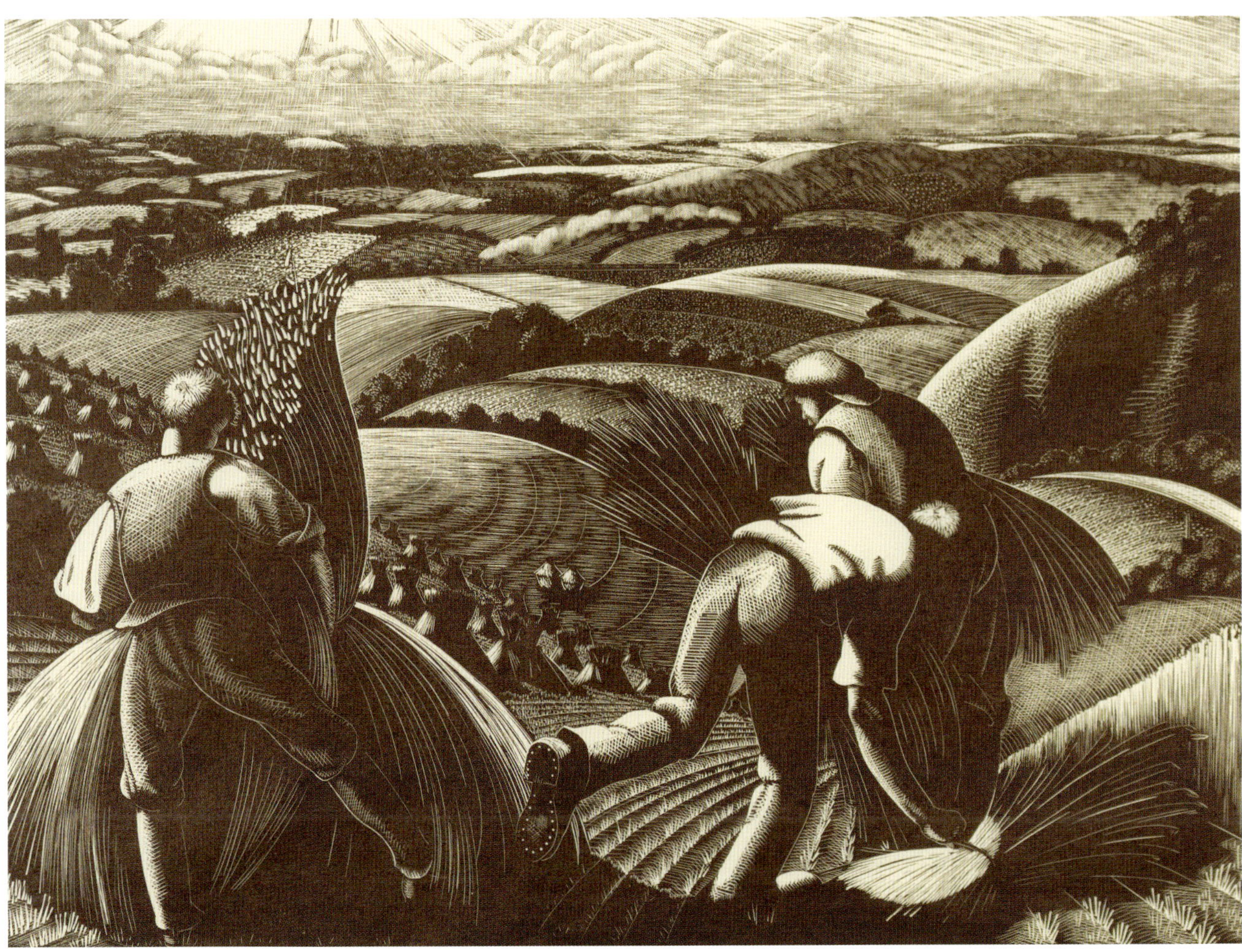

Clare Leighton (1898–1989)

August

1933 • wood engraving • 204 x 273 mm
from *The Farmer's Year*

Stuart Southall Collection • Clare Leighton's
wood engravings are reproduced courtesy
of the artist's estate

Clare Leighton's affinity with rural workers runs through her engravings, *Harvesting* is no exception. She remarked:

> *The harvesting draws all men to it. Ploughboy and cowman, carter and shepherd, all are in the fields. Strange farmhands have appeared, too: vagrants tramping the countryside for work. These are gathered warmly into the fellowship of harvesting, and no questions asked. For the glamour of the sheaves blends all.*[1]

Three men take advantage of the dry weather and radiant sun to tie the oats into sheaves, Leighton explains that the number of sheaves used to make a stook depends on local custom. Inscribed on the engraving in the Ashmolean underneath the mount was written 'Stooking (incorporating views from Whiteleaf Cross)'.[2] The view of rolling hills and varying shapes of fields was well known to Leighton who lived nearby in Peter's Lane, Whiteleaf, on a hill above Monks Risborough in Buckinghamshire. She shared the cottage with her partner (Henry) Noel Brailsford (1873–1958) the left wing intellectual and radical journalist whose ideals of political and social justice she shared and with whom she bought the plot of land in 1930 in the Chiltern Hills, on the edge of the ancient Icknield Way. The location gave Leighton insights and knowledge of traditional farming methods (she had stooked corn at harvest) and country crafts and customs, and direct experience of the challenges of creating a garden from the rough and exposed chalky meadowland. *Four Hedges* first published in 1935 lovingly chronicled the trials and tribulations of a year in the life of the garden. **GC**

1. Leighton, C. (1933/2018), *The Farmer's Year: A Calendar of English Husbandry*, Little Toller Books, p. 43
2. Leighton quoted in Stevens A. and D. Leighton D., *Clare Leighton Wood Engravings and Drawings*, Ashmolean Museum, Oxford, 1992, p. 26

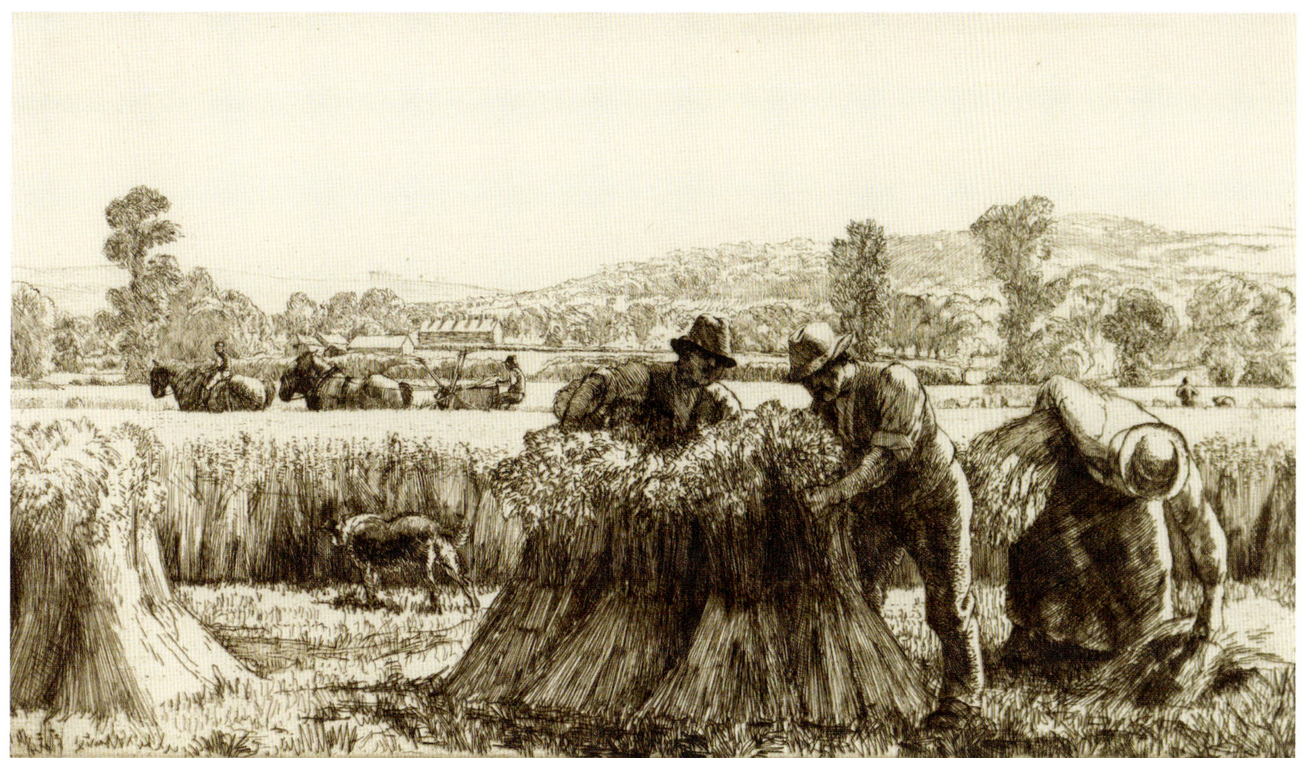

Charles Tunnicliffe
(1901–1979)

The Wheat Field

1927 · etching · 158 x 278 mm

Stuart Southall Collection · image reproduced by
kind permission of The Estate of C.F. Tunnicliffe

Tunnicliffe's father William had taken on the running of Lane Ends Farm, Sutton in 1903 and it was very much a family enterprise from that point on. Tunnicliffe notes that by the time he was ten he was 'up in the morning with the earliest, milking the cows'.[1] William died in 1925 leaving his wife Margaret to run the farm until 1927 when she gave it up and moved to a house in Macclesfield paid for by the proceeds of her son's etching sales. Although Tunnicliffe felt that his mother was due a long earned rest, he was somewhat lost on returning from his studies in London to find the centre of his early life gone and much of his subject matter with it. He would have to discover his country anew.

This etching looked back on memories of life on the family farm during the critical summer work of gathering the corn harvest. In the foreground the farmhands are arranging the cut wheat into stooks in such a way that the wind can pass through and finish the drying process before threshing can begin. The number of sheaves in a stook varied from region to region, in some places a 'shock' was made up of six sheaves while a stook was made up of twelve. In Cheshire where the Tunnicliffes were farming twenty-four sheaves made up a 'threave'.[2] In the background four horses are drawing the reaper-binder which cuts the corn and binds it into sheaves, a far quicker process than the old method of cutting by hand with scythes. **SM**

1. Tunnicliffe, C.F. (1942), *My Country Book*, The Studio, p. 10
2. Hennell, T. (1936), *Change in the Farm*, republished 1977 by EP Publishing, pp. 117–8

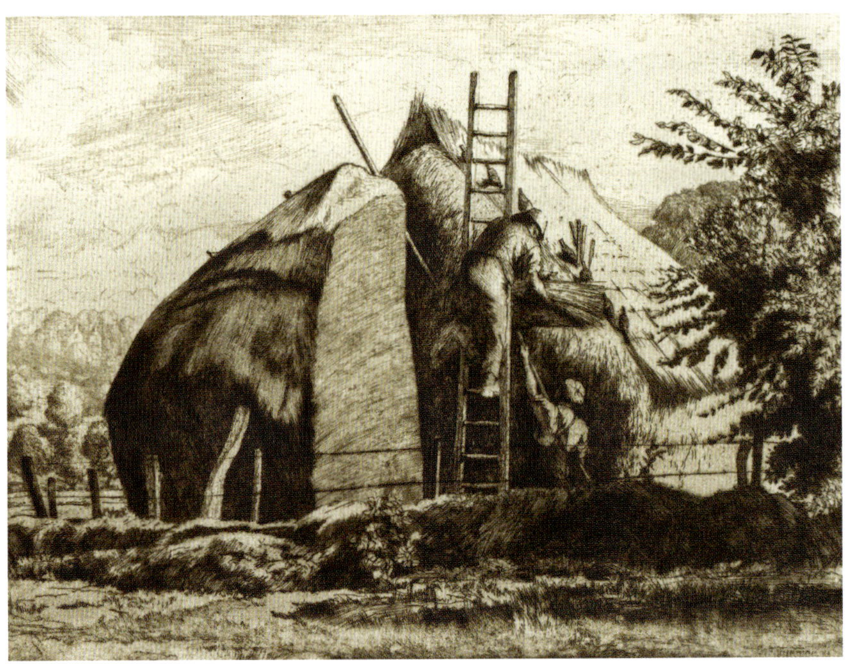

Charles Tunnicliffe
(1901–1979)

The New Rick

1927 • etching • 206 x 267 mm

Stuart Southall Collection • image reproduced by
kind permission of The Estate of C.F. Tunnicliffe

This etching shows Tunnicliffe and his father William at work thatching a new rick next to the remains of an old one, which has been neatly sliced by a hay knife over the preceding year. Since William had died two years earlier this subject must have been prepared from memory or previous drawings. If the rick was for hay it would be loaded on to carts with pitchforks and then moved to the farmyard where the feed would be needed during the winter. There it was built up in levels which were carefully tramped down; there was an art to making sure the structure did not collapse since it was narrower at the bottom than the top. Once it was finished a thatched roof would be added to protect it from the rain. On larger farms a journeyman thatcher might be employed but for smaller operations like the Tunnicliffe farm it was a skill they developed for themselves.

Hay would have been built into ricks immediately after the harvest in June so that it was safely stored against the weather. The straw from corn could also be stored in this way and if corn was not threshed immediately it could be kept whole in a rick during the winter. In his diary for 21 October 1920 Tunnicliffe recorded that he came 'home at 4 o'clock and helped father to thatch the corn stack which we finished'.[1] On a small farm, like this one of twenty acres, jobs such as rick thatching might drift well into autumn especially further north where the corn harvest might be gathered in later. The finished ricks were a symbol of readiness and supplies for the winter to come. **SM**

1. Meyrick, R. and Heuser, H. (2017), *Charles Tunnicliffe Prints: A Catalogue Raisonné*, Royal Academy of Arts, p. 75

AUTUMN

Thus harvest ends its busy reign,
And leaves the fields their peace again;
Where Autumn's shadows idly muse
And tinge the trees in many hues:
Amid whose scenes I'm fain to dwell,
And sing of what I love so well.
But hollow winds, and tumbling floods,
And humming showers, and moaning woods
All startle into sudden strife
And wake a mighty lay to life;
Making amid their strains divine,
Unheard a song so mean as mine.

John Clare · The Shepherd's Calendar · 1827

The shift from summer towards winter as September's calm gives way to October's storms, is deftly described by Clare, but it is probably John Keat's poem *To Autumn*, written in September 1819, which has indelibly characterised this time of year as the 'Season of mists and mellow fruitfulness'. These poems reflect Autumn's dual character as a time of plenty and ease after the rigours of the harvest, but also as the harbinger of winter, marking an end to growth and fruitfulness. The splendour of autumn foliage precedes the fall that will expose the bare and apparently lifeless forms beneath. In this sense it is often seen as a melancholy time when the corn fields are reduced to stubble, flowers wither, leaves turn and days shorten. There is a tendency to ponder on mortality and the ephemeral nature of life and its pleasures. Yet autumn is also the fulfilment of spring and summer's promise and merely a pause in the cycle of life rather than its end.

The autumn equinox falls around 22 September when the hours of daylight and night are once again equal. The harvest moon is full within two weeks of this date. Harvest Home was a traditional end to the farming cycle, the date depending on the work and the weather. Farmers would lay on a substantial feast for their workers and afterwards there would be toasts, games, singing and dancing. These might degenerate into drunken revels as was the case in Thomas Hardy's *Far From the Madding Crowd* (1874) when Bathsheba and Gabriel are left to secure the ricks from a storm while the rest of the farmhands are comatose in the barn.[1] The harvest festival was an altogether more seemly way to give thanks for nature's abundance (fig. 25). These church-sponsored events were a relatively new tradition dating from the 1830s onwards and were the subject for one of Robin Tanner's most evocative etchings (p. 95). A vital date in the agricultural calendar was Michaelmas on 29 September, one of four quarter days, when rents were due and people changed jobs. The Celtic festival of Samhain (31 October– 1 November), falls roughly halfway between the autumn equinox and the winter solstice. It marked the end of the harvest season and the start of winter. Cattle were brought in from summer pastures, livestock was slaughtered and protective bonfires were lit as this was felt to be a time when the boundary with the spirit world was weak. Hallowe'en perpetuates the idea of witches and evil creatures being abroad until All Saints Day on the 1 November brings relief and heavenly protection. The tradition of lighting fires to brighten dark nights is continued in Guy Fawkes bonfires and the torchlight processions and effigy burnings of the Sussex Bonfire Societies (p. 99).

High pressure in September may bring clear skies and temperatures higher than the average for July. Such hot weather is known as an Indian Summer, the phrase arising in America where early settlers observed Native Americans using these spells to harvest and prepare stores of food for the winter, avoiding the exhausting heat and humidity of high summer. The autumn mists immortalised by Keats are likely after a day of sunshine when moist air rising from the ground quickly cools under clear night skies. As the nights lengthen these mists get thicker and may last until well into the day in sheltered areas. Heavy dews are also expected in September and there may be frosts on high ground. John Aldridge's painting *First Frost* (Royal West of England Academy Collection) shows garden flowers wilting after this sudden shock. October

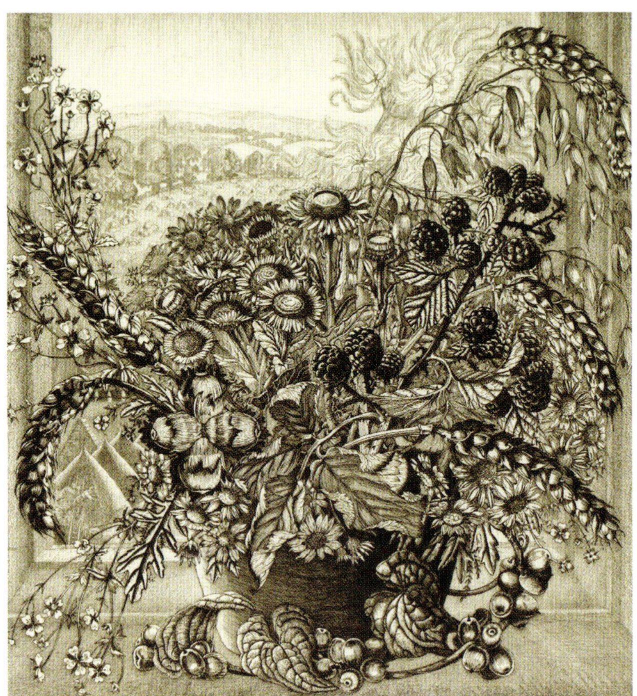

FIG. 24 · **Robin Tanner** (1904–1988) · *Autumn* 1932 · etching
St Barbe Museum and Art Gallery Collection

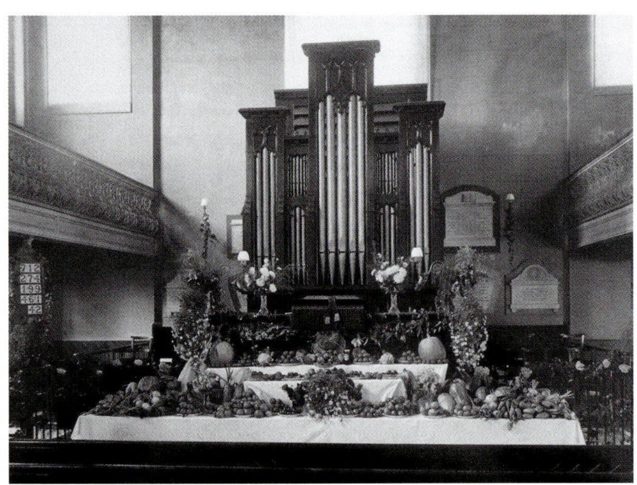

FIG. 25 · Harvest Festival display at Lymington Baptist Church, 1912
St Barbe Museum and Art Gallery Collection

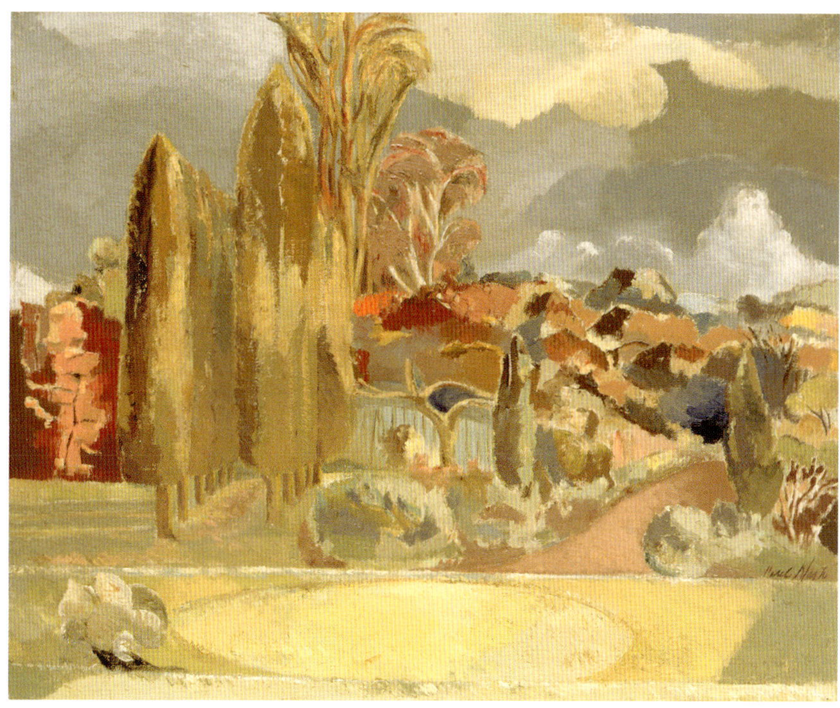

FIG. 26 · **Paul Nash** (1889–1946)
Michaelmas Landscape
1943 · oil on canvas
Ferens Art Gallery, Hull Museums/Bridgeman Images

is usually warmer than April, but south or south westerly winds can bring cloudy and damp weather which may linger. The end of the month is known for the storms alluded to in John Clare's poem, created when cold arctic air meets warmer winds from the Atlantic. Falling temperatures mean that rain-dampened fields will not now dry out properly before the spring. Good weather around Martinmas (11 November) was known as a St Martin's Summer and this is referenced in William Rothenstein's (1872–1945) painting of the same name (Manchester Art Gallery Collection) which shows a leafless tree against a brilliant blue sky at Iles Farm, Far Oakridge in the Cotswolds, his home from 1912.

By October the colours of autumn can be seen in their full glory. Each species of deciduous tree brings its own tint: beech is coppery, oaks are yellow and orange, hawthorn can be red, rowan is golden, elms turn bright yellow, wild cherry a deep crimson. This seasonal spectacle occurs as trees put waste products into their leaves, replacing the green of chlorophyll. All this extravagant colour does not last and in November when winds and frost bring the leaves down, their cells die off and oxidation turns them brown. Dora Batty's Underground poster (p. 94) reminded Londoners that it was still worth travelling out to the countryside at this time of year to experience the changing colours and bracing winds. W. H. Allen was acutely aware of the agricultural landscape around his home in Farnham and in *Work on the Land* (p. 92) he shows a farmhand and plough team labouring under the varying hues of oak, elm and birch. Ivon Hitchens' woodland home near Petworth in Sussex provided constant inspiration and he would paint the same view across different seasons and weather conditions producing a series of variations on a theme (p. 91). British artists' approach to autumnal colour has largely been marked by a muted palette that perhaps matches both the national climate and character. These restrained colour combinations

are evident in the paintings of Alfred East (1844–1913), one of the country's most noted landscape painters before the First World War, for whom Autumn was a favourite season, typical examples being *Golden Autumn* (*c.* 1904, Tate Collection) and *Autumn in Gloucestershire* (Alfred East Gallery Collection). Paul Nash's *Michaelmas Landscape* (fig. 26) is one of several portrayals of Wittenham Clumps in Berkshire. Nash was fascinated by their changing appearance across the seasons and linked works in this series to the spring equinox and the phases of the moon. The warm browns and ochres of the vegetation are offset by a somewhat ominous grey sky and Nash would have been aware of the symbolism of autumnal decay as he neared the end of his life. A sharp contrast can be found in the work of Wilhelmina Barns-Graham (1912–2004) who, during the 1990s, produced a series of studies of autumn trees in vibrant colours in her garden at Balmungo House in St Andrews (Wilhelmina Barns-Graham Trust Collection).

It is not just the leaves that turn in Autumn; as Heywood Sumner's *The Fern Cart* (p. 93) shows, grasses and heather are fading, as is the dun-coloured bracken being gathered for winter bedding. There are still splashes of colour to be found in the bright pink lantern-like fruits of the spindle and the reds of sycamore keys, hawthorn berries and rose hips. The hedges have their own harvest in autumn that provides for birds, mice, voles and humans alike. In *The Seasons* (1953), Ralph Wightman surveyed the plants growing on the field boundaries of his Dorset farm noting that 'The blackberries, the hips, the haws, the elderberry, the woody nightshade and the bryony have their fruits as their great glory'.[2] These seasonal pickings are celebrated in Gertrude Hermes' wood engraving *Autumn Fruits* (p. 96), which features teasels, conkers, blackberries and mushrooms. Robin Tanner's etching *Autumn* (fig. 24) shows a vase overflowing with wheat, oats, nuts, berries and wild flowers while in the background stooks line the fields and ricks are built. Folklore tells us that the blackberry should not be eaten after Michaelmas (29 September) because when the devil was cast out of heaven by St Michael, he landed on a bramble bush, cursed it and spat on it. Damson and sloe fruits were thought to need a frost to sweeten them before picking. The horse chestnut is one of the first trees to lose its leaves, often before its conkers fall in late September, ushering in time-honoured playground games and the occasional bruised knuckle. Hazelnuts are a favourite meal for the nuthatch, which wedges them into crevices in tree bark and then hammers away with its beak until it can reach the kernel within. Sweet chestnuts are ready for eating in September and October, while beech mast falls in November providing food for birds, squirrels and pigs out for pannage.

In the animal world autumn is a time when many creatures born in the spring and summer are reaching maturity and independence. It is also a time for hoarding and feeding up for the winter to come. Badgers gather bedding for their earths and hedgehogs hunt for slugs and beetles to sustain them during hibernation. Jays and squirrels gather stores of acorns, snails seek out a handy stone, log or watering can to hibernate beneath, while butterflies such as the red admiral are feeding on the last flowers before heading for the Mediterranean. For the birds it is a time of arrivals and departures. Swallows, house martins and swifts gather and leave for Africa (p. 103) where they will find fresh supplies of insects to feed on. Many move at night so their disappearance once seemed sudden and mysterious, their absence noted as a sure sign that summer was over. Meanwhile redwings and fieldfares arrive from Scandinavia (p. 102). Starlings appear from Eastern Europe, supplementing the resident birds and creating huge flocks. This gives rise to one of the wonders of autumn: starling murmurations where thousands of birds wheel and swoop together creating hypnotic patterns in the sky, the inspiration for Colin See-Paynton's intricate wood engraving *Starlings* (fig. 27). Brent geese journey from Arctic Russia to southern and eastern coasts where they will feed on eelgrass and newly sprouting winter corn. In November whooper swans make an appearance and will remain until April when they depart once again for the Arctic.

In the New Forest the drifts which began in August continue through to November. These annual pony rounds-ups were memorably depicted in Lucy Kemp-Welch's (1869–1958) painting *Colt Hunting in the New Forest* (1897, Tate Collection). It was unheard of for a woman to take part in those days, but Kemp-Welch insisted that it was the only way to convincingly capture the action. Drifts are still conducted on horseback – the best way to cover the rough terrain, sometimes at breakneck speed. The ponies are driven to pounds where they are given a health check and may be fitted with life-saving fluorescent collars that make them more visible to motorists at night. New foals are branded with their owner's identifying mark: they all belong to commoners who exercise their right to graze animals on the Forest. Some ponies may be returned to commoners' holdings for the winter or offered at one of the Beaulieu Road sales. Those being let loose again will have their tails cut in distinctive patterns by the Agisters to show that the owner has paid their annual fee. Another feature of the New Forest in autumn is the sight of pigs wandering free when they are let out for pannage (another of the commoners'

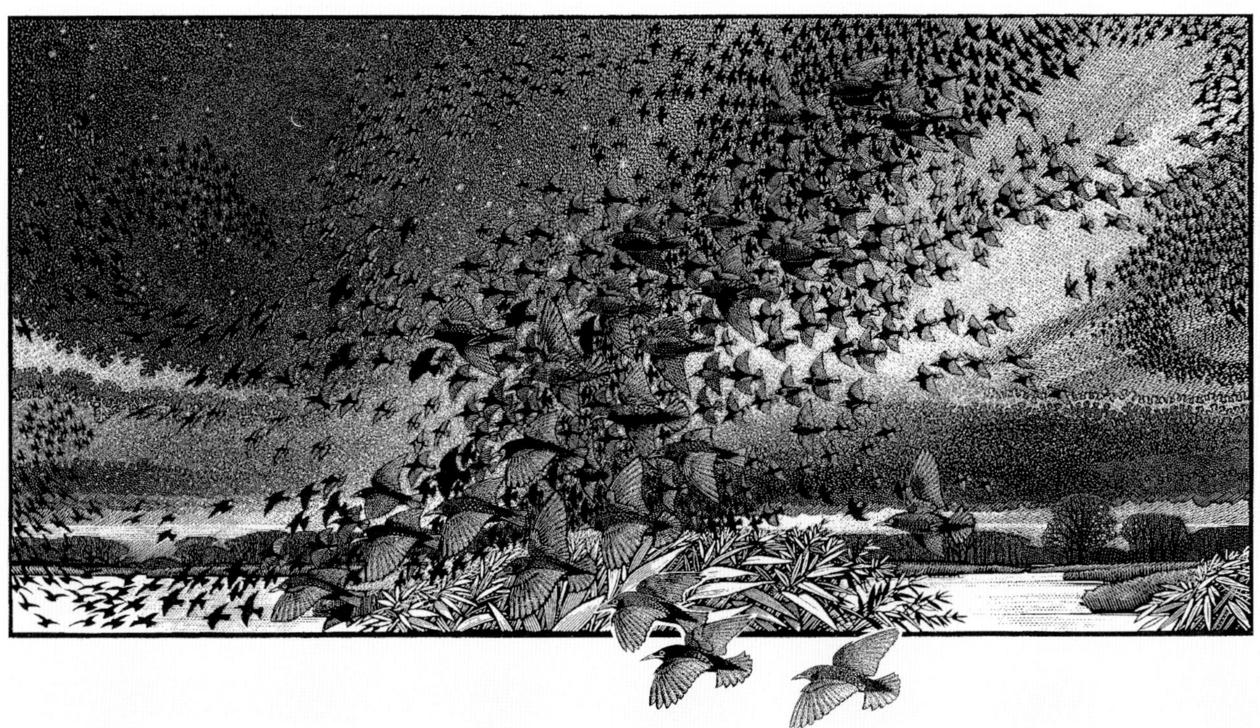

FIG. 27 · **Colin See-Paynton** (b. 1946) · *Starlings* · wood engraving
© the artist

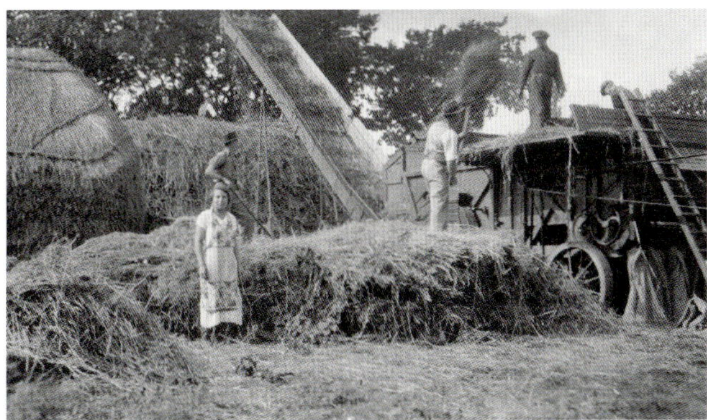

FIG. 28 · Threshing at Flanders Farm, Hordle in the 1930s
St Barbe Museum and Art Gallery Collection

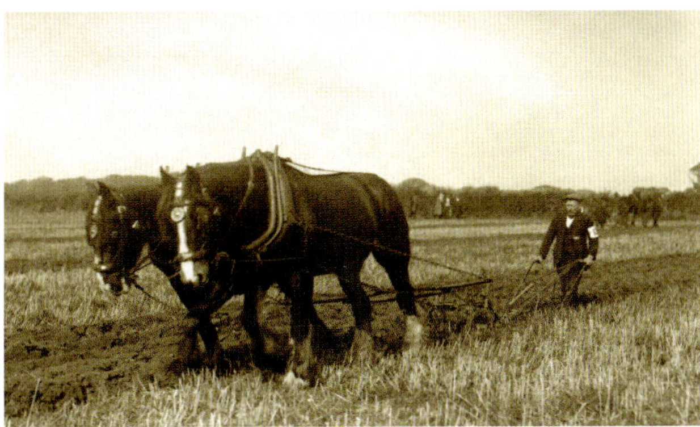

FIG. 29 · Ploughing match at Manor Farm, Lower Pennington, 1932
St Barbe Museum and Art Gallery Collection

historic rights). They will fatten up on chestnuts, beech mast and, most importantly, acorns which can be toxic when eaten by ponies and cattle.

September on the farm would see the harvest mostly brought in, at least in the south. Threshing by hand once took up most of the winter but labour-saving machinery meant that this could now be done immediately (fig. 28). Gwen Raverat's engraving (p. 109) shows how the farm workers came together to get the job done while the weather held. The agricultural landscape was in transition again, fields of waving golden corn had given way to bleached stubble and now the colours changed again as ploughing commenced. This was the main task for autumn, breaking up the stubble, ploughing in manure and preparing for the sowing of winter corn. At the start of the twentieth century a plough team was expected to manage an acre a day, and on larger farms the task would last most of the season. Clare Leighton's nostalgic take on the subject for November in *The Farmer's Year* (p. 107) shows the young ploughman already at work as the sun rises, making the most of the daylight hours. Stanley Anderson's *Three Good Friends* (p. 108) refers to the special bond between the ploughman and his horses. The bare trees and the need for a warm coat during a feed break suggest that autumn is now giving way to winter. Both of these prints portray a strong connection with the land and chime with A.G. Street's comment that: 'No matter which the motive power, ploughing in November is still a lovely job, with only the birds for company. Peewits, rooks, starlings and seagulls by the hundred wheel and swoop around the plough-man's head, or strut drunkenly on the newly turned fallows in search of worms and grubs'.[3] As if the ploughmen had not spent enough time trudging behind their horses, autumn was also the traditional time for ploughing matches (fig. 29) where they could compete with their neighbours and be judged on the neatness, straightness and depth of their furrows.

From August onwards it was hopping time, particularly in Kent and Worcestershire, hops being a vital flavouring ingredient for beer. The harvest relied on an influx of casual labour: East Enders in their thousands flocked to the Kent hop fields, where they were joined by Gypsies and itinerant agricultural labour-ers. Workers would tear down vines from the poles and strip the hops into bins, as seen in John Minton's painting from

1945 (p. 104). This was piece work and pickers were paid by the bushel. George Orwell spent a couple of weeks picking hops in September 1931 and commented that: 'on hot days there is no pleasanter place than the shady lanes of hops, with their bitter scent – an unutterably refreshing scent, like a wind blowing from oceans of cool beer. It would be almost ideal if one could earn a living at it'.[4] He found it hard on the hands and impossible to make even one pound a week.

September was also time for the potato harvest. Before mechanisation a potato plough was used to lift the tubers and workers had to hunt through the soil to uncover the whole crop. John Stewart Collis (1900–1984) was an academic but worked on the land during the Second World War. In *The Worm Forgives the Plough* (1973) he recalled: 'This potato harvest calls for really dry weather. And one seldom gets it … The mud was terrific. It clung to one like glue. I soon qualified not only as a clod-hopper but also as a clod-lifter. With such a soil potato picking in rain provides considerable discomfort. It was so extreme in sheer wetness, slipperiness and muddiness that I enjoyed it'.[5] During the war any available labour was drafted in for this critical task, school children were even given a week off to help. By 1960, when C.F. Tunnicliffe was illustrating *What to Look For in Autumn*, a tractor-drawn potato spinner would fling the potatoes from the soil. They still needed to be gather-ed by hand and the constant stooping was hard on the back.[6] Mangels, an important source of winter feed, were harvested in October. This had to be done carefully to avoid damage and all the leaf stalks were removed by hand before they were stored in clamps. It was also time for the sugar beet harvest, a popular crop in East Anglia. In the 1950s the beets were lifted by plough but still pulled and topped manually. Sugar beet had been important during the war when it was the sole source for Britain's sugar. All of these tasks have been mechanised over the last fifty years or so.

One job which is still largely done by hand is fruit picking. Clare Leighton's engraving for September in *The Farmer's Year* (p. 105) shows pickers climbing ladders with their baskets in a method unchanged for centuries. Paul Drury's etching *September* (p. 97) focuses on a family gathering fallen apples beneath a tree laden with fruit. The evening light, grazing sheep and oast houses give a sense of plenty and tranquillity that owes something to the work Samuel Palmer and Edward Calvert (1799–1883). Along with Palmer, Calvert was one of 'The Ancients', a group of young artists who were inspired by the work of William Blake to create visions of an idealised rural world. Calvert's wood engraving *The Cyder Feast* (1828, Tate Collection) presents the apple harvest and cider making as a kind of archaic bacchanal. In contrast Clare Leighton's wood engraving of cider making (p. 106) conveys the strenuous physical work involved in turning the winch and manoeuvring the heavy barrels.

September was also a time for buying and selling sheep. Charles William Taylor's wood engraving (fig. 30) shows the fair held at Findon, West Sussex on 14 September each year. This view from the 1930s shows sheep penned in the foreground with their canine minders looking on, but also the rides and amusements that made fairs such as this an eagerly anticipated event for the whole community.

The harvest marked the end of the farming year, but there was little time to rest, for Michaelmas on 29 September ushered in the start of the new one. Farm tenancies and workers' contracts traditionally began on this date. Decisions now had to be made about what to plant where and when. On mixed farms this usually revolved around a scheme such as the Norfolk or 'four-course' rotation which included break crops like field beans that were less demanding than cereal crops and helped the soil to recover.[7] A.G. Street saw this as

an 'unalterable law' resulting from centuries of experience and believed that the use of such systems relied on an attitude that: 'One didn't farm for cash profits, but did one's duty by the land'.[8] It is these decisions that, as the seasons unfold, dictate the appearance of the network of fields that still makes up much of the rural landscape. Changing demand and fashions in the food we eat, the rise of the globalised economy and the development of farming technologies have dictated the size and content of our fields. This will undoubtedly change again as government and farmers respond to the challenges of climate change, soil loss and declining fertility. New agricultural and rural stewardship regimes will also have to protect the biodiversity on which we rely, not only for our survival, but for the richness in nature and landscape that make the changing seasons such an emotive and rewarding aspect of our lives. **SM**

1. Hardy, T. (1874), *Far from the Madding Crowd*, Folio Society edition, 1985, illustrated with wood engravings by Peter Reddick, pp. 250–5
2. Wightman, R. (1953), *The Seasons*, Cassell & Co. Ltd., p. 22
3. Street, A.G. in *Nature Through the Seasons in Colour*, 1953, Odhams Press Ltd., p. 153
4. Orwell, G. (1931), 'Hop Picking', *New Statesman & Nation*, 17 October 1931. Adapted from Orwell's hop-picking diary, www.orwellfoundation.com/the-orwell-foundation/orwell/essays-and-other-works/hop-picking/ (accessed 9 April 2020)
5. Collis, J.S. (1973), *The Worm Forgives the Plough*, 2009 edition, Vintage, p. 44. This section was originally published as part of *While Following the Plough* in 1946.
6. Watson, G.L. (1960), *What to Look For in Autumn*, Ladybird Books, p. 23
7. Brown, J. (2009), *The Edwardian Farm*, Shire Books, pp. 27–8
8. Street A.G. (1932), *Farmer's Glory*, Faber and Faber, 1934 edition, p. 32

FIG. 30
Charles William Taylor (1878–1960)
Findon Fair · *c.* 1934 · wood engraving
Stuart Southall Collection · © The Estate of C.W. Taylor

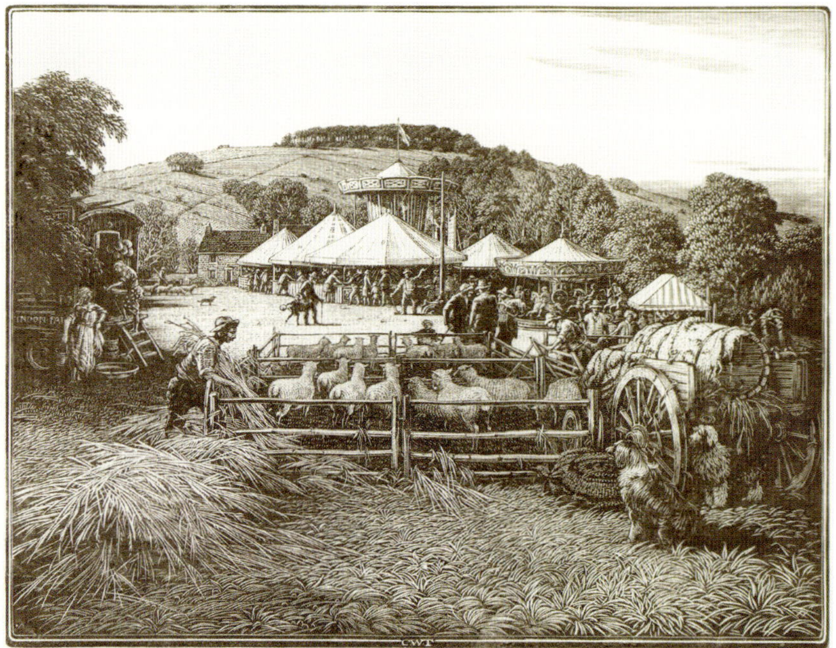

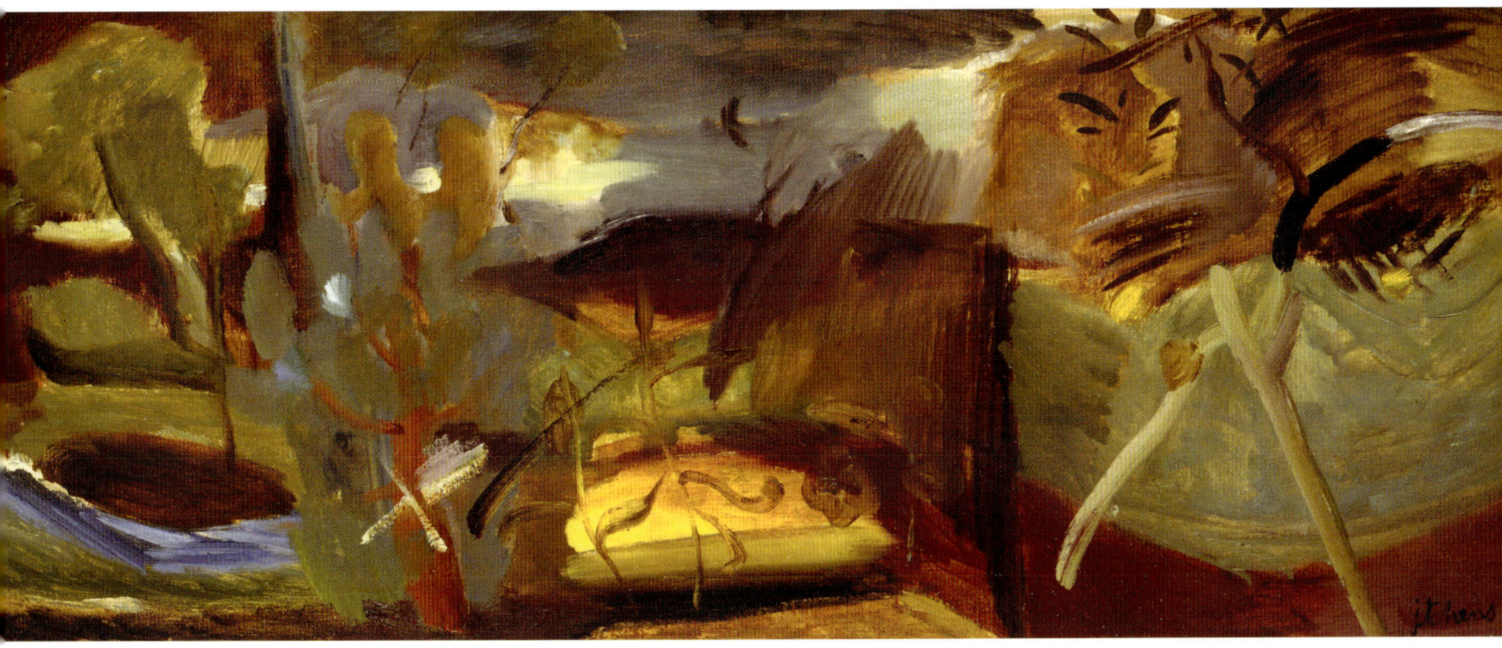

Ivon Hitchens (1893–1979)

Autumn Trees with Distant Hill

1947–48 · oil on canvas · 535 x 1300 mm

The bombing of Ivon Hitchens' Hampstead home during the early years of the Second World War prompted his move in 1940 to Lavington Common amongst the silver birch trees and the bracken, just south of Petworth in West Sussex. The move was to be a turning point, revitalising his work and providing material for a lifetime. Hitchens had earlier written to the civil servant and patron of the arts Edward Marsh (1872–1953) expressing his horror of making a meaningless smear, explaining:

I do try to say clearly and directly by tone and colour what I feel is the essence of the object, and I see no point in building this up with many little strokes … where one will suffice and be more vital.[1]

Autumn Trees with Distant Hill is assured and full of vitality, the harmonious tones and colours reflecting aspects of the forms of the natural world directly around him. Hitchens would often return to the same subject matter seeking new ways of expressing its totality, its 'depth, spaces and objects' rather than topographical accuracy.[2] The ordered, fluid sweeping brushstrokes of *Autumn Trees with Distant Hill*, are employed to effect on his preferred long and shallow canvas shape. Hitchens' marriage to Mary (Mollie) Coates, a pianist in 1935 helped him: 'to consolidate his views on the links between painting and music, which he felt shared a common language of harmony, rhythm, tempo, pulse and structure'. He said: 'My paintings are painted to be listened to'[3] and as in *Autumn Trees with Distant Hill* which captures his affection for painting woodland scenes, it should be scanned from left to right. **GC**

1. Hitchens cited in *The Swindon Collection of Twentieth Century British Art* (1991), p. 66
2. See 'The Forties' in Khoroche, P. (1990), *Ivon Hitchens*, André Deutsch Limited, p. 53
3. Collins, J. and Hamlyn, R. (1982), catalogue notes in *Within these Shores: A Selection of Works from the Chantrey Bequest, 1883–1985*, Tate Gallery & Sheffield City Art Galleries, p. 73, and see Clarke, G. (ed.) (2016), *The Bishop Otter Art Collection: A Celebration*, Sansom & Company, p. 81

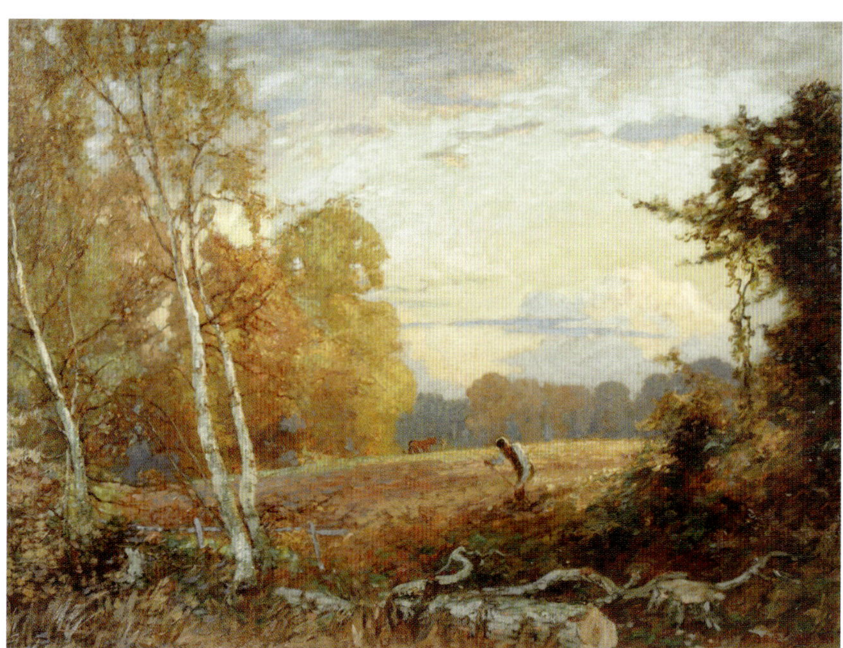

William Herbert Allen
(1863–1943)

Work on the Land, Farnham

oil on canvas • 330 x 430 mm

Hampshire Cultural Trust
image © Hampshire Cultural Trust

W.H. Allen won a scholarship to the Royal School of Woodcarving in 1880 but studies at the Royal College of Art from 1884 set him on a path to becoming a prolific painter in watercolour and oil. In 1889 he joined the staff of the Farnham School of Art later becoming its director and a key figure in the cultural life of the town where he remained for the next thirty-nine years. The surrounding countryside provided his principal subject matter, although he also worked in Italy on commissions from the V&A and other British museums.[1] Towards the end of his life he moved to Bradford-upon-Avon where he concentrated on subjects in Wiltshire and Dorset. Allen would venture out in all weathers making drawings and watercolour studies and returned repeatedly to the same areas to capture the landscape and farming activity across the seasons.

Allen's interests were wide-ranging and encompassed the agricultural landscape, buildings and traditional crafts. Recurring motifs included fields of stooked corn, oast houses, barn interiors and tranquil village scenes. Allen must have been conscious that this quiet rural world was increasingly under threat from mechanisation, development and the rise of motor traffic. His great niece commented: 'Now when I look at his pictures the vanished world of rural crafts and agricultural practices of a past era are recreated in my mind. And at the same time a nostalgic wish to return to the world of "gentlemanly values" and romantic ideas for which my great uncle always seemed to stand'.[2] *Work on the Land, Farnham* with its autumnal colours presents a timeless scene of agricultural work, in the distance a plough team is at work preparing the soil for the new season's sowing. **SM**

1. Penfold, A. and Gillett, J. (1989), *W.H. Allen 1863–1943 Landscape Artist*, Hampshire County Council, unpaginated.
2. Ibid.

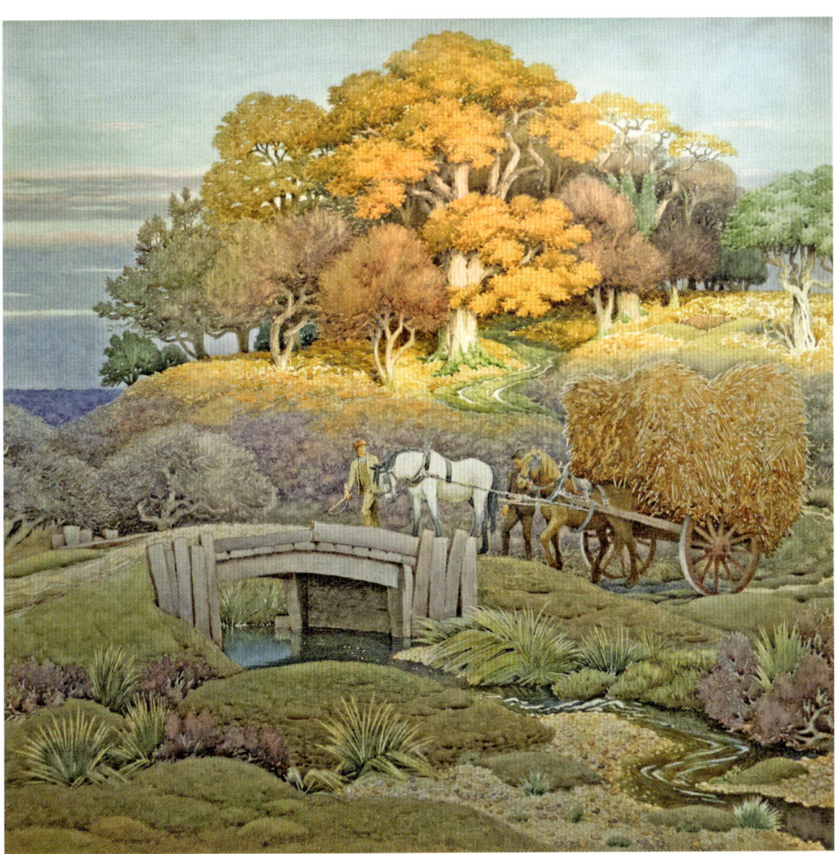

Heywood Sumner
(1853–1940)

The Fern Cart

watercolour • 750 x 750 mm

Hampshire Cultural Trust
image © Hampshire Cultural Trust

Heywood Sumner seemed destined for a career as a barrister but, inspired by the writings of William Morris (1834–1896), John Ruskin (1819–1900) and Edward Burne-Jones (1833–1898), he instead became an artist although he had no formal training. Asked to provide etchings for the 'Artist's Edition' of John Wise's book on the New Forest he spent the early part of 1882 in the area making drawings and then, clearly captivated, returned the following year for his honeymoon. The Sumners settled in London and Heywood became an active, if lesser known, figure in the Arts and Crafts movement producing book illustrations, posters, designs for wallpaper, stained glass and textiles and sgraffito decorations for houses and churches. In 1904 he moved to Cuckoo Hill, near Gorley in the New Forest. There he immersed himself in local culture and heritage as an artist, archaeologist and countryman.

Sumner recorded his experiences and discoveries in a beautifully hand-written and illustrated commonplace book that combined local history, topography and observations on rural life accompanied by his distinctive stylised watercolours. It was published in 1910 as *The Book of Gorley*. This painting is a development of an illustration called *Splash Bridge – Near Holly Hatch*. Sumner explains:

> *The two harvests of the Forest are fern and holly – ferning in the autumn and holly in the winter. The fern is cut by the Forest men, and carried by the buyers at 8 shillings a load: and the loads are full measure! Twelve feet high from the ground, bonded in the loading, corded, and then the moving brown stacks creak slowly homeward along the rutty Forest tracks to supply litter for the small farmers who are not men of straw.*[1]

Sumner has placed much of the landscape, with its fading heather and grasses, in deep evening shade while the bright sunlight illuminating the tree-covered knoll gives it an almost supernatural appearance. **SM**

1. Sumner, H. (1987), *Cuckoo Hill: The Book of Gorley*, facsimile edition published by J.M. Dent, p. 116

Dora M. Batty (1891–1966)

There is Still the Country

1926 · poster · 1016 x 635 mm

London Transport Museum
image © TfL from the London Transport Museum collection

There is Still the Country was one of at least 60 posters
that leading woman designer Dora Batty produced for
the Underground Group and London Transport between
1921–38; these successfully 'mixed motifs from folk art
with modernist design.'[1] Batty like other women artists
of the period was paid less than her male colleagues
and also received limited critical attention.

Batty's versatile and bold designs included a number
of posters celebrating the seasons, *Kew Gardens, Fox-
gloves* (1924, London Transport Museum) for instance
depicted brightly coloured flowers blooming tall in the
summer sun. Although it was one of her early designs
it was selected to appear in the *Design and Industries
Association Yearbook* (1924) as an example of high-
quality modern design and effective advertising.[2]
There is Still the Country differs markedly with its
highly stylised art deco autumn landscape featuring
in the foreground a young athletic looking woman with
short cropped hair, sporting a blue patterned stylish
top over a grey skirt, she stands powerfully in profile,
avoiding engagement with the viewer instead she
stares, self-assured into the distance. Batty cleverly
suggests through her composition the idea of a plea-
surable daytrip to the country for an independent
woman to enjoy the seasonal sights and sounds of
autumn. From 1932, Batty taught textile design at the
Central School of Arts and Crafts until retiring in 1958.
She also worked as a book illustrator and designed
ceramics for Poole Pottery, most notably the Nursery
Toys patterned ware for children. Her work was included in the government backed 'Britain Can Make It'
exhibition in 1946 featuring the top designers. **GC**

1. Bownes, D. (2018), *Poster Girls*, London Transport Museum, p. 42
2. Ibid., p. 43

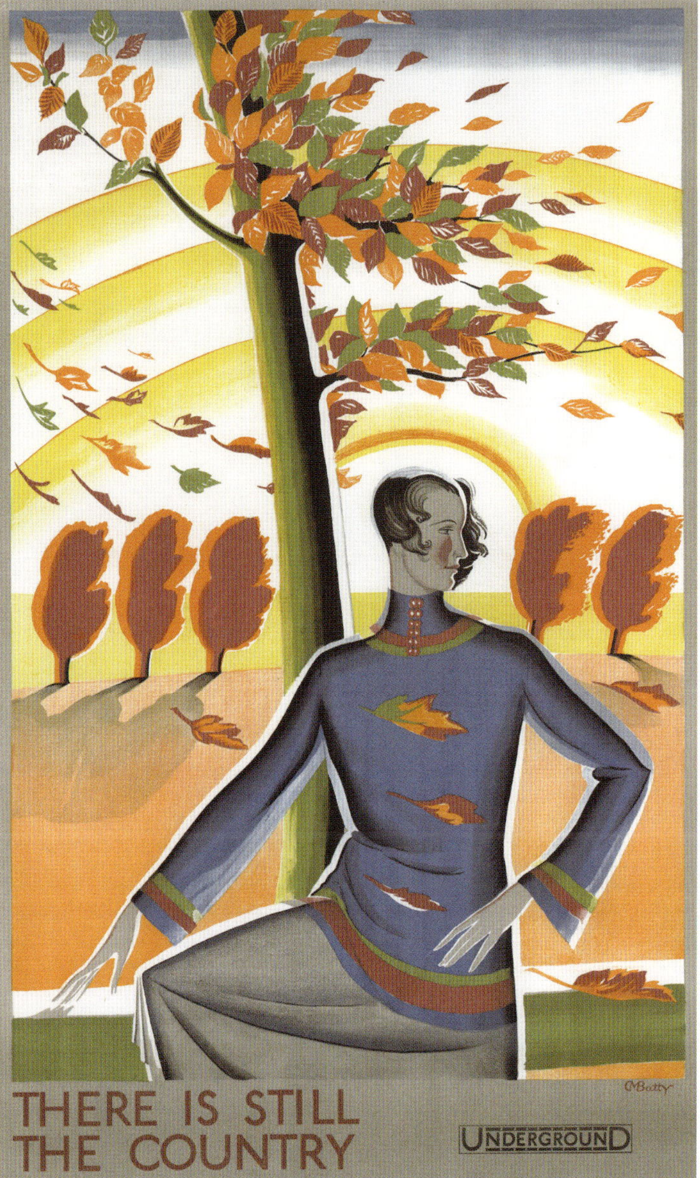

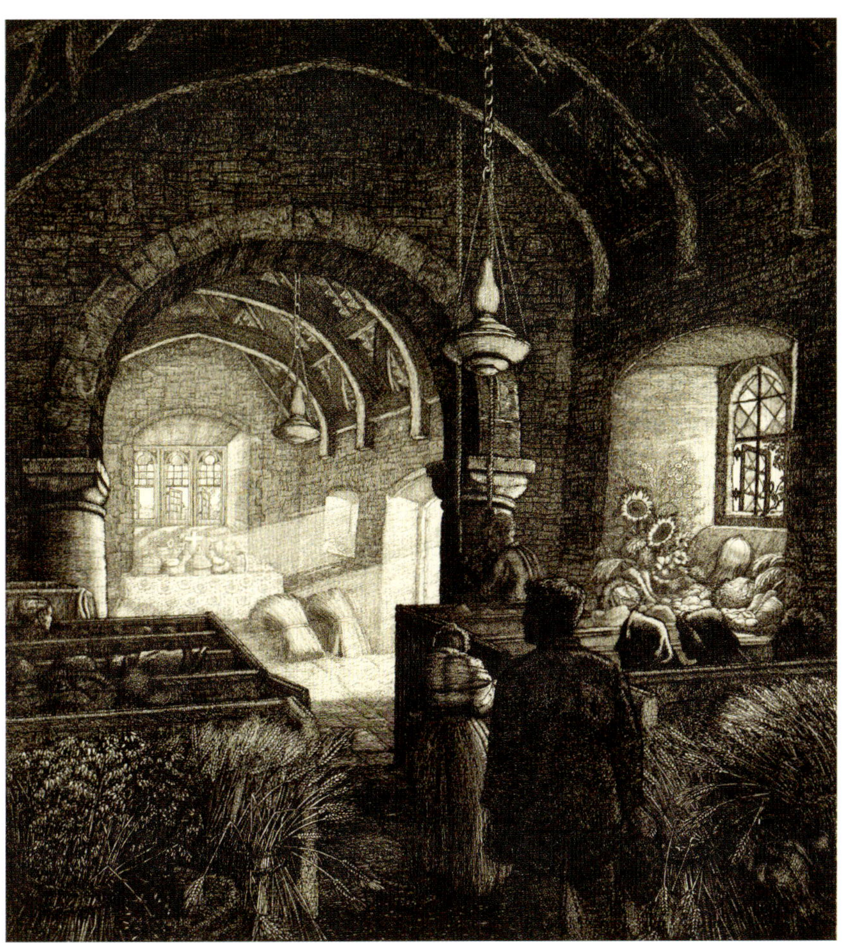

Robin Tanner (1904–1988)

Harvest Festival

1930 · etching · 341 x 308 mm

Stuart Southall Collection
image © The Estate of Robin Tanner

Harvest marks an important date in the British farming calendar as the crops grown for food and animal feed are gathered. *Harvest Festival* celebrates this success; in Britain, such ceremonies have since pagan times been held annually in Autumn during the month of September. Robin Tanner's scene was based on studies made at Harvest Festival time at three churches located close to Chippenham, including Draycot Cerne, which was predominant, he also drew on features from St Peter's, Langley Burrell, and the medieval St Nicholas, Biddestone.

Tanner's freshly decorated church interior in *Harvest Festival* focuses on the 'fruits' of the farmers' labours, a shaft of light from the stained-glass window illuminates the sheaves of wheat stacked under the wagon roof in front of the altar table on which are cottage loaves. In front of the boxed pews piles of apples and other fruit and well-scrubbed vegetables are placed alongside large cabbages with Michaelmas daises and giant sunflowers visible to all attending the service. As the congregation enter the church, they are met by wheat roughly stacked against the back of the rows of pews. The figures in the pews were posed for by Tanner's family including his mother and one of his brothers and several friends. Following the service the vegetables were sent to the nearest hospital.

Harvest Festival was printed by David Strang (1887–1967) younger son of the re-nowned painter and printmaker William Strang (1859–1921), who was well-known as a printer and for getting good results from the plate. Strang also a talented etcher wrote *The Printing of Etchings and Engravings*, in the same year. Despite the quality of Tanner's work, none of the edition of fifty priced at 5 guineas were sold. It was as he said, 'the time of "The Great Slump", when many etchers decided to abandon the craft … I gave away most of them to my friends.'[1] **GC**

1. Tanner, R. (1980) *The Etcher's Craft*, Friends of Bristol Art Gallery, p. 56

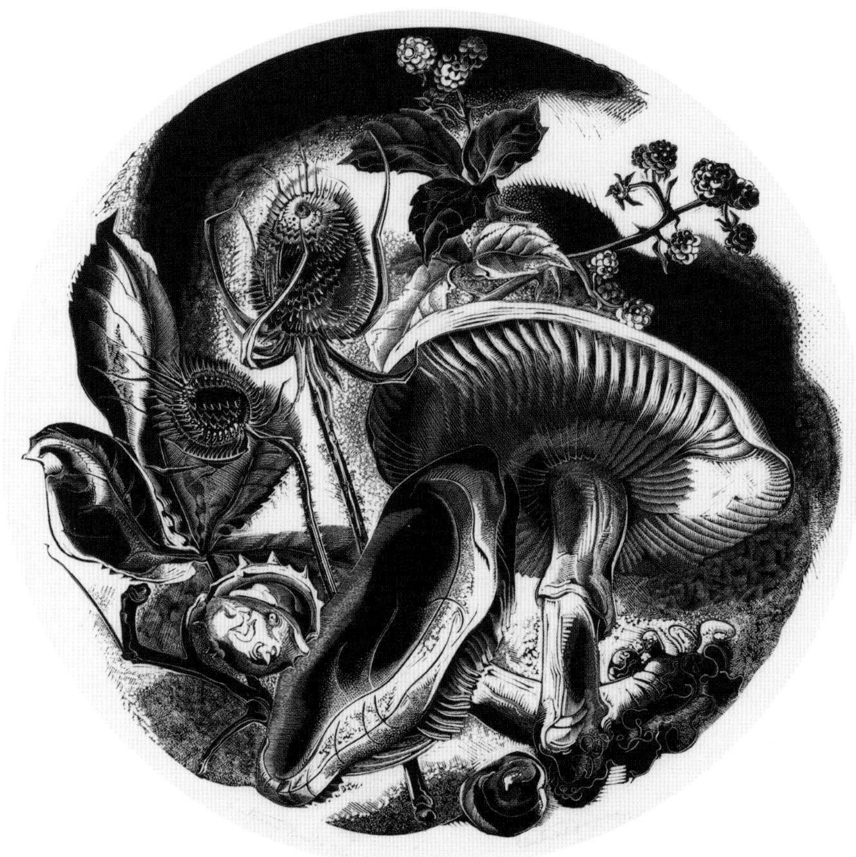

Gertrude Hermes
(1901–1983)

Autumn Fruits

1935 · wood engraving · 345 x 345 mm

Julian Francis Collection
image © The Estate of Gertrude Hermes

In October 1930 Hermes and her husband Blair Hughes-Stanton moved to Tregynon in Montgomeryshire to work for the Gregynog Press, providing illustrations for their high quality limited edition books. They were joined by the wood engraver Agnes Miller-Parker (1895–1980) who would also provide illustrations and her artist husband William McCance (1894–1970) who became the press manager. This proved to be an extremely difficult time for Hermes as Hughes-Stanton's infidelity led to their separation and eventual divorce in 1933. She had been commissioned to engrave thirty illustrations for an edition of Gilbert White's *Natural History of Selborne*, but was only able to complete six and in the difficult financial climate of the early 1930s the book was never published.[1] However, freed from the constraints of working to the Gregynog programme she began producing larger engravings intended for exhibition and in a burst of creativity and renewed confidence produced some of her most striking work.

Hermes' affinity for nature and awareness of its changing face across the seasons can be traced in a number of her engravings. *Spring Bouquet* (1929) shows daffodils, primroses, crocuses and catkins, while its pair *The Harvest* (1929) is a study of oats, barley and hops. Two stylistically contrasting colour linocuts *Winter: Rooks and Rain* (1950) and *Spring Trees* (1957) portray rooks swirling above their treetop nests and the appearance of fresh new leaves. *Autumn Fruits* celebrates the seasonal harvests of fungi, blackberries, teasels and conkers. The startling contrasts of black and white seen in the engravings for *A Florilege* (p. 32) have been replaced by more nuanced variations of mark making and incredibly fine hatching on the gills of the mushroom and the background patterns. When it was exhibited in the Society of Wood Engravers exhibition in 1935 *The Times* commented that: 'the most striking print among 130 is the large circular design by Gertrude Hermes'.[2] SM

1. Katherine Eustace in *Underwood's Children* from *The Wood Engravings of Gertrude Hermes and Blair Hughes-Stanton*, 1995, Ashmolean Museum, Oxford, p. 16
2. Russell, J. (1993), *The Wood Engravings of Gertrude Hermes*, Scolar Press, p. 116

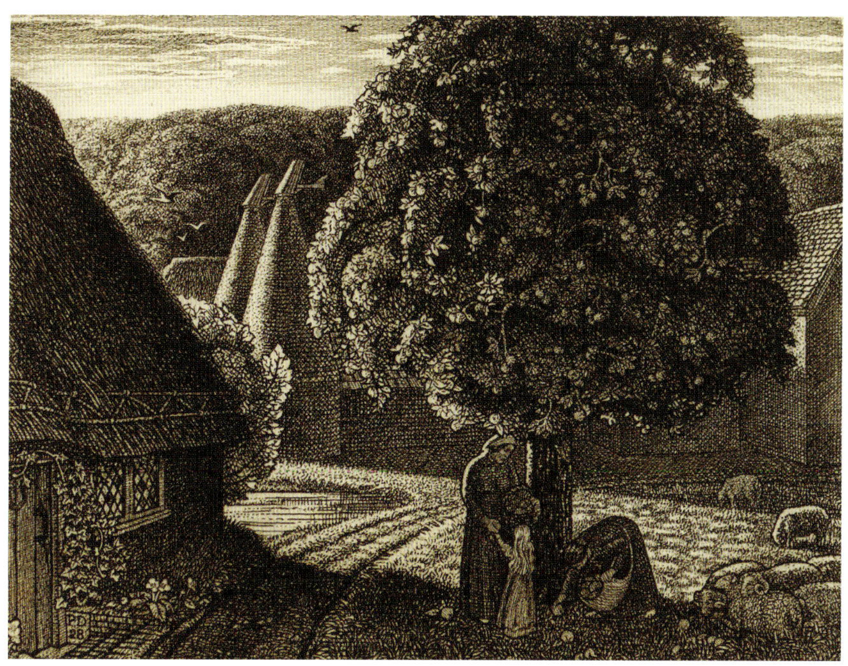

Paul Drury (1903–1987)

September

1928 · etching · 102 x 131 mm

Paul Drury entered Goldsmiths' School of Art in 1921 and with Graham Sutherland, Edward Bouverie Hoyton and William Larkins became part of a coterie of gifted young students who were inspired by the pastoral visions of Samuel Palmer. The excitement they found in etchings like *The Herdsman's Cottage* (1850) and *The Sleeping Shepherd* (1854–7) was such that they even dressed in cloaks in imitation of Palmer and the Ancients during their Shoreham heyday a hundred years previously.[1] The densely worked plates they produced in response were not appreciated by their tutor Stanley Anderson and went against the prevailing fashion for working *en plein air* which precluded too much detail, achieving a more painterly effect by 'omission'. Drury remains best known for his landscape etchings although they only represent about a quarter of his output, portraiture was a far more common subject for him.[2]

The most Palmeresque of Drury's etchings are *After Work* (1926) which shows a weary labourer on his way home hand in hand with his daughter, and his masterpiece *September*. This plate was begun in 1927 and completed the following year. Having settled on the composition Drury developed the etching's beautifully evoked lighting through a sequence of twelve states in which the initial sun beams were removed so that the evening glow is created only by subtle variations in the density of line. The figures perhaps owe more to Jean-François Millet's paintings *The Angelus* (1859) and *The Gleaners* (1857) than they do to Palmer. What Drury achieved was to make a simple scene of evening apple picking into an image that symbolises autumn and the month of September in particular – it is Keats' 'mellow fruitfulness' made manifest. **SM**

1. Drury, J. (2006), *Revelation to Revolution – The Legacy of Samuel Palmer: The Revival and Evolution of Pastoral Printmaking by Paul Drury and the Goldsmiths School in the 20th Century*, Jolyon Drury, p. 34
2. Garton, R. (1992), *The Catalogue Raisonné of the Prints of Paul Drury 1903–1987*, Robin Garton, p. 7

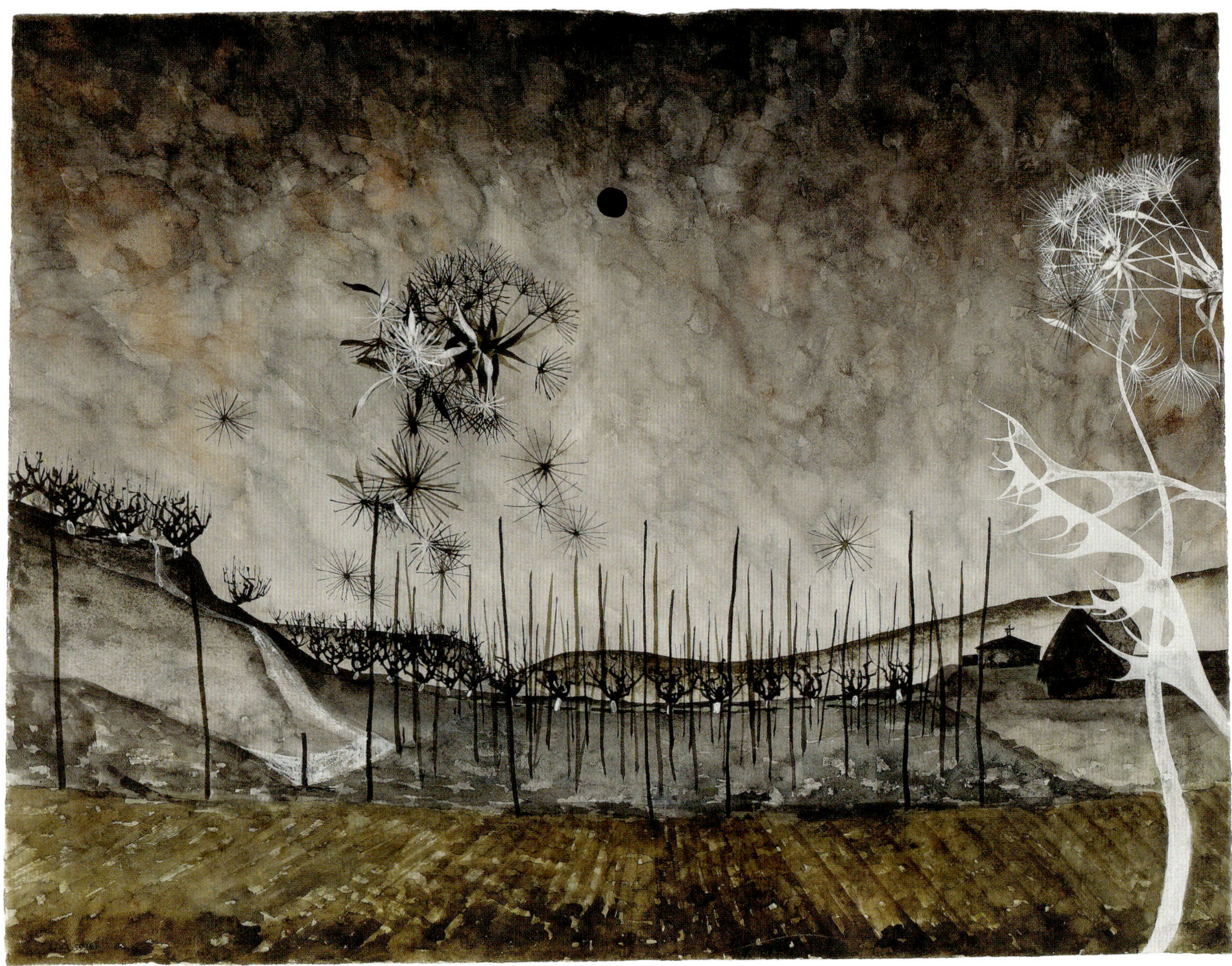

Alan Reynolds (1926–2014)

Bleak November

1955–6 ink · watercolour and gouache
475 x 615 mm

Ingram Collection · image courtesy of The Ingram
Collection of Modern British Art · © Kettle's Yard,
University of Cambridge

The sombre landscape of *Bleak November*, with its simplified forms is one of
Alan Reynolds' remarkable botanical watercolours. Reynolds viewed the landscape
as an inexhaustible subject and here his focus is on a hop garden in late autumn;
winter is not far away. The highly stylised composition like *Summer: Young
September's Cornfield* (p. 76) is indebted to the manner of Paul Klee (1879–1940)
and his 'semi-geometrical signs for natural phenomena'.[1] Reynolds first came across
Klee at the end of the war when stationed in Hanover; he described the experience
as a 'baptism' and this influence combined with Palmeresque elements creates
a disquieting landscape.

The bare pointed black hop poles in *Bleak November* rise up from nowhere and
appear like spears embedded in the ground. They stand starkly behind the ploughed
field, threatening against a mottled and foreboding sky. The low perspective Reynolds
adopts renders the spiky ghost like silvery leaves of the dandelion gargantuan, as
they reach menacingly into the bleak landscape. The earthy and muted palette
of muddy brown and black washes naturally eschews the vibrancy of his earlier
painting *Summer: Young September's Cornfield*.

Reynolds became dissatisfied with his work and feeling he was repeating himself[2]
started his move into greater abstraction between 1958 to 1959 leaving behind
landscape painting and botanical motifs and those critics and collectors who
longed for a revival of the English watercolour tradition. **GC**

1. Robert Melville (1956), preface in *The Four Seasons*, The Redfern Gallery
2. See Hodin, J.P. (1962), *Alan Reynolds*, The Redfern Artists Series

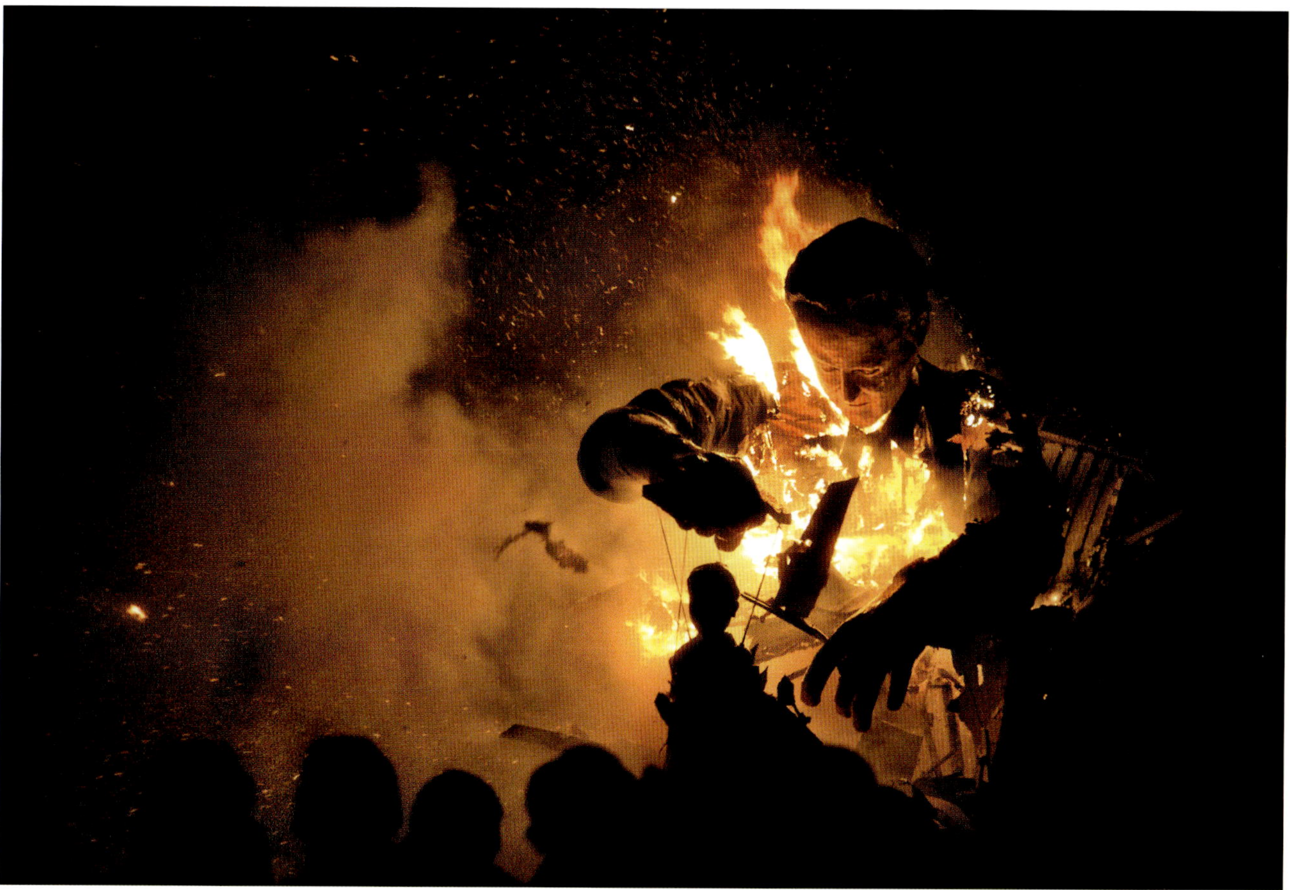

Sara Hannant (b. 1964)

*Burning effigy of
David Cameron with
Nick Clegg as his puppet,
Cliffe Bonfire Society,
Lewes, Sussex*

2010 • archival pigment print
297 x 420 mm

collection of the artist • image © Sara Hannant

Traditionally, at the end of the harvest when all the work on the land was finished, pastoral communities would slaughter weak animals before the winter, and light the dark nights with fires and feasting. Sussex Bonfire Societies seemingly echo this practice by staging costumed torch lit parades throughout Sussex from September to November. In Lewes, tar barrels are dragged through the streets on sledges as part of the bonfire celebrations. Later the barrels are thrown blazing into the River Ouse. Lewes is well known for the controversial practice of burning effigies of 'unpopular' characters, including politicians, known as 'Enemies of the Bonfire'. It is also customary to burn an effigy of the Pope, which is in reference to the burning of seventeen Protestant Martyrs in the mid-1500s. Most Bonfire Societies stage firework displays, and many societies also include remembrance services for lives lost in armed conflict. **Sara Hannant**

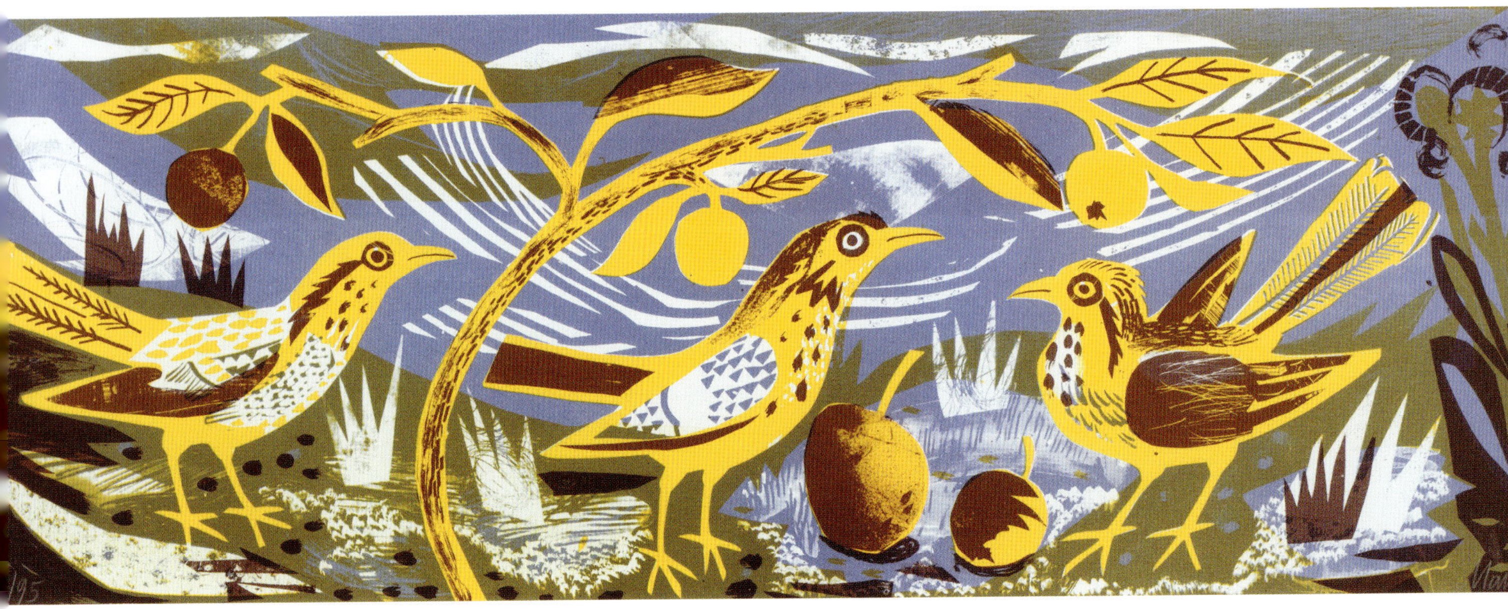

Mark Hearld (b. 1974)

Thrushes and Crab Apples

2010 • lithograph • 260 x 690 mm

Julian Francis Collection • image © the artist

Mark Hearld has described himself as a 'collagist, printmaker, designer of this and that, and collector of tat'.[1] His enthusiasm for the kind of everyday nature seen in gardens, streets and country lanes is reflected in work that celebrates sometimes unloved species like mice, pigeons and starlings. His prints, collages and designs for ceramics and textiles bring these familiar creatures to vibrant life, capturing their innate characters in arresting stylised forms. Hearld studied illustration at the Glasgow School of Art with Mick Manning who shared his love of nature and encouraged him to draw outside. He then moved on to the Royal College of Art to take an MA in natural history illustration with John Norris Wood who had worked with Edward Bawden and Cedric Morris. Hearld's admiration for artists of that generation including John Piper (1903–1992), Eric Ravilious and Edward Burra is evident from his work, as is an interest in folk art shared with Enid Marx (1902–1998) and Barbara Jones (1912–1978).

Thrushes and Crab Apples shows how Hearld's work as a collagist has informed his approach to lithography, the birds appearing almost as cut-outs layered against the abstracted setting. His keen observation of the world around him is reflected in convincing portraits of the behaviour and quirks of his subjects. The landscapes in which they flit and strut are also full of seasonal references, here an autumnal feast of crab apples. In other works thrushes are found minding a nest of speckled blue eggs, a blackbird pecks at a crop of strawberries, partridges scurry through ripe corn, spindle fruits brighten an autumnal hedgerow, rust-coloured leaves blow around a passing fox and owls flit among bare, snow-dusted trees. **SM**

1. Martin, S. (2012), *Mark Hearld's Work Book*, Merrell Publishers Limited, p. 6

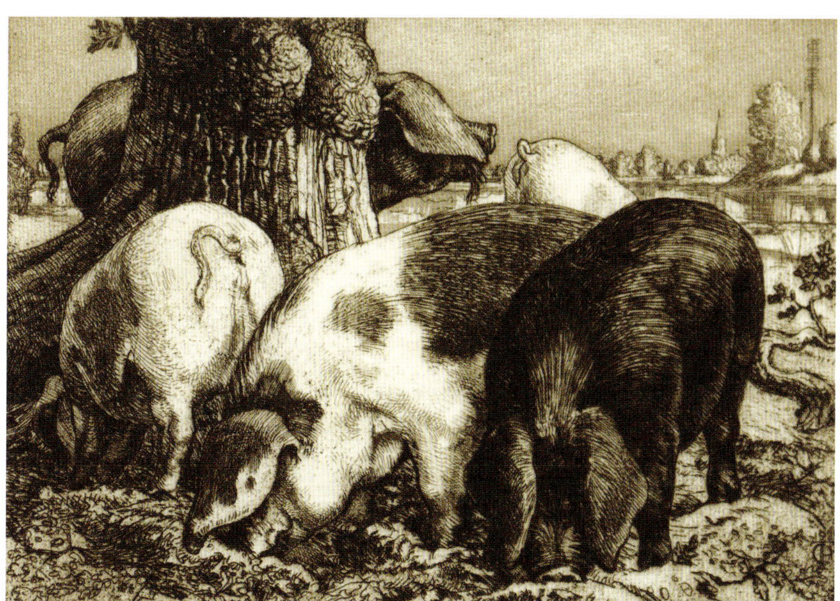

Charles Tunnicliffe
(1901–1979)

The Acorn Hunters

1929 · etching · 120 x 170 mm

Autumn traditionally saw the release of domestic pigs to roam in forests to forage for fallen acorns which if left in large quantities were poisonous to horses and cattle. The custom known as Pannage or 'Common of Mast' was granted to local people on common land or in royal forests and dates to the time of William the Conqueror, who founded The New Forest in 1079 and where the practice continues today lasting for not less than 60 days. The pigs are marked, have rings put through their snouts to lessen the damage caused by rooting and are turned out on a start date determined by the Court of Verderers who administer commoning rights and practices.

Charles Tunnicliffe's early upbringing on a farm in East Cheshire gave him first-hand experience of many traditional agricultural practices including working with pigs and importantly for the young would-be artist, opportunities to draw them on any scrap of paper he could find. These early sketches were later used in his etchings. Tunnicliffe was taken by the 'interesting form' of pigs finding them 'quite beautiful'.[1] *The Acorn Hunters* is characterised by his trademark precision and accuracy, variously titled *'Pigs Foraging'*, *'Pigs Rootling'*, and *'Pigs under Oak'*, the composition of a group of pigs foraging under an old oak tree was envisaged following him making notes about an etching on 14 November 1929. The same day Tunnicliffe transferred 'the drawing on the plate and started the needling.'[2] Subsequently he made a study of the gnarled base of an oak tree and finished the needling and biting of the plate. By 19 November Tunnicliffe was satisfied that he had 'managed to get a good even tone over the sky and get good prints' from the sixth and final state.[3] **GC**

1. Tunnicliffe, C.F. (1942), *My Country Book*, The Studio, p. 41
2. Meyrick, R. and Heuser, H. (2017), *Charles Tunnicliffe Prints: A Catalogue Raisonné*, Royal Academy of Arts, p. 110
3. Ibid., p. 110

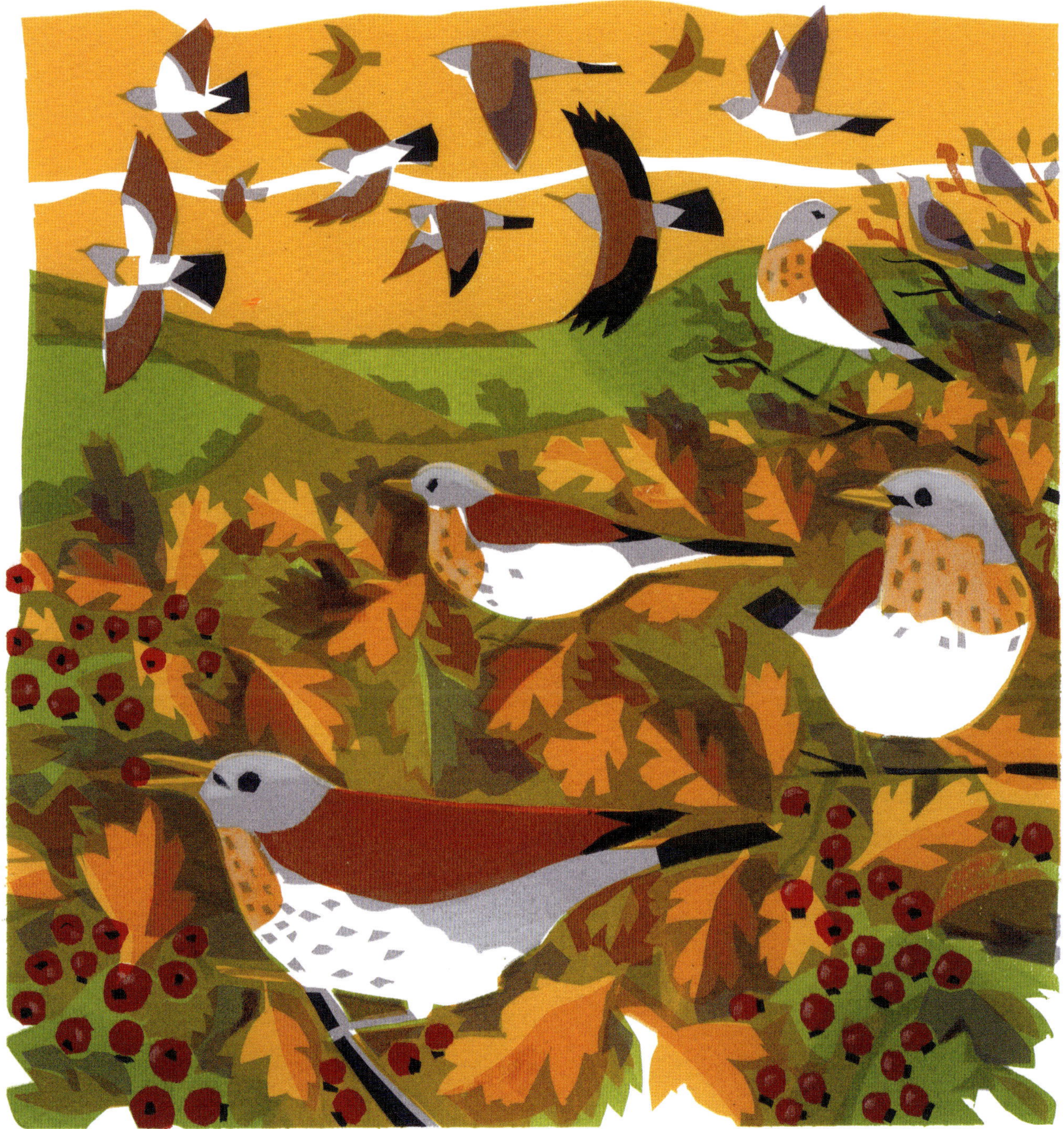

Carry Akroyd (b. 1953)

Fieldfares

2019 • screenprint • 200 x 200 mm

collection of the artist • image © the artist

The date when these winter thrushes arrive depends on conditions in Scandinavia, but suddenly there will be a gathering of them moving down the hedgerows feeding on the autumn berries, or calling to each other as they fly towards a buffet on other bushes. They fly with a hesitation, a moment with the wings held still. As winter comes on, they must feed on the ground, faring over frosty fields. I never see them leave in spring, I just notice one day that they have gone. **Carry Akroyd**

Charles Tunnicliffe (1901–1979)

Swifts and Swallows

1960 • watercolour • 270 x 180 mm

During the Second World War Tunnicliffe and his
wife Winifred took a much-needed break on the Isle
of Anglesey in North Wales. He spent time observing
and drawing the island's rich bird life and having fallen
in love with the place they both agreed to move there
as soon as a suitable property became available.
In 1947 they took possession of a bungalow called
Shorelands on the Cefni Estuary. The move and his
early experiences on Anglesey were the subject for the
book *Shorelands Summer Diary* (1952) which featured
full colour reproductions of watercolour paintings and
a wealth of monochrome scraperboard vignettes.

This illustration is based on a view of the village of
Malltraeth and is a variation on one of the scraperboard illustrations from *Shorelands Summer Diary*.
Tunnicliffe's diary entry for 5 September describes
swallows gathering in preparation for their migration:

> *They came in hundreds, twittering excitedly all
> about the roof and the garden, and in the after-
> noon the slates of the roof as well as the ridge
> tiles were populated with them as they basked
> in the bright sunlight … some of them rested on
> their sides with one wing and tiny foot turned
> skywards as if revelling in the warmth. Others
> preened vigorously, and some young birds
> crouched and asked for food whenever a
> flying bird approached them.*[1]

SM

1. Tunnicliffe, C.F. (1952), *Shorelands Summer Diary*,
Orbis Publishing edition 1985, pp. 123–4

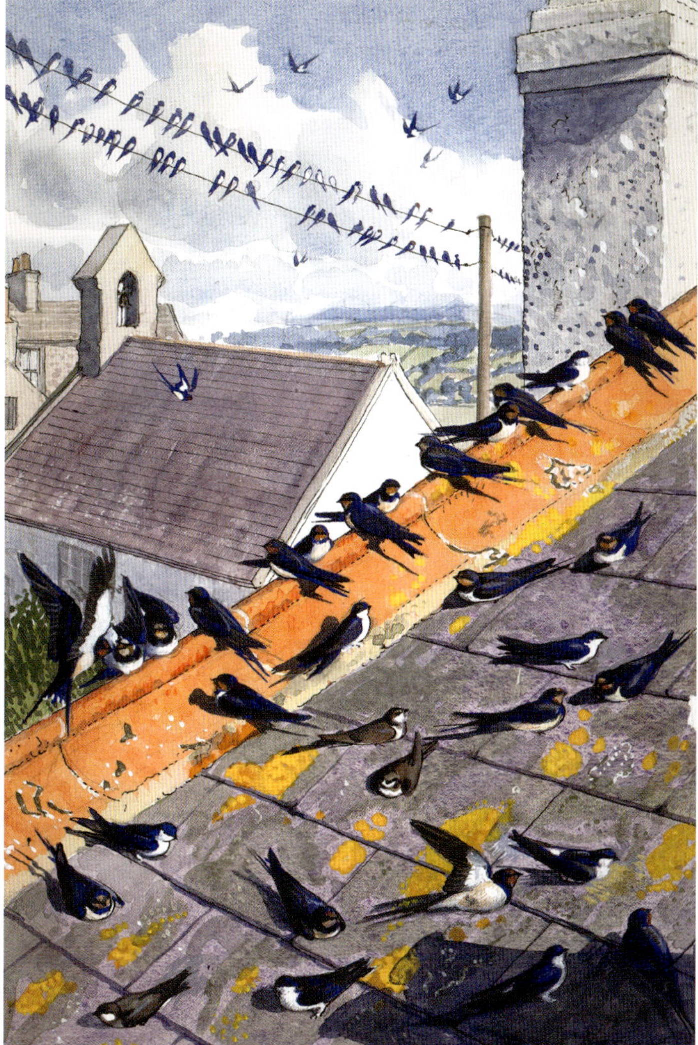

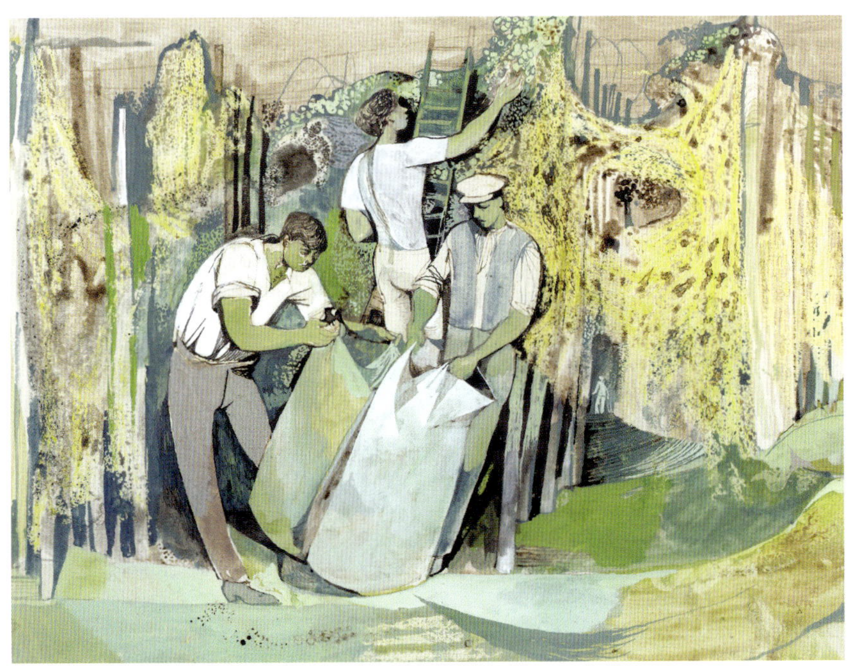

John Minton (1917–1957)

The Hop Pickers

1945 · gouache, chalk, pen, watercolour
260 x 335 mm

The Ingram Collection of Modern and Contemporary British Art · image © The Royal College of Art/ Bridgeman Images

Hop Picking required considerable labour, its value depended on being harvested quickly and at the right moment, a task that required an additional work force. East Enders in their droves left London by special trains each September for Kent for the annual hopping season where they would stay in rudimentary farm huts for four to six weeks, many regarding it as a rural holiday with pay. John Minton was familiar with the task having regularly visited the Weald of Kent from 1945–54 staying in Chart Sutton with fellow St John's Wood Art School student Edie Lamont and Newton her husband, making numerous drawings of the countryside.[1]

Minton's lyrical and highly individual painting *The Hop Pickers* was completed in the mid 1940s when he was teaching illustration at Camberwell School of Art and living with and sharing the two Roberts', (MacBryde and Colquhoun) studio. He had obtained the teaching post in Autumn 1943 having been discharged from the Army in June.[2]

> *There is a strong reminiscence of neo-romanticism in* [The Hop Pickers], *but it is blended with a much greater interest in the visible world and the activities going on within it. The dark accents, suggestive of shadow, around the figures offset the lighter colours in their clothing and sharpen attention on this central group.*[3]

This central group of three male workers are engrossed in their various tasks. One is perched halfway up a ladder stripping the hop bine growing up a 10-foot-high pole, while the other two prepare to move the full hop bins for measurement so that payment can be calculated. At the far end of the row, in the shadows, can be glimpsed a diminutive male figure beneath 'the net' of hops. Minton's interest is not only with observing the actions of the workers but also in conveying the abundance of the luxuriantly coloured hops and the dense patterning created by their richness.[4] *The Hop Pickers* was reproduced in *The English People* by George Orwell as part of the series *Britain in Pictures*, publication was delayed until 1947 owing to the wartime paper shortage. **GC**

1. See https://www.bonhams.com/auctions/17824/lot/59/ catalogue entry compiled by Frances Spalding for sale of John Minton's *The Hop Pickers* accessed 5 May 2020)
2. See Clarke, G. (2018), *Conflicting Views: Pacifist Artists*, Sansom & Company, p. 101 re Minton's discharge
3. Spalding, op. cit.
4. See Mr John Minton. 'The Lyrical Touch', *The Times*, 22 January 1957, p. 12, and Spalding, F. (1991), *John Minton: Dance till the Stars Come Down*, Hodder & Stoughton

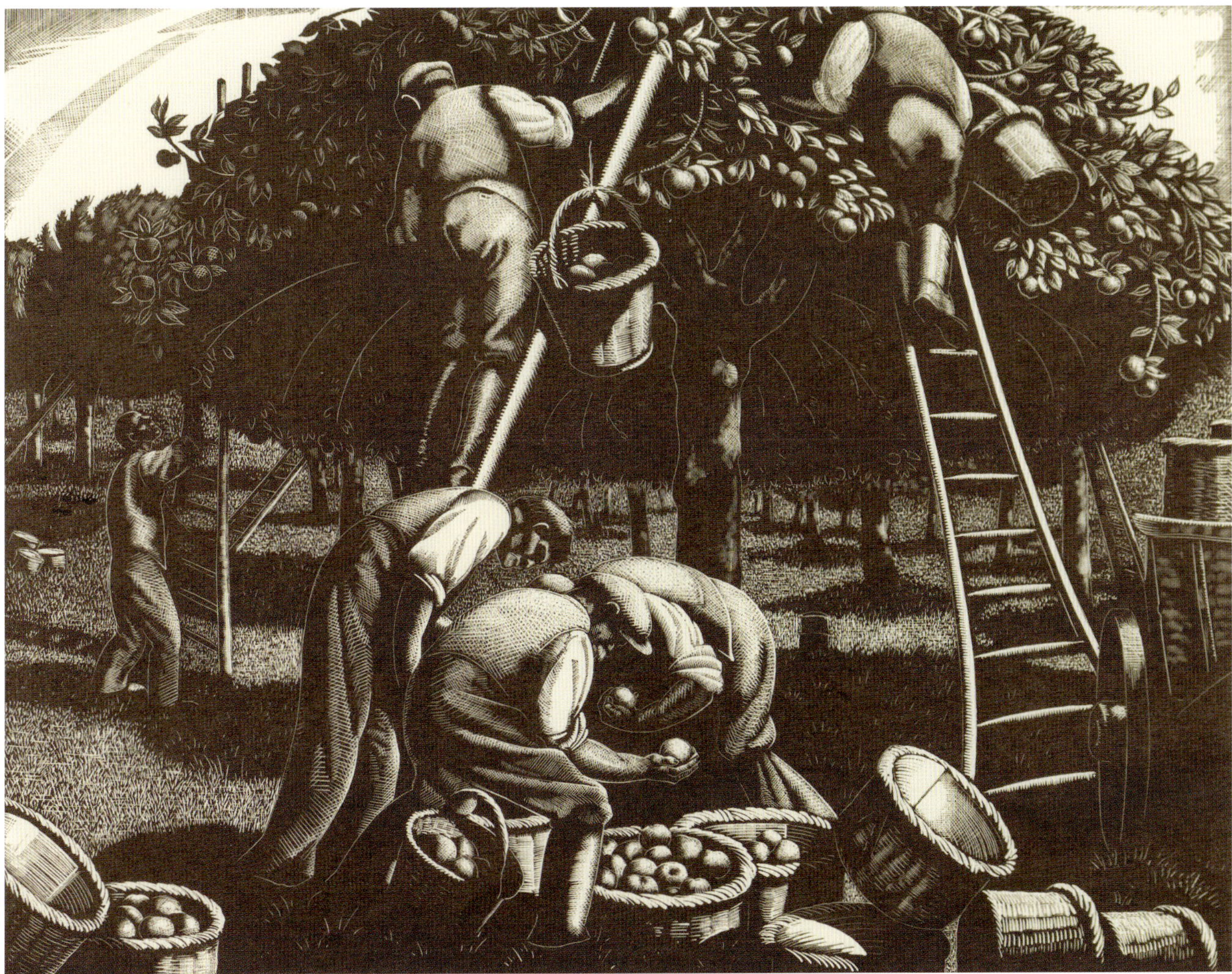

Clare Leighton (1898–1989)

September

1933 · wood engraving · 221 x 280 mm
from *The Farmer's Year*

For her September subject in *The Farmer's Year* Leighton travelled to the apple orchards of Kent, 'the Garden of England'. Both the engraving and accompanying text are clearly based on direct experience of the apple harvest as she follows the work through the day from early morning dew through midday heat and on to the peace of evening. It is all underpinned by an appreciation of the significance this event held for the fruit growers. Everything has been leading to this moment from late winter pruning to attempts to protect the spring blossom from frost and bull-finch and a summer of watching the fruit develop. In keeping with her approach throughout the book the focus falls on the endeavours of the workers. It is their quiet skill in these ageless tasks that will provide food for a nation largely un-aware of their existence. The engraving shows men on stout ladders picking the fruit while below another group have the important task of checking and sorting them ready to be transported as Leighton imagines 'for grey-faced people in the cities who never saw an apple shine upon the top most bough against the blue of a September sky'.[1] **SM**

1. Leighton, C. (1933/2012), *The Farmer's Year: A Calendar of English Husbandry*, Little Toller Books, p. 46

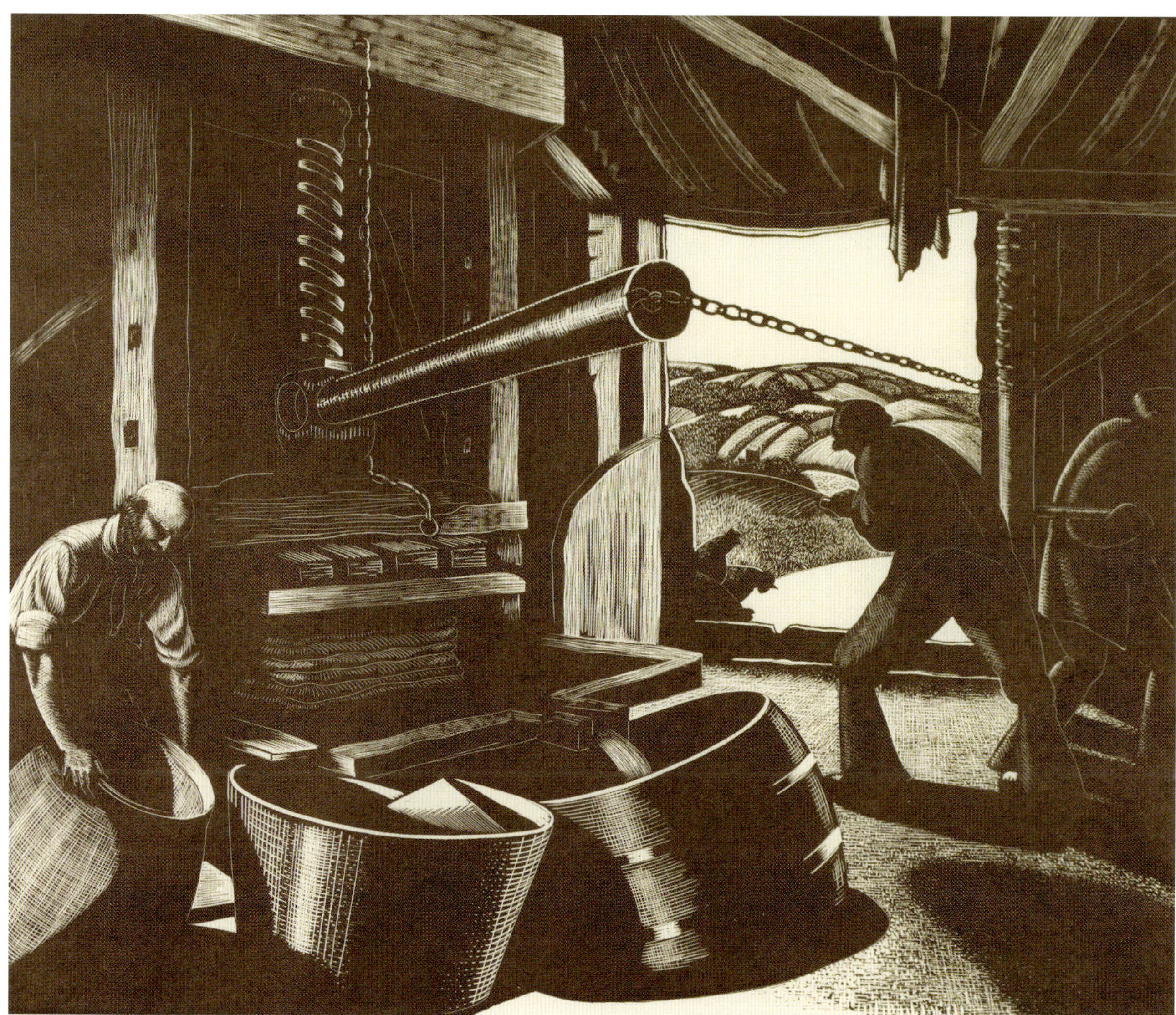

Clare Leighton (1898–1989)

October

1933 · wood engraving · 216 x 254 mm
from *The Farmer's Year*

Stuart Southall Collection · Clare Leighton's
wood engravings are reproduced courtesy
of the artist's estate

A logical step from the apple harvest is cider making, but here Leighton has moved her subject from Kentish orchards to a Devon barn. Her preference for large areas of black is well-suited to portraying the shadowy interior in contrast to the bright light beyond. Each incision the wood engraver makes on their block will be a white line in the print, they are cutting light from darkness. Here Leighton with a single faint line reveals the form of the upright support on the cider press and with a few more tiny marks shows the screw. Once again she depicts the labour involved in the process as in the corner two bent figures trudge round and round turning the winch that will crush the juice from the apples.

> *As hour after hour the winch turns the screw, the sacks of apple pulp flatten and diminish, and after a time the trickling gurgle of juice grows feeble and uncertain. Creaking and groaning, the press plays a sleepy bass to the grunts of the two old men and the shuffle of their earth-caked boots. Age is upon it all; we are outside of time. These men must have been trudging round and round before our grandsires were born; and they will be trudging still when we ourselves are dead.*[1]

SM

1. Leighton, C. (1933/2012), *The Farmer's Year: A Calendar of English Husbandry*, Little Toller Books, p. 49

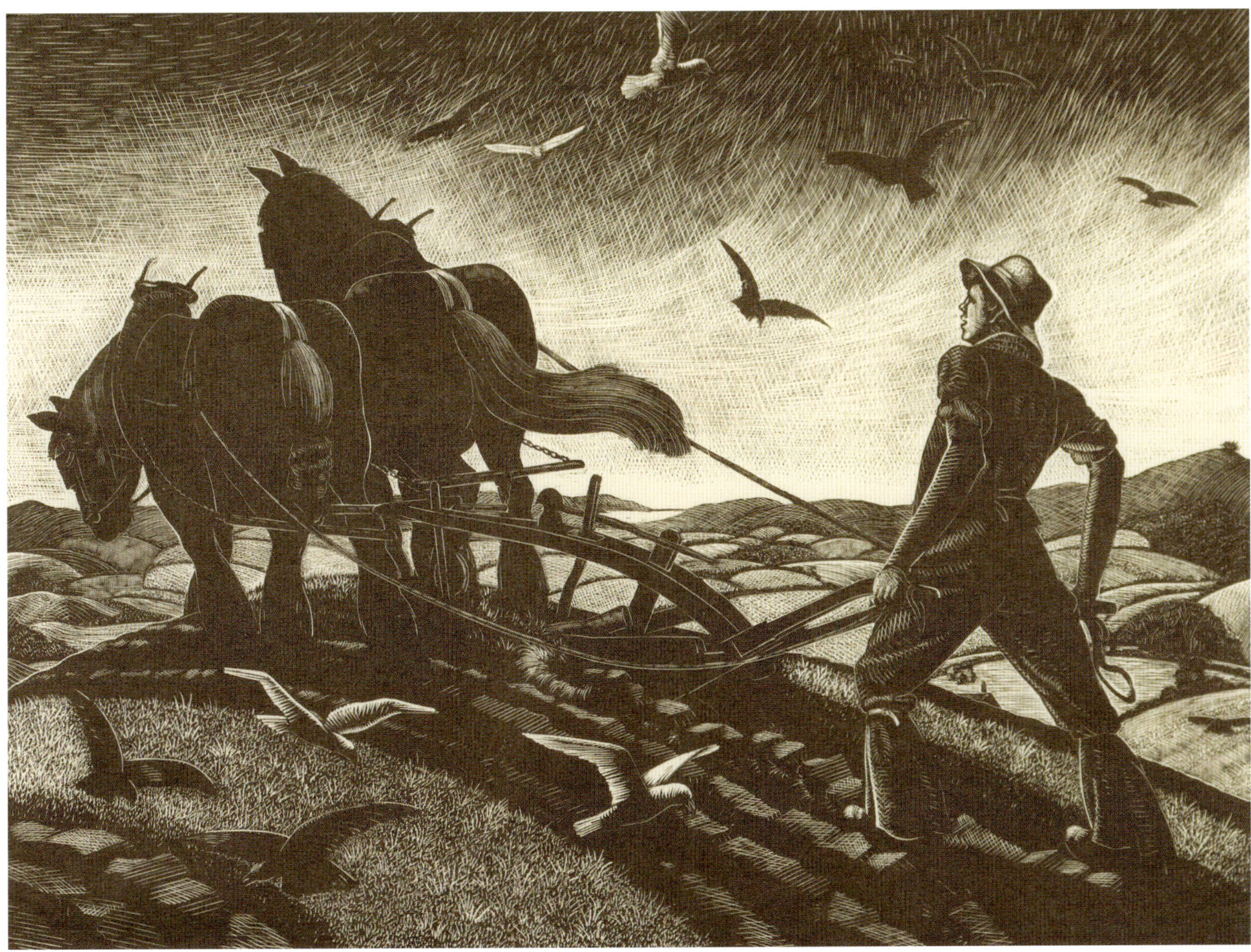

Clare Leighton (1898–1989)

November

1933 · wood engraving · 190 x 254 mm
from *The Farmer's Year*

Stuart Southall Collection · Clare Leighton's
wood engravings are reproduced courtesy
of the artist's estate

Clare Leighton's illustrations for *The Farmer's Year* are an unsentimental record of agricultural work in the 1930s. However, the engraving for November is an unashamedly romantic vision of the ploughman at work. He breasts the hill just as dawn is breaking, illuminating the patchwork of fields laid out below. Gulls swirl around him as his team plods on, breaking up the soil in preparation for sowing next year's crops. So the farming seasons roll on, as soon as one planting and harvesting cycle has finished another begins.

Yet Leighton is still very much aware of the practical details of this task. Ploughing in late autumn will give the winter frosts a chance to break up the clods to provide an even tilth suitable for planting in the spring and the work requires care and skill:

> *Firmly the ploughman holds the handles, taking care not to press too much or too little on them, lest the depth of his furrows should vary. Keenly he keeps his eye on the end of the furrow so his line may be straight, and turning his team and his plough at the field's edge, he must make the right curve lest it be too sharp and he get pitched into the ditch, or too wide and he miss the next furrow.*[1]

Despite working in monochrome, Leighton's text also reveals an artist's sensitivity to colour as she notes the transformation of autumn's gold to the greys and browns of winter. **SM**

1. Leighton, C. (1933/2012), *The Farmer's Year: A Calendar of English Husbandry*, Little Toller Books, p. 53

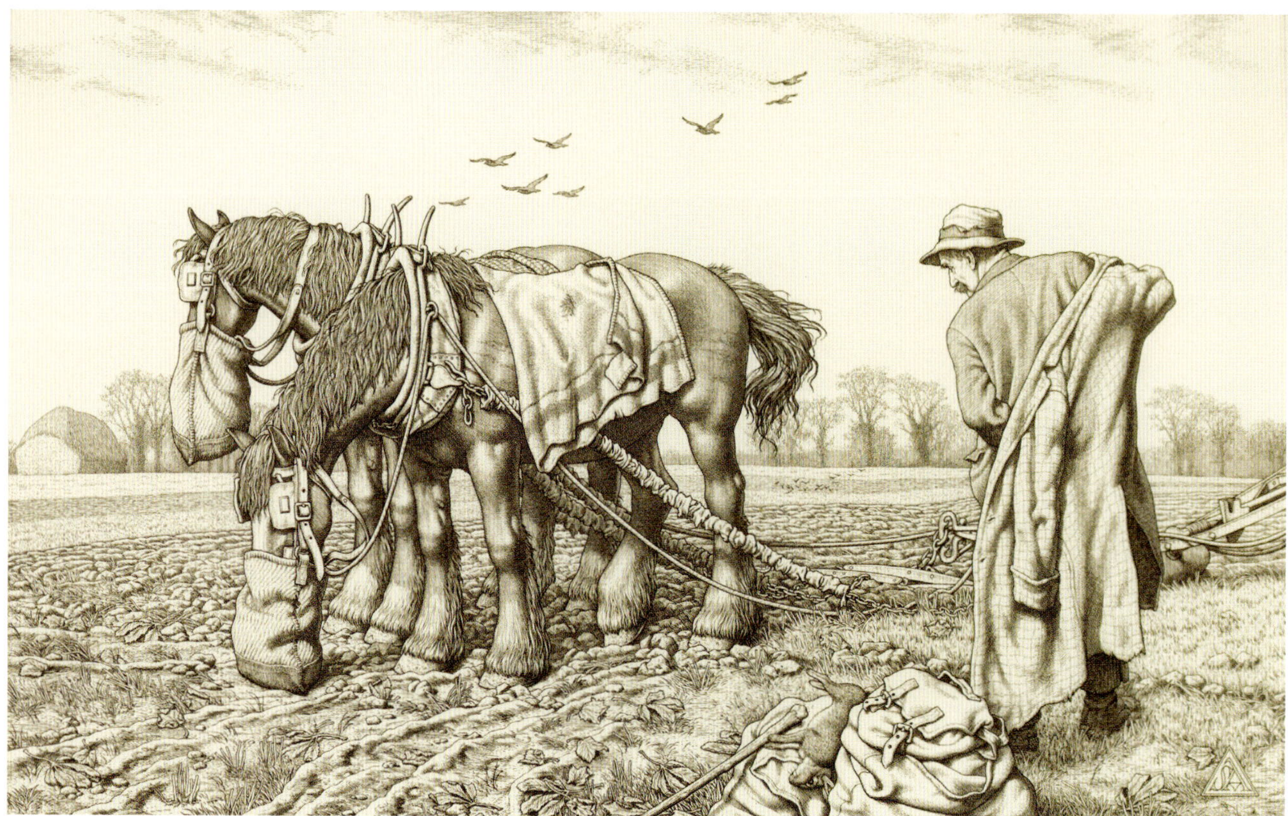

Stanley Anderson
(1884–1966)

Three Good Friends

1950 · line engraving · 172 x 268 mm

Ploughing with horses was a skilled job but like other traditional ways of working it was threatened by increasing mechanisation. Stanley Anderson had great sympathy and admiration for rural workers and concerned by the pace and impact of these changes he sought to painstakingly record English country crafts and seasonal farming practices before they disappeared from the landscape. It was for this body of work that he was made a CBE in 1951.

Over some twenty years Anderson produced many minutely detailed line engravings, based on his acute and loving observation including those of thatching, hedge-laying, basket and lace making. He often knew the craftspeople personally, how-ever neuritis in his right hand and arm forced him from 1953 to concentrate on his evocative watercolours of country scenes that had been an important part of the Recording Britain project during the Second World War.

Three Good Friends demonstrates Anderson's mastery of engraving, a skill he had helped to revive in the inter war years. It was the only print he produced in 1950. Highly disciplined in his approach it was based on his customary practice of under-taking detailed preliminary sketches. These commenced in 1945 and were inscribed 'Darkie and Prince in the Orchard'. Anderson was by then living permanently in Buckinghamshire in the cottage 'Old Timbers' he purchased in 1933 in Towersey, about two miles east of Thame. He had moved there from London during the Blitz following the bombing of his home and studio.

Anderson's work avoids nostalgia for some bucolic golden age rather it reflects his concern for manual workers whom he championed and viewed as equals. *Three Good Friends* shows his keen understanding of the rural environment and the harsh reality of agricultural labour together with the close bond established between man and beast. Here the ploughman and his trusted team of horses take a well-earned rest. The rooks having followed the plough and feasted on wireworms and other soil pests return to the treetops where old nests remain. **GC**

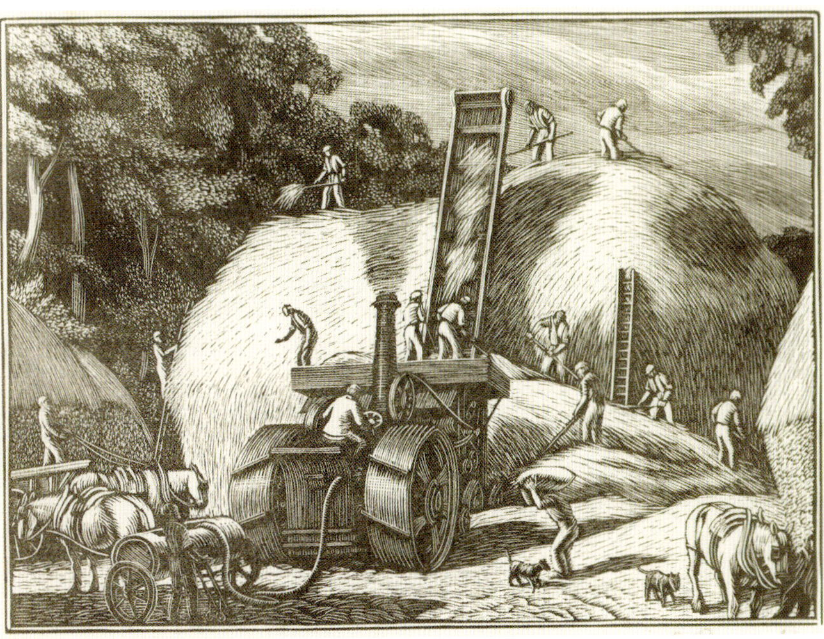

Gwen Raverat (1885–1957)

The Threshing Machine

1930 • wood engraving • 132 x 177 mm

Gwen Raverat became widely known as the author of *Period Piece* (1952) an account of her childhood in late Victorian Cambridge. She studied painting at the Slade School of Art but as a wood engraver she was largely self-taught. In 1911 she married Jacques Raverat and from 1920 they lived at Vence in the South of France. When Jacques died in 1925 after a long illness she returned to Cambridge-shire. As an engraver Raverat had a painterly and naturalistic style quite different from the more formal precision seen in the work of some contemporaries. Many of her engravings are based on life and landscapes around her French and English homes, but after working on Kenneth Grahame's *Cambridge Book of Poetry for Children* (1932) she was much in demand as a book illustrator. One of her finest achievements were the wood engravings for A. G. Street's *Farmer's Glory* (1932) a memoir of farming practices in England and Canada. Although *The Threshing Machine* was engraved several years earlier it would have been a perfect fit with the book's nostalgic scenes of traditional harvesting and haymaking.

With increasing mechanisation threshing became a task that could be completed as soon as the harvest was brought in. Traditionally it had been something to occupy the farm workers through the lean winter months but might now be performed in the warmth of late summer or early autumn. Raverat's engraving shows a steam engine powering the threshing machine, beyond which is a conveyor carrying straw up to the top of the stack where men with forks are organising it into a regular and stable structure. Down below another worker is carrying a sack of grain which has been separated and bagged by the labour-saving thresher. Even with machinery this task still brought together all available hands to get the corn threshed and ricked before the weather could turn. **SM**

ACKNOWLEDGEMENTS

The Coronavirus outbreak created a number of challenges during the development of this book and exhibition. For the authors the inability to directly access libraries, archives and collections made research more challenging. Planning and implementing the loans for the exhibition also became a very uncertain process and we would particularly like to thank all our lenders for their patience and support and for honouring their commitments during this difficult time.

We would like to thank Stuart Southall for his crucial role in the development of this exhibition. We have drawn heavily on his outstanding collection of prints and could have generated an entire exhibition from its content, such was the range of artist and seasonal subject matter it contains. Stuart's generous sponsorship also made this publication possible. His support and enthusiasm throughout the process was also greatly appreciated.

Thanks to our lenders: Chris Beetles Gallery, The British Council, Julian Francis, Hampshire Cultural Trust, The Ingram Collection of Modern and Contemporary British Art, Ladybird Books and University of Reading Special Collections, London Transport Museum, Southampton City Art Gallery, St Barbe Museum and Art Gallery, Tate, the UK Government Art Collection and the private collectors. Our appreciation also extends to the contemporary artists who provided work and kindly wrote texts to accompany them: Carry Akroyd, Keith Grant, Sara Hannant, Andrew Haslen, Mark Hearld, Kurt Jackson, James Lynch, Annie Ovenden, Howard Phipps, Colin See-Paynton and George Tute.

For images and copyright permissions we are grateful to Julia Berlin, Bridgeman Images, DACS, Jolyon Drury, Kettle's Yard, John Huddlestone, David Leighton, Penguin Random House, Tim Russell, Science and Society Picture Library, Tom Willingham and John Hammond (photography) and the various lenders and artists' estates. Every effort was made to contact copyright holders and we would be happy to hear from any we were unable to trace.

The exhibition and book would not have been possible without the support of St Barbe Museum and Art Gallery. We would like to thank the trustees, staff and volunteers, in particular Maria Ragan, Director, Rosalyn Goulding, Collections and Engagement Manager, Mark Haswell, Collections and Engagement Assistant and Jackie Millard, trustee, volunteer and conservator.

It has been a pleasure, as always, to work with Clara Hudson at Sansom and Company and Ian Parfitt at E&P Design on the development of this book.

For support, advice and information we express our gratitude to Sonia Aarons, Jo Baring, Guy Baxter, Chris Beetles, Caroline Benson, Sam Butcher, Clive Chatters, Gracie Cooper at Common Ground, Pete Durnell at Hampshire County Council Countryside Service, Becky Fisher at Hampshire & Isle of Wight Wildlife Trust, Jane Fisher, Sarah Gilroy, Sara Glenn, Eliza Gluckman, Anthony Green, Nicola Heald, Stelina Kokarida, Amy Marshall, Robert Meyrick, Clare Mitchell, Jim Mitchell at New Forest National Park Authority, Hannah Murray, Alison Price, Jasmine Rodgers, Lyndsey Stride, Edward Twohig and David Wootton and the staff at the London Library.

INDEX